LINCOLN'S GREATEST CASE

LINCOLN'S GREATEST CASE

*The River, the Bridge, and
the Making of America*

Brian McGinty

LIVERIGHT PUBLISHING CORPORATION

a division of **W. W. Norton & Company** • NEW YORK • LONDON

For information about permission to reproduce selections from this book,
write to Permissions, Liveright Publishing Corporation,
a division of W. W. Norton & Company, Inc.,
500 Fifth Avenue, New York, NY 10110

For information about special discounts for bulk purchases, please contact
W. W. Norton Special Sales at specialsales@wwnorton.com or 800-233-4830

Manufacturing by RR Donnelley, Harrisonburg, VA
Book design by Brooke Koven
Production manager: Anna Oler

ISBN 978-0-87140-784-9

Liveright Publishing Corporation
500 Fifth Avenue, New York, N.Y. 10110
www.wwnorton.com

W. W. Norton & Company Ltd.
Castle House, 75/76 Wells Street, London W1T 3QT

1 2 3 4 5 6 7 8 9 0

To the memory of my grandfather
Lucius Frank McGinty Jr.,
a Southerner who revered Lincoln, and encouraged
my earliest efforts at writing

CONTENTS

LINCOLN'S GREATEST CASE

INTRODUCTION

On September 8, 1857, a tall and eerily thin lawyer from the prairies of central Illinois rose in the crowded courtroom of the United States Circuit Court in Chicago to address the judge and jury. Abraham Lincoln, already a well-known courtroom attorney in the lakeside city, had come north from his home in downstate Springfield because of an incident that occurred in the spring of the previous year on the Mississippi River between Rock Island, Illinois, and Davenport, Iowa. On May 6, 1856, a steamboat known as the *Effie Afton* had crashed into the first railroad bridge ever built across the Mississippi River, erupted in flames, and sunk in the river waters. No one was killed in the crash, but the steamboat was a total loss, and the bridge itself—called the Rock Island Bridge—was badly damaged. The owners of the steamboat had filed suit against the owners of the bridge to recover damages sustained in the collision. Lincoln had been retained as one of the lawyers for the defense of the suit, and the trial was now about to begin.

Officially titled *Hurd et al. v. The Railroad Bridge Company,*[1] but better known to newspaper reporters as the *Effie Afton* case, the trial in the United States Circuit Court was recognized from the outset as one of the most important ever heard in Illinois, for the transportation future of the state, of the Middle West, and of the nation depended in large measure on its outcome. Could a railroad bridge be built across the greatest river in North America without violating the navigation rights of steamboats? Could the Rock Island Bridge remain standing in the face of a great lawsuit for damages, or would the decision of the jury force it to be torn down? Historians of Lincoln and America's transportation history have called the

1

trial the most significant in Lincoln's nearly twenty-five-year career at the Illinois bar. His participation in the trial was, they have said, his "finest hour" as a lawyer.[2] Of the thousands of cases he handled in his legal career, "none was more important."[3] It showed him "at his most forward-looking and innovative as a legal practitioner."[4] It had "transcendent importance in the rivalry between the railroads and the river interests."[5]

This book tells the story of the *Effie Afton* case, the dramatic series of events that led up to it, Lincoln's key role in it, and the equally dramatic events that followed. It traces the history of steamboat traffic on the Mississippi in the first half of the nineteenth century, follows the progress of railroads west of the Appalachians in the middle of the century, and describes the epochal clash of the railroads and the steamboats at the river's edge. It explains how the Rock Island Bridge carried the first iron rails across the great river and details the determined efforts of the steamboat owners and their supporters to bring it down. It tells how the *Effie Afton* trial and Lincoln's participation in it saved the bridge from destruction, how the trial contributed to Lincoln's meteoric rise to the presidency only four years later, and how the bridge helped Union military forces achieve victory over Confederate armies in the Civil War.

Lincoln had a close relationship with the western rivers and riverboats when he was a young man, and as an adult he was never far from the railroads, which came into Illinois as he was beginning his legal and political careers. He was a river man in his early years, and a railroad attorney of sorts in his middle years (he never worked exclusively for railroads, but took cases both for them and against them). The river and the railroads form an indispensable background to the story of the Rock Island Bridge, the *Effie Afton*'s demise at its base in 1856, and Lincoln's career as a lawyer and politician, both before and after the *Effie Afton* trial.

Given its importance, it is curious that historians have not focused more attention on the trial and its place in the transportation history of the nation. It has, of course, been mentioned in almost every serious book and article about Lincoln's legal career, sometimes as a mere footnote to the main narrative, more often as the subject of a few paragraphs outlining its contours. And, in recent years, more and more light has been focused on Lincoln's life as a lawyer and the influence it had on his political life and his ultimate service as president, thanks in large part to the momentous Lincoln Legal Papers project, which has uncovered tens of thousands of documents from his law practice.

Yet, for all the attention given Lincoln the lawyer, the *Effie Afton* case has been strangely neglected.[6] Perhaps this is at least in part because it does not have the raw appeal of a sensational murder trial (Lincoln and his partners participated in at least twenty-six homicide trials in their careers)[7] or one that touched on the knotty issue of slavery, the great political, moral, and legal issue of Lincoln's day (Lincoln was involved in a handful of such cases).[8] Students of the man history reveres as the Great Emancipator and the Savior of the Union deserve to know the real facts about the trial he participated in in Chicago in 1857, the pivotal role it played in the advance of the railroads from east to west, and the facts that gave it its "transcendent importance."

The *Effie Afton* case, like most other civil lawsuits, was a contest between private litigants with private economic interests. The three plaintiffs—Jacob S. Hurd, Alexander W. Kidwell, and Joseph W. Smith—were the owners of the steamboat that was lost in its crash with the Rock Island Bridge. The defendant Railroad Bridge Company was an Illinois corporation created and controlled by railroad corporations in Illinois and Iowa: the Chicago and Rock Island Railroad Company in Illinois and the Mississippi and Missouri Railroad Company in Iowa. The plaintiff boat owners and the defendant corporation all had significant "skin" in the contest, in the form of the money they had invested, the property they owned, and the losses that had been suffered—and potentially might be suffered in the future. If the decision was in favor of the steamboat owners, they stood to recover $50,000, perhaps even more, in damages—an enormous sum in the 1850s—and the Railroad Bridge Company stood to lose that sum. If the decision was in favor of the Railroad Bridge Company, it would not only be absolved of any obligation to pay damages to the owners of the *Effie Afton*, but more importantly, future lawsuits brought by other owners whose boats had been damaged in collisions with the Rock Island Bridge would be discouraged—perhaps totally stifled.

Unlike many other lawsuits, however, the *Effie Afton* trial also had enormous legal, economic, and political implications for the public. As the first railroad bridge to span the largest and most important river in North America (a bridge for pedestrians, carriages, and wagons had opened a year earlier in Minnesota, but no span with rails had previously crossed the Mississippi),[9] the Rock Island Bridge permitted trains of the Chicago and Rock Island and the Mississippi and Missouri railroads (and potentially other railroads as well) to cross the great river, significantly increasing their capacity to move passengers and freight from east to west. At the same time, however, the bridge threatened the economic supremacy of the steamboats that had, for almost half a century, been the most important, most lucrative, and politically most influential mode of transportation in the trans-Mississippi region—perhaps in the entire nation. Chicago was an up-and-coming railroad center on Lake Michigan, recently connected to the Atlantic states by railroads that ran through New York, Pennsylvania, Ohio, Michigan, and Indiana. Chicago stood to gain enormously from the Rock Island Bridge, for it provided the first railroad connection between Lake Michigan and the rapidly expanding farmlands of Iowa and Nebraska, while St. Louis, the throbbing center of steamboat traffic on the Upper Mississippi (and a much bigger and richer city than Chicago), stood to lose significantly from the Rock Island Bridge. If the bridge was allowed to stand, farm products that had previously passed on steamboats through the Missouri city to markets in the South and East would be diverted to Chicago.

Before and after the *Effie Afton* suit was filed, railroad interests in Chicago complained that St. Louis steamboat owners, acting through the St. Louis Chamber of Commerce, were the real parties in interest in the litigation. The St. Louis interests denied the charge, but effectively admitted its truth by gathering witnesses for the trial and raising money to pay the prestigious lawyers who were hired to represent Hurd, Kidwell, and Smith. *Hurd et al. v. The Railroad Bridge*

Company was the official title of the litigation, but it might as well have been *St. Louis v. Chicago.*

The trial was a landmark in the development of the law governing America's navigable waters. It had long been conceded that states had the right to control the use of the lakes, rivers, and streams within their borders. It was also understood, however, that Congress, as the legislative authority of the federal government, had the power to regulate interstate commerce.[10] Where waterways crossed state lines, Congress's power to regulate the commerce on them was superior to the conflicting laws of any state.[11] But another basic law, the so-called Northwest Ordinance, by which the territory north and west of the Ohio River had become part of the United States in 1787, also played a part in the legal puzzle. That law declared that the navigable waters leading into the Mississippi and St. Lawrence were "common highways and forever free" to inhabitants of the territory, as well as to citizens of the United States and any states created out of the territory.[12] Ohio, Indiana, Illinois, Michigan, Wisconsin, and part of Minnesota eventually occupied Northwest Territory land, so all of those states were subject to the Northwest Ordinance. But what would happen when a state (or states) authorized a bridge to be built over a navigable river (both Illinois and Iowa had authorized the Rock Island Bridge) and the boats that had long had the exclusive use of the river labeled the bridge an "obstruction" and a denial of their legal rights to free navigation? The American courts, led by the Supreme Court of the United States, had tried to delineate an answer to this difficult question.[13] By the time of the *Effie Afton* trial, however, it was still unclear whether the owners of a steamboat that collided with a bridge over the Mississippi could force the bridge owners to compensate them for the damage to their steamboat, and even demand that the bridge be demolished to eliminate the possibility of future collisions. This was the overriding legal question that Lincoln and his fellow attorneys wrestled with in Chicago in September 1857, and the reason the *Effie Afton* trial was, in the words of the noted railroad historian Albro Martin, recognized as a "milestone in the vast changes in American law and jurisprudence."[14]

It is ironic that the *Effie Afton* trial and the Supreme Court's famous (and to some infamous) *Dred Scott* decision both occurred in 1857. Both cases had factual roots at Rock Island, Illinois, and both are to this day closely associated with Lincoln, although in strikingly different ways. Rock Island, of course, was the site of the Rock Island Bridge, the subject of the intense legal battle waged in the *Effie Afton* trial. But it had also been the home of an obscure slave named Dred Scott during an important part of his early life, and his residence there had given rise to his history-making claim to be a free man. Scott's legal bid for freedom began in a St. Louis court in 1846 and ended in the Supreme Court in Washington, D.C., in 1857, when Chief Justice Roger Taney ruled that blacks were ineligible for American citizenship and thus unable to bring suit in federal court. Taney declared in bold terms that Americans of African descent were not included in the Declaration of Independence's soaring assertion that "all men are created equal" and went on to make equally draconian assertions about the inability of Congress to make laws excluding slavery from any American territories or depriving slaveholders of the right to take their slaves anywhere in the country they wished.[15]

Lincoln was outraged by Taney's *Dred Scott* decision. He called it "an astonisher in legal history"[16] and embraced the dissenting opinions filed by Associate Justices John McLean of Ohio and Benjamin Curtis of Massachusetts. Then he went on to formulate his own theories of the case and the deference it was (or was not) entitled to under the Constitution.[17] The *Effie Afton* trial, fought out in Chicago in September 1857, was the most important courtroom battle of Lincoln's legal career, the one that best displayed his legal skills and had the greatest economic and political consequences for the country, while the *Dred Scott* decision, announced in Washington in March 1857, gave rise to one of Lincoln's most powerful political arguments. Both, however, contributed to Lincoln's growing reputation as a rising star on the nation's political horizon.

Historian Kenneth M. Stampp called 1857 "a crucial year in the antebellum American sectional conflict."[18] It was, he wrote, a year that "encompassed a political crisis which proved to be decisive in the coming of the Civil War." It was the year in which conflict over the admission of Kansas to the Union as a slave state split the national

Democratic Party. It was also a year in which a panic in the financial institutions of eastern cities, beginning in New York and rapidly
spreading across the nation, plunged the country into economic
turmoil.[19] Stampp believed that the conflict in Kansas, the Supreme
Court's *Dred Scott* decision, and the economic depression that followed the financial panic all contributed to the growing rupture
between the North and the South. "As a result, 1857 was probably
the year when the North and South reached the political point of no
return—when it became well nigh impossible to head off a violent
resolution of the differences between them."[20]

The struggle over the Rock Island Bridge that was the subject of
the *Effie Afton* trial may not have appeared to be as earthshaking as
the Kansas conflict, the *Dred Scott* decision, or the financial panic,
although it contributed significantly to the widening sectional gulf.
At the end of the trial, thanks in large part to Lincoln's efforts, the
Rock Island Bridge stood tall and erect. The iron rails that spanned
the river remained intact, binding together the eastern and western
banks of the Mississippi on a northern (not a southern) latitude,
providing a powerful spur to the growth of the northern city of
Chicago and stifling (for the time being at least) the transportation aspirations of southern cities like Memphis, Vicksburg, and
New Orleans. It handed Chicago, a city free of slaves in a state free
of slavery, a victory at the expense of St. Louis, a city where slaves
toiled in the streets and in the warehouses, hotels, restaurants, and
factories that led back from the crowded waterfront. It provided a
vital rail link across the Mississippi, inviting anti-slavery settlers to
make new homes in Iowa and adjacent territory, where they tilled the
land and built up a substantial population that, during the Civil War,
made significant contributions of men and supplies to the Union
war effort. If, as Stampp argued, 1857 was a crucial year in the history of pre–Civil War America, the *Effie Afton* trial made a powerful
contribution to that history.

Although this is not a book about Lincoln's legal career (other
writers have paid due attention to that fascinating part of his life),[21]
it touches in many places on his long and eventful life at the bar. Historians' opinions of Lincoln's legal abilities, and of the importance

that his legal career had in preparing him for his duties as president, differ widely. Among recent writers, Phillip Shaw Paludan, author of a widely read study of Lincoln's presidency, has expressed the view that Lincoln's legal experiences helped him develop skills that were "imperative in the crisis of disunion."[22] "Thinking like a lawyer," Paludan wrote, "was a profound part of his makeup."[23] But Mark Neely Jr., author of important books about Lincoln's career as a political leader, has written that "the law did not offer especially good training" for Lincoln's "constitutional thinking in a political context" and that Lincoln was successful in large part because he "was able to escape the habits of thinking like a lawyer."[24] "Lawyers," Neely wrote, "are paid to come up with clever arguments,"[25] and Lincoln's presidential triumphs were certainly not the result of "clever arguments." Lincoln was successful, Neely said, because he was able to escape the "straightjacket" of his legal background.[26] Brian Dirck, author of books about Lincoln's legal career and his views on the Constitution (and a student of Phillip Shaw Paludan), has written that "as a whole the Lincoln law practice was unremarkable."[27] "Lincoln the great American," Dirck wrote, "was in reality a pretty ordinary attorney."[28] In contrast, the prolific Lincoln scholar Harold Holzer has written that "Lincoln's life as a lawyer informed nearly every aspect of his future, a future that became inseparable from the nation's future." "Nothing," Holzer added, "was ever more sacred to Lincoln than the rule of law."[29]

Lawyer, judge, and Lincoln scholar Frank J. Williams has expressed a high opinion of the legal skills that Lincoln brought to the presidency. Williams made a list of the traits that every good lawyer must possess, including honesty, industriousness, meticulousness, confidence, rhetorical skill, courage, zealousness, persistence, and fair-mindedness, and found that Lincoln possessed all of them.[30] But Lincoln had "something more" than just the traits of a good lawyer, Williams wrote. "Put simply, Lincoln is still great today because he is remembered as a truly good person.... This 'goodness' cannot be reduced to any simple list of attributes, it just is."[31]

If "goodness" was the key ingredient in Lincoln's presidency, it had very little to do with the *Effie Afton* case, considering that neither side could lay exclusive claim to being the "good" side. Persuasive arguments could be—and were in fact—made by both the plaintiffs' and the defendants' lawyers that they should prevail. Lincoln's approach relied less on his innate sense of virtue than on his intelligence, analytical instincts, powers of persuasion—and, most important of all, his judgment. He allied himself with the Rock Island Bridge, and with the railroads that had built and operated it, in opposition to the steamboats. But this alliance implied no hostility to the steamboats. It was his considered judgment, as expressed in his closing argument in the *Effie Afton* case, that there was room both for steamboats on the Mississippi and railroads passing over it, though he realized what history would soon demonstrate, that the future belonged far more to the railroads and the bridge than to the steamboats. And he believed that, in the final analysis, it was essential that the law accommodate the future—that the Rock Island Bridge should not be held liable for the damages suffered by the owners of the *Effie Afton*, that the bridge should be allowed to stand and the railroads permitted to cross over the Mississippi.

Railroads represented the future, of course. But they represented something else that was important in Lincoln's mind. River traffic mostly led from the northern part of the country into the southern reaches of the republic. Both the Ohio and the Mississippi bordered slave states along their banks. Steamboats traveled from Pittsburgh and St. Paul, in the North, through St. Louis, a slaveholding city, and New Orleans, home of the largest slave-trading market in the United States, in the South. From its origins in Minnesota to its mouth in the Gulf of Mexico, the Mississippi, symbolically if not quite physically, divided the country east from west. The railroads mostly ran from east to west (railroads in the southern states were rudimentary compared to those in the rest of the country). Lincoln believed in the essential unity of the United States. He opposed the idea of secession and the consequent dissolution of the great republic that had been founded in the revolutionary generation by men who believed in the ideals of liberty and equality. In his closing argument in the *Effie Afton* case, Lincoln referred to the idea (broached by one of the opposing lawyers) that strife caused by the bridging of the Mississippi might lead to "a dissolution of the Union."[32] This, of course, was anathema to Lincoln, for the Union was his guiding light, his ideal, the vessel that would protect liberty and equality far into the future. By establishing ties between the East and the West to match those that already ran from the North to the South, Lincoln believed that the railroads, and the bridges that would eventually carry them across the Mississippi, would help to bind the sections of the country together. They would help to unite people and commerce in far-distant parts of the nation, and ultimately help to preserve the Union of the United States.

All modern studies of Lincoln's legal practice are indebted to the Lincoln Legal Papers project, begun in the 1980s as a comprehensive search in courthouses, libraries, private collections, and archives for documents from Lincoln's legal career. The search (which is ongoing) has, according to a recent count, uncovered more than 97,000 documents from more than 5,200 cases in which Lincoln and his law partners participated.[33] Now part of the larger Papers of Abraham Lincoln,[34] the Legal Papers are indispensable sources of information about the law practice of America's greatest president. This book could not have been written, nor could the story of the *Effie Afton* case have been told—or told as well—without them.

ONE

A Great Highway of Nature

≈

The Mississippi River and the streams that feed into it form one of the greatest river systems in the world. From its source in northern Minnesota to its mouth below New Orleans, the Mississippi itself measures 2,350 miles from end to end, but when its principal tributary, the Missouri, is added in, its length grows to 3,710 miles.[1] The Mississippi-Missouri combination is generally ranked as the fourth-longest river system in the world, behind only the Nile, the Amazon, and the Yangtze. The watershed of the Mississippi extends from the Appalachian Mountains in the East to the Rocky Mountains in the West and covers all or parts of thirty-one of the United States and two provinces of Canada. The Missouri and the Ohio are the principal tributaries of the Mississippi, though there are countless other rivers, streams, rivulets, lakes, and even ponds that link with the major rivers and contribute to an unending flow that passes down from the mountains and through the prairies on its way to its ultimate destination in the Gulf of Mexico. One of the early historians of the western rivers called them "the great highways of nature, given for man's use."[2] With the acquisition of the Louisiana Territory and the invention of the steamboat, it became clear that man was determined to make use of them.

History would soon demonstrate, however, that using the great streams would not always be easy, for, despite their obvious advantages, they had some notable drawbacks. They were wide and straight and deep in places, but twisting and narrow and shallow in others. Mark Twain, who spent his boyhood along the Mississippi, called it "the crookedest river in the world, since in one part of its journey it uses up one thousand three hundred miles to cover the same ground that the crow would fly over in six hundred and seventy-five."[3] The Mississippi, Twain said, had a "disposition to make prodigious jumps by cutting through narrow necks of land, and thus straightening and shortening itself. More than once it has shortened itself thirty miles at a single jump!"[4] Even where a stretch of river was straight, it could present hazards to navigation. There were sandbars, reefs, rapids, falls, overhanging trees, snags (broken trees that had anchored themselves to the river bottom), and rocks that posed formidable challenges to even the most skillful steamboat pilots. Islands dotted the streams in unexpected places, sometimes forming in a single season of high (or low) water and disappearing just as quickly in the next. And when the weather turned bitterly cold, ice formed and brought all navigation to a halt. The ice could be thick enough in some places to support teams of horses pulling wagons from shore to shore; but when it began to break up, it formed floes that moved down the river with deadly destruction, menacing boats, barges, rafts, and shoreline structures as well.

If navigation on the broad Ohio and the Lower Mississippi was hazardous, it was even worse on the Mississippi north of St. Louis, for much of that part of the river was clogged with sandbars, and in dry weather the water was sometimes only a few inches deep. About two hundred miles upstream from St. Louis the river was obstructed by the Des Moines Rapids (so named for the nearby confluence of the Des Moines River), which ran for more than eleven miles over a slab of limestone between two rocky bluffs. Without a discernible channel, water in the Des Moines Rapids flowed fast and furious when the river was high but slowed to barely a trickle when water levels dropped.[5] Another hundred or so miles upriver brought boats to the Rock Island Rapids, a short distance above Fort Armstrong, a U.S. Army post built between 1816 and 1817 to defend settlers along the river from the Indians who still claimed the region as their own. There the river ran for eighteen miles over sharp ridges (or chains) of rock that twisted from shore to shore, forming narrow channels (sometimes called chutes) and raising strong and unpredictable cross-currents. Steamboat passage through the Rock Island Rapids was treacherous, even at high water; during low water the underwater obstructions were covered with less than thirty inches of water and passage was sometimes impossible.[6] Some of the river channels twisted so dangerously that boats had to make hairpin turns to avoid running aground on the rocks, and in others the channels were no more than a hundred feet across.[7]

No steamboat ventured north of the Des Moines or Rock Island Rapids before the spring of 1823, when a small vessel called the *Virginia* left St. Louis bound for Fort Snelling, at the confluence of the Minnesota and the Mississippi.[8] The *Virginia* had a few passengers on board (including a chief of the Sauk Indians) and a cargo of supplies for the military post at Snelling. It moved slowly but safely through the Des Moines Rapids, but when it reached the Rock Island Rapids, it got stranded on a rock, where it remained for two days before rising water permitted it to resume its voyage.[9]

Despite the treacherous rapids, steamboat traffic on the Upper Mississippi experienced a healthy growth after 1823. Lead was being mined around Galena, in the northwestern corner of Illinois, and thousands of miners and their families were flocking to the area. With a silver content of about 5 percent, the lead ore in the local mines constituted the largest and richest mineral deposit found in the United States up to that time.[10] By the close of the season in 1828, a hundred steamboats had docked at Galena to pick up some thirteen million pounds of lead and bring them downriver. Seven years later, the number of boats engaged in the same operations had increased to 176.[11]

Congress was repeatedly asked to appropriate funds for the improvement of the western rivers, but the southern senators and representatives who held the balance of power in the national capital limited their help to the southern sections of the waterways. In 1829, a survey of the Des Moines and Rock Island Rapids was carried out in the hope that canals could be built around the obstacles, but that hope was soon abandoned in favor of a program of blasting and rock removal.[12] It was not until 1837, however, that any effort was made to do this. In that year, the U.S. Army sent a young lieutenant of engineers from Virginia by the name of Robert E. Lee to survey the St. Louis waterfront and both the Des Moines and Rock Island Rapids, and recommend improvements.

The harbor at St. Louis at that time was menaced by a large bar of accumulated sand and silt called Duncan's Island. Already a mile long, Duncan's Island was growing larger every year, threatening to wholly obstruct the harbor and divert the main river channel across the river to the Illinois side.[13] Lee was accompanied by another army engineer named Montgomery Meigs, and the pair worked with a German mapmaker named Henry Kayser to prepare accurate maps of the river obstructions. Their report recommended blasting rock to open channels in the two rapids and building dikes in the river at St. Louis to deflect the main course of the river toward Duncan's Island and wash it away. Work was done at St. Louis and on the Des Moines Rapids in 1838 and 1839, but congressional appropriations soon ran out, and Lee was summoned back to Washington in 1840. A channel five feet deep and two hundred feet wide had been cut through the Des Moines Rapids, but the Rock Island obstructions remained untouched. Duncan's Island was not finally removed until other engineers returned to the river in later years and finished the work begun by Lee and Meigs.[14]

As steamboat design developed, it became apparent that a practical river craft needed some essential features. First, it had to have a shallow hull, one that spread the weight of the boat and its cargo widely over the water and penetrated only a few feet—or in the case of smaller craft only a few inches—below the surface. Second, its propulsive power had to stay close to the surface so that underwater obstructions would not disable it. This resulted in the almost universal use of paddle wheels instead of propellers, which had to ride much lower in the water to move the boats forward. Third, it had to have guards, or sections of the main deck that projected beyond the hull and protected it from any collisions the boat might be subject to. Fourth, it had to have several decks—at least two, sometimes three or even four—so cabin passengers could enjoy some separation from the bellowing steam engines and the unsavory cargos (coal, farm products, cotton bales, even livestock) that crowded the main deck.

Fifth, it had to have a pilot house that was elevated well above the river surface, so that the men responsible for navigation could see the river ahead and spot potential trouble before it was too late to deal with. Finally, it had to have iron chimneys that extended high above the boat, so that the smoke and soot produced by the steam engines would not obscure the pilots' vision and the red-hot cinders that rose from the fireboxes would be scattered over the river before they could land on a deck and start a potentially catastrophic fire. Chimneys sometimes rose to a height of ninety feet above the water, where they belched black clouds of smoke, soot, and embers that could be seen (and smelled) for miles around.[15]

Lincoln was only two years old when the first steamboat was put into service west of the Appalachians.[16] Built just outside Pittsburgh in 1810 and 1811, the 116-foot-long *New Orleans* was a joint venture of Robert Fulton, Robert R. Livingston, and Nicholas Roosevelt, a great-uncle of Theodore Roosevelt and a distant relative of Franklin D. Roosevelt. It became the first steamboat on the Ohio when, in October 1811, it sailed downstream from Pittsburgh with Roosevelt and his wife, Lydia Latrobe, daughter of architect Benjamin Latrobe, aboard. The Great Comet of 1811 was visible to the naked eye for most of the trip, and the first of the New Madrid earthquakes occurred just as they were to leave the Ohio and enter the Mississippi, causing the great river to flow backward for a time. Indians along the banks thought that the *New Orleans* was the comet come to earth and attacked it in war canoes, but the boat was too fast for them to catch. Although the steamboat eventually made it all the way to New Orleans, its engine was not strong enough to power it back upstream to Pittsburgh, so it spent the rest of its short life making trips between New Orleans and Natchez. It struck a snag and sank in 1813 or 1814.[17]

Lincoln was five years old when, in 1814, a boat called the *Enterprise* became the first steamboat to engage in regular commerce on the Ohio and Mississippi Rivers. When it reached New Orleans, General Andrew Jackson pressed it into service delivering munitions and other supplies for the Battle of New Orleans.[18] Lincoln was seven when, in 1816, his family crossed the Ohio from Kentucky into Indiana. That was the year in which a New Jersey–born inventor and steamboat captain named Henry Shreve sailed the first double-decked steamboat down the western rivers to New Orleans and back to Louisville. Shreve's steamboat, called the *Washington*, followed up this trip with a round trip from Louisville to New Orleans and back in 1817, covering the distance in forty-one days.[19]

The year after the Lincoln family took up residence in Indiana, the first steamboat designed exclusively for passenger service was built at Cincinnati and christened the *Zebulon Pike*. It became an official U.S. mail carrier on the western rivers and the first steamboat to navigate the Mississippi above the mouth of the Ohio, completing a voyage all the way to St. Louis in August 1817.[20] In 1818, the year Lincoln marked his ninth birthday, six steamboats were built at Cincinnati, which was then emerging as the chief boat-building port on the western rivers.[21] Between 1826 and 1830, the Louisville and Portland Canal was built to bypass the Falls of the Ohio and allow cargo and passengers to travel all the way from Pittsburgh to New Orleans without changing boats or waiting for high water. The Falls of the Ohio were a stretch of two and a half miles in which the river dropped a total of twenty-six feet. For about ten months every year, boats were unable to make it through this dangerous obstruction, so it became a location for portage—with keelboats and rafts unloading their cargos and carrying them around the falls to be loaded again onto keelboats or rafts. The portage gave rise to the city of Louisville, but the falls were such an obstruction to paddle-powered boats that the bypass canal became a necessity, and eventually a blessing.[22]

The completion of the Louisville and Portland Canal helped fuel a great expansion of boat-building and river commerce. Steamboat construction flourished along the Ohio River, with much of it concentrated in Cincinnati. For twenty years beginning in the late 1830s, thirty or more steamboats were built every year in the self-styled "Queen City of the West." In one year alone (1843) forty-eight boats left Cincinnati boatyards bound for service on the western rivers.[23] Meanwhile, the line of steamboats that crowded the New Orleans waterfront grew longer each year. In 1840, New Orleans was the fourth-most-populous city in the United States and the fourth-busiest port in the world, exceeded only by London, Liverpool, and New York.[24]

Lincoln's birth near Hodgenville, Kentucky, and the fourteen youthful years he spent on his father's farm at Little Pigeon Creek, Indiana, gave him a good deal of experience with rivers. His father, Thomas Lincoln, who spent most of his life as a carpenter and farmer, also did some work on the rivers. At least once (and possibly several times) Thomas floated a flatboat all the way down the Mississippi to New Orleans, where he sold both his boat and his cargo. In New Orleans, he sold his goods on credit and was cheated when the buyers failed to pay him, forcing him to come home empty-handed.[25] Lincoln was aware of his father's failures on the rivers, but they did not dissuade him from trying his own hand at river work, for he was anxious to better his condition in life and willing to take whatever opportunities presented themselves. Young Abraham resented the fact that his father rented him out to neighbors for the most menial kind of physical labor and kept the meager earnings for himself. He later complained that this practice, which continued until he turned twenty-one, made him a slave, since he was forced to work without receiving anything in return but a bare subsistence.[26]

In 1827, Abraham was hired to operate a ferry on a local creek for the miserable wage of twenty cents a day, and the money all went to his father. About this time, however, he also experimented with a little private enterprise. He built a small boat and took it down to the Ohio River (about fifteen miles from Little Pigeon Creek). There two men asked him to ferry them out to a steamboat in the middle of the river. When Lincoln obliged them, they responded by throwing two silver half-dollars into his boat.[27] Lincoln was astonished that he could make a whole dollar in just one day. "The world seemed wider and fairer before me," he later wrote. "I was a more hopeful and thoughtful boy from that time."[28] Encouraged by his initial experience, he turned his little boat into a ferry business, regularly rowing people out from the shore to riverboats in the Ohio. When the operator of a competing ferry had him arrested and taken to Kentucky for operating a ferry without a license, he defended himself before a justice of the peace by arguing that, although the Kentucky license law authorized ferry boats to carry passengers across the river, it did not forbid others to convey passengers to steamboats in the middle of the river. This episode was, in later years, described as one of Lincoln's earliest experiences with the law, and one that helped him develop an interest in a legal career.[29]

In 1828, when Lincoln was nineteen, he and another young man built a flatboat, loaded it with farm products from the area, and floated it twelve hundred miles down the Ohio and Mississippi to New Orleans.[30] They found buyers for their goods along the river and sold the flatboat in New Orleans, then returned north as deck passengers on a steamboat, thus qualifying for the lowest available fares.[31]

Thomas Lincoln moved his family to central Illinois in 1830, the year that Abraham turned twenty-one and was at last free of the duty to work for his father without compensation.[32] After helping his family fence off a ten-acre plot of ground with rails (this was the work that later gave him his nickname of "the Rail-Splitter"), he began his life as a free man by heading down the Sangamon River in a canoe, a "friendless, uneducated, penniless boy."[33] When he met a businessman who proposed that he and two other young men take a flatboat down the Ohio and Mississippi to New Orleans, he gladly took on the job, felling trees with which to build the boat, loading it with farm products and livestock, and acting as pilot of the craft. When, early in the trip, the boat became impaled on a milldam and filled with water, Lincoln showed his enterprise and ingenuity by boring a hole in the hull, draining the water over the face of the dam, then plugging up the hole and getting the boat back on the journey to New Orleans.[34]

In 1832, Lincoln took a job helping to clear the Sangamon River of overhanging trees so that a steamboat called the *Talisman* could come up the river, take on a cargo of local crops, and return downstream to St. Louis and New Orleans. When the boat arrived in New Salem, the village Lincoln then called home, he went on board as pilot. But the water level in the Sangamon quickly dropped, forcing the *Talisman* to retreat. With Lincoln still at the helm, the boat was ultimately brought to rest on the same milldam that had impaled his flatboat a year earlier.[35]

After Lincoln entered politics in the early 1830s, he demonstrated a friendly disposition to river traffic, as well as other developing forms of transportation in Illinois. Most of the people who lived in the southern and central parts of the state were Democrats and supporters of President Andrew Jackson. Many had come to Illinois from Kentucky and Virginia, hoping to recapture on the Illinois prairies the agricultural lifestyle they had enjoyed in their southern homes. Although Lincoln, too, hailed from a southern state, he believed in the idea of progress and embraced the values of enterprise and energy.

Lincoln's "beau ideal of a statesman" was Henry Clay, leader of the Whig Party.[36] The central plank of Clay's political philosophy was the so-called American System, which called for tariffs to protect and promote American manufacturing and create a home market for American products, a national bank to provide a sound and uniform currency, and federal support for roads, canals, and river improvements.[37] On the other side, the Democrats, heirs to the agrarian philosophy of Thomas Jefferson, believed that the federal government should have only the most minimal involvement in the lives of the people. The Democrats (particularly Jackson) were bitter foes of the Bank of the United States, which they believed to be unconstitutional.[38] They opposed federal roads and canals as further violations of the Constitution[39] and were quite satisfied for Americans to sell their agricultural products to England and France and, in turn, use the profits to buy European manufactured goods.

Henry Clay wanted the American economy to grow and become more unified. He believed that roads, canals, and river projects, financed in large part from federal tariff revenues, would bring greater prosperity to the nation. The Bank of the United States would provide the credit needed to finance the improvement projects and, in the process, help to knit the disparate regions of the country together. Taken together, the American System would promote interdependence and, according to Clay's biographers David and Jeanne Heidler, "make disunion not only unlikely but unthinkable."[40]

Lincoln embraced the Whig philosophy, believing that the "legitimate object of government, is 'to do for the people whatever needs to be done, but which they can not, by individual effort, do at all, or do so well, for themselves.' There are many such things—some of them exist independently of the injustice in the world. Making and maintaining roads, bridges, and the like; providing for the helpless young and afflicted; common schools; and disposing of deceased men's property are instances."[41]

Seeking to emulate Henry Clay's American System on the state level, Lincoln urged state support for straightening and deepening river channels, for building roads, and for raising bridges over creeks and rivers. He supported state financing for one of the biggest construction projects then under way in Illinois, the nearly one-hundred-mile-long Illinois and Michigan Canal that linked the Chicago River near Lake Michigan with the Illinois River, which in turned flowed into the Mississippi. Begun in 1836 and not completed until 1848, it was an expensive and time-consuming project, but it was the first great leap forward on Chicago's road to becoming the principal commercial center of the Middle West. The completion of the canal turned the lakeside city into a major market for the grain products of the Illinois River Valley at the same time that it severely limited St. Louis's participation in that market.[42]

Lincoln was also an enthusiastic supporter of the "General System of Internal Improvements" that was approved by the Illinois legislature on February 27, 1837.[43] This was an even more ambitious project than the Illinois and Michigan Canal, and much more expensive, for it aimed to support canals, railroads, and other improvement projects throughout the state. But coming just before the Panic of 1837, which shook the financial foundations of the nation, it proved to be too much. While voters were eager to have the improvements built, they were loath to fund them with increased tax dollars, and without tax increases, the state could not pay for all of the promised improvements.[44] Lincoln, who was a Whig leader in the General Assembly at the time, was widely blamed for the extravagance of the internal improvements scheme, but he continued to defend the law and another measure that ordered the removal of the Illinois state capital from Vandalia to Springfield, where he then lived.[45] Carried out in 1839, the move proved to be a great boon to Springfield, bringing not only the statehouse to the town but also the governor and the legislature, the state Supreme Court, the state library, the United States courts, and the U.S. Marshal.[46] The move also benefited the state generally, for Springfield occupied a more central location in Illinois, making it easier for people from the northern as well as the southern parts of the state to conduct their business there.

Lincoln continued to support internal improvements after he entered national politics. Shortly before he went to Washington to take his seat in the U.S. House of Representatives in 1847, he spoke at a convention called in Chicago to respond to President James K. Polk's recent veto of an act of Congress appropriating federal moneys for the improvement of rivers and harbors in New York, Ohio, Illinois, and Wisconsin. Polk took the position, originally advanced by Thomas Jefferson, that internal improvements were unconstitutional, since Congress had power to regulate commerce between the states but not within them. Polk also argued that federal aid to internal improvements was an unwarranted drain on the federal treasury, that the improvements favored certain parts of the country at the expense of others, and that the federal government could have nothing to do with them unless the Constitution was first amended.[47] Lincoln touched deftly on the constitutional issue, modestly disclaiming any expertise as a constitutional lawyer, but expressing warm approval for federal action. David Dudley Field, a prominent New York lawyer and Democrat, had just spoken before the same convention, arguing that federal aid to internal improvements was unconstitutional. In his own speech, Lincoln acknowledged that Field "loves the Constitution." Lincoln said he also loved it, although "in a different way." Field looked upon it "as a network, through which may be sifted the seeds of discord and discussion," Lincoln said. "I look upon it as a complete protection to the Union. He loves it in his way; I in mine."[48]

When Lincoln got to Congress, he delivered a much longer speech in favor of federal aid to internal improvements, in which he addressed the whole panoply of the Democratic arguments against them. On the issue of their constitutionality, he quoted from Chancellor James Kent's *Commentaries on American Law*, one of the leading legal treatises of the time. Kent thought the arguments in favor of the constitutionality of internal improvements were "vastly superior" to those against it. Lincoln agreed.[49]

Both before and after his service in Congress, Lincoln continued his busy law practice. The cases that he handled included a healthy sprinkling of disputes that arose out of rivers, river navigation, and bridges.[50] Some of the cases had modest implications; they were disputes about streams that were obstructed by mill or fish dams, or the loss of cargos in flatboat accidents.[51] But at least two cases that he participated in before the *Effie Afton* case were potentially more important.

One case arose in 1849 when a canal boat carrying a load of wheat struck part of a privately owned wagon bridge that had been built over the Illinois River at Peoria. The canal boat and the wheat were both lost. The boat's insurance company paid the boat owners' claim and then brought suit against the stockholders of the bridge company. Under the law of subrogation, an insurance company that pays a claim is entitled to all of the rights and remedies its insured could assert against third parties responsible for the underlying loss.[52] An attorney for the insurance company asked Lincoln to join him in prosecuting its claim. The issues to be decided in the case were similar to those that later arose in the *Effie Afton* trial. First, was the bridge a "material obstruction" to navigation of the river? Second, was the collision caused by negligent operation of the boat? And third, did the fact that the building of the bridge was expressly authorized by law (in this case an act of the Illinois legislature) exempt the bridge owners from responsibility for the collision? Lincoln successfully argued in *Columbus Insurance Company v. Peoria Bridge Company* that the legislative authorization did not immunize the bridge owners from claims.[53] Beyond that, the issues were hotly disputed, and the case was eventually settled.

A second case arose from the sinking in the Ohio River of a large flat-bottom boat that was transporting sixty very valuable railroad cars to a railroad construction project in 1854. Eads and Nelson, a salvage firm from Missouri that had contractual rights to salvage sunken boats and claim payment from the owners or their insurance companies, raised fifty-two of the cars and turned them over to their owners. Soon a dispute arose among the salvagers, the railroad company, and the insurers as to how they would be compensated. A judgment in favor of Eads and Nelson and against the railroad company was initially obtained in the U.S. District Court in Missouri, but since the company had no assets in Missouri, a second suit in admiralty was begun in the U.S. District Court in Springfield, Illinois. Lincoln joined with two attorneys from St. Louis to represent the railroad and its officers. The resulting case of *Eads and Nelson v. The Ohio and Mississippi Railroad* raised complicated questions of admiralty jurisdiction, salvage rights, and insurance law. Samuel Treat, the district judge in Springfield, entered a judgment allowing the salvagers to foreclose a lien on the rescued railroad cars. The railroad appealed the judgment to Supreme Court Justice John McLean, sitting as a circuit justice in Springfield, but before McLean could decide the case there was a settlement and the appeal was dismissed.[54]

Lincoln's close involvement with the rivers and riverboats was attested to by an event that occurred in 1848, when he was serving as a Whig congressman from Illinois. The first session of the Thirtieth Congress came to an end on August 14 of that year, and the second session was not due to begin until December. During the intersession, Lincoln came home by way of New York, New England, and the Great Lakes, using some of his time to campaign for General Zachary Taylor, that year's Whig candidate for president. While a passenger on a steamboat traveling on the Detroit River, he saw another steamboat that had gone aground on an island. The captain ordered the passengers to get out and put loose planks, empty barrels, and boxes under the hull of the stranded craft in an effort to refloat it.[55] Lincoln thought about the problem of the stranded boat and, when he got back to Illinois, worked on an invention he thought would help in such a situation. Using his skill at whittling wood (and with the aid of a Springfield mechanic named Walter

Davis) he made a model of it and took it back to Washington when he returned to Congress.[56] There he hired an attorney to apply for a patent in his behalf.[57] In his application, he wrote:

> Be it known that I, Abraham Lincoln, of Springfield, in the county of Sangamon, in the state of Illinois, have invented a new and improved manner of combining adjustable buoyant air chambers with a steam boat or other vessel for the purpose of enabling their draught of water to be readily lessened to enable them to pass over bars, or through shallow water, without discharging their cargoes.[58]

The invention was never built, and it is by no means certain that it would have worked if it had. Still, it occupies a unique place in American history, for it was (so far as is known) the first and only patent ever awarded to a president of the United States.[59] The inspiration for the patent (no. 6,469) came from a problem frequently experienced on the western rivers—boats running aground on sandbars—and the inventive idea for a solution to it had its birth in the mind of a lawyer from Illinois named Abraham Lincoln.

TWO

No Other Improvement

~≈~

The earliest railroads in America were short, horse-drawn tramways that hauled building materials from one point to another. The Granite Railway, which opened in Massachusetts in 1826, was one of these roads. Running for a distance of four miles from the town of Quincy to Milton on the Neponset River, it carried granite for the construction of the Bunker Hill Monument in Charlestown.[1]

The first commercially successful, steam-powered railroad in the country was the Baltimore and Ohio, which began building west from the Maryland city in 1828 with the goal of crossing the Appalachians to the Ohio River. The B&O was touted as a faster and cheaper route for moving passengers and freight from the eastern seaboard to the states of the Old Northwest than the Erie Canal, which was built across upper New York State between 1817 and 1825 to connect the Hudson River to Lake Erie. A branch of the B&O was extended to Washington, D.C., in 1835, but the Ohio was not reached until 1852, when the rails were finally brought into Wheeling, Virginia (now West Virginia).[2]

The first rails laid north and west of the Ohio River were short lines designed to connect established waterways—the Ohio River in the south, Lake Erie in the north, and canals in between—with agricultural marketing centers. Ohio's first line was the Kalamazoo and Erie, which ran a modest thirty-six miles from Toledo to Adrian, Michigan, in 1836.[3] Springfield, Ohio, was connected to Cincinnati by the Little Miami Railroad, built between 1837 and 1848. By 1850, thanks in large part to these midwestern roads, the United States led the world with nine thousand total miles of railroads.[4]

Although Lincoln was an early and determined proponent of water transportation in Illinois, he recognized that railroads were a marvelous innovation and that the day was not far off when rail transportation would come to his state. In 1832, in his first campaign for election to the Illinois state legislature, he publicly proclaimed his support for railroad construction. "No other improvement that reason will justify us in hoping for," he said then, "can equal in utility the rail road. It is a never failing source of communication, between places of business remotely situated from each other. Upon the rail road the regular progress of commercial intercourse is not interrupted by either high or low water, or freezing weather, which are the principal difficulties that render our future hopes of water communication precarious and uncertain."[5]

Lincoln did not win his 1832 election, but he was successful in four subsequent elections and held his seat in the legislature until March 1841. He was one of the leaders of the Whigs in the Illinois General Assembly when it passed its "General System of Internal Improvements" in February 1837.[6] This ambitious program envisioned state support for railroad construction as well as continued work on the Illinois and Michigan Canal, which had already begun. Rail lines were to be built from Galena in the far northwestern corner of the state to Cairo at the southern tip; from Alton, an important shipping point on the Mississippi opposite St. Louis, to Mt. Carmel on the Indiana line; from Quincy on the middle Mississippi to Wabash, again on the Indiana line. Other railroads were to be constructed to connect towns and villages in between.[7] If taxes adequate to finance these ambitious projects had been raised, they might have been completed, but the voters were as firmly opposed to tax increases as they were in favor of internal improvements. So, by 1840, the legislature called for an end to the railroad projects.[8]

Before the state wholly abandoned its efforts, however, it embarked on the construction of one of the railroads called for in the Internal Improvements Act. Dubbed the Northern Cross, the road was originally intended to cross the state from the Mississippi River in the west to the Indiana border in the east, but in its straitened circumstances the state could only afford to lay sixty miles of track extending from the Illinois River to Springfield on the Sangamon.[9] As part of the construction work, a small locomotive was brought in to haul construction materials along the line. According to John W. Starr, who studied Lincoln and the railroads closely, it was the first locomotive ever put into operation anywhere in the Mississippi Valley.[10] The people of Springfield celebrated when the Northern Cross arrived in their midst on May 13, 1842, but their celebration soon crumbled into disappointment. The road itself was poorly built, and its equipment was inadequate to carry all of the products Springfield and its environs wanted to send to New Orleans. What's more, economic conditions had so glutted New Orleans with the products of the Mississippi and Ohio River Valleys (mostly wheat, corn, vegetables, and fruits) that the market for products from Illinois was nearly nonexistent. The Northern Cross soon ceased operations, and in April 1847, the state sold the road and its equipment at auction.[11] The new owners changed its name to the Sangamon and Morgan Railroad, and in 1853 changed it again to the Great Western Railroad Company.[12]

Lincoln left Springfield to attend his first (and only) term in Congress in October 1847, traveling with his wife and two sons. It is difficult to trace the family's route all the way from Springfield to the national capital, although parts of it are known. They went by stagecoach from Springfield to Alton and from there crossed the Mississippi to St. Louis, where they boarded a riverboat for a trip downriver to the Ohio. They then proceeded up that river to its junction with the Kentucky River, which in turn brought them to Frankfort. There they boarded the Lexington and Ohio Railroad for a short trip to Lexington, where they visited Mrs. Lincoln's family.[13] Their journey east from Lexington probably included a return to the Ohio River and a trip upstream to Wheeling, Virginia, or Pittsburgh, Pennsylvania, although at least part of it would have been made by stagecoach and a part on the partially completed Baltimore and Ohio Railroad to Washington, where they arrived in December 1847.[14] Lincoln returned to Illinois after the congressional adjournment in August 1848, traveling through New York and New England by train and by boat through the Great Lakes to Chicago. Returning to Washington in December 1848, he remained until March 1849. His trip back home undoubtedly included some travel on the Baltimore and Ohio, some travel by stagecoach, and a long trip by boat down the Ohio and up the Mississippi to St. Louis, where he arrived on March 26, 1849.[15] The journeys both to and from the nation's capital were difficult in 1847, 1848, and 1849, much slower and more involved than Lincoln's trip to the national capital would be twelve years later, after he was elected president.[16]

Before he left on his first visit to Washington, Lincoln had joined his neighbors in central Illinois in urging the construction of a railroad between Springfield and Alton.[17] The railroad was to be called the Alton and Sangamon and provide a valuable connection between two of the most important cities in the south-central part of the state. Financing was, as usual, difficult, so work on the project did not begin until 1850, and the first train did not arrive in the capital until September 9, 1852. Hundreds of Springfielders were on hand to cheer the arrival of the cars. "It was a glorious sight," the editor of a local newspaper wrote, "—the careening of the passenger train over our prairies! The railroads of Illinois will hasten our state to her brilliant destiny!" From Springfield, the railroad continued north to Bloomington, where it arrived in 1853.[18]

The construction of a central railroad that would connect the northern and southern extremities of Illinois had been discussed for years. As early as 1836, the Illinois legislature chartered a corporation to lay rails from "the mouth of the Ohio river, and thence north to a point on the Illinois River, at or near the termination of the Illinois–Michigan Canal,"[19] but the money necessary to build the road could not be raised. When Sidney Breese, a sometime Illinois circuit judge and state Supreme Court justice who had presided over cases that Lincoln argued, was a member of the United States Senate in the mid-1840s, he tried to get the federal government to subsidize the construction of a railroad through central Illinois, but Congress would not act. Things went differently, however, when one of Breese's Senate colleagues, Lincoln's later arch political rival Stephen

A. Douglas, formed an alliance with Senator William R. King of Alabama and successfully steered a bill through Congress granting not only Illinois but also Mississippi and Alabama large tracts of federal land to finance the building of railroads.[20]

Congress called for a north-south railroad running through Illinois from the southern terminus of the Illinois and Michigan Canal to Cairo at the junction of the Ohio and Mississippi Rivers, with branches to Chicago and Galena; there was also talk that the Illinois railroad would connect with another north-south line extending all the way to Mobile, Alabama.[21] Illinois received nearly 2.6 million acres of federal land to help it finance construction of the Illinois stretch of the railroad.[22] The state in turn chartered the Illinois Central Railroad, authorized it to build the Illinois road Congress called for, and gave it the federal land to finance the project.[23] Construction began in late 1851 and was completed in September 1856. The road covered the then-astounding distance of 705 miles, ran through thirty counties, and was reported to be the longest single railroad in the world.[24]

The railroads stimulated business in Illinois, making it easier (and cheaper) for farmers to bring their crops to market and thus encouraged more extensive planting. The railroads also promoted the growth of towns in the interior part of the state; no longer did villages and hamlets have to depend on wagon shipments to riverboats to make their markets.[25] The railroads also invigorated legal business in Illinois, for railroads were complicated business entities with extensive commercial and property interests that touched the lives of people everywhere. Lawyers were needed to provide legal guidance for railroad entrepreneurs, to protect the interests of stockholders, and to enforce the rights of those with whom they came into contact.

Lincoln accepted many cases involving the railroads, although he never represented railroad interests to the exclusion of other clients: he was always as willing to file lawsuits against railroads as to defend them from suits filed by other lawyers.[26] Lincoln and his law partner, William H. Herndon, sued the railroads in behalf of individuals who had been injured on or about the rails.[27] They handled at least twenty-nine cases involving railroad stock subscription payments,[28] and Lincoln himself participated in at least six cases involving the corporate charters of railroads.[29]

One of Lincoln's most important railroad cases tested the power of counties to tax the property of the Illinois Central Railroad. The state constitution gave all counties "power to assess and collect taxes" and provided that the taxes were to be "uniform in respect to persons and property."[30] But when the state legislature chartered the Illinois Central it exempted the railroad from taxation for six years on condition that it pay the state 5 percent of its gross proceeds every six months during the same six-year period.[31] The case was begun in the McLean County circuit court when an attorney employed by the railroad sought an injunction barring the county from collecting any tax against the railroad. The case would ultimately have to be decided in the Illinois Supreme Court, so the attorney asked Lincoln to join him in taking the case up on appeal.

Lincoln first checked with the county to make sure that it was not going to engage him, and then agreed to represent the railroad. In the supreme court, he presented an elaborate argument to uphold the constitutional power of the legislature to exempt a corporation from taxation upon the payment of a portion of its earnings. He cited four cases from the United States Supreme Court and twenty-two from different state courts as authority for his argument. When the Illinois Supreme Court issued its decision (in favor of the railroad) it cited thirteen of those cases in its opinion.[32]

After the case of *Illinois Central Railroad Company v. County of McLean* was concluded, Lincoln presented a bill for his services. Years later, Herndon recalled that the amount was originally $2,000 but that the railroad refused to pay. Herndon said that the railroad official in Chicago exclaimed, "Why, sir, this is as much as Daniel Webster himself would have charged. We cannot allow such a claim."[33] Stung by the rebuff, Lincoln increased his bill to $5,000, and in January 1857, filed suit against the railroad for that amount. He submitted to the court a written opinion signed by six highly respected lawyers stating that his services in behalf of the railroad were reasonably worth $5,000, and on June 23, 1857, the court awarded him judgment in that amount. After the sheriff was given a writ to collect the judgment, the railroad relented, paying Lincoln $4,800, the amount of the judgment less Lincoln's initial retainer of $200.[34] Since his agreement with Herndon called for equal division of all of their fees, Lincoln promptly gave his partner one-half of the money he received.[35]

The following year, in his famous campaign for the United States Senate against Stephen A. Douglas, Lincoln answered reports (possibly originating with Douglas) that he had once received a fee of $5,000 from the Illinois Central and that this represented public money to which he was not rightfully entitled. In a public statement, Lincoln admitted that he and Herndon had received the fee but insisted that it was fairly earned. He thought that his services in the McLean County tax case were worth $5,000, for he had saved the railroad half a million dollars, but they only wanted to pay him about $500. "I sued them and got the $5,000," Lincoln explained. "This is the whole truth about the fee; and what tendency it has to prove that I received any of the people[']s money, or that I am on very cozy terms with the Railroad Company, I do not comprehend."[36]

In addition to his legal work for and against railroads, Lincoln did important work for businessmen who hoped to take advantage of the advent of the railroads. In 1853, he acted as attorney and adviser for a group of promoters who wanted to start a new town in Logan County, northeast of Sangamon, along the projected route of the new railroad from Springfield to Chicago. Lincoln helped the promoters meet the legal requirements for the establishment of the town, used his influence with the legislature in Springfield to help the town become the new seat of Logan County, and drafted necessary papers. When the promoters told him that they wanted to name the town for him, Lincoln professed modesty—he was later quoted as saying, "I know of nothing named Lincoln that ever amounted to very much," but he was clearly proud of the honor they had bestowed on him. Years later, a story was told that Lincoln was in the new town when lots were first put on sale. He is supposed to have cut a watermelon open with his pocketknife, squeezed the juice into a cup, and poured it on the ground, saying: "I now christen this town site. Its name is 'Lincoln' and soon to be named the permanent capitol of

Logan County."[37] The story may be apocryphal, but Lincoln's important role in the establishment of the town is not. Lincoln did in fact become the new Logan County seat, the site of the Logan County Courthouse, and a prosperous stop on the Chicago and Alton Railroad between Springfield and Chicago. It also acquired a historical distinction that no other town could equal, for it was the first and only town named for America's most famous president before he assumed his high office.[38]

While Illinoisans were encouraging the construction of railroads within the state, investors from the East Coast were eyeing the feasibility of lines that would enter the state from outside. In 1851, under the leadership of a New York investor named Thomas C. Durant and a construction engineer from Connecticut named Henry Farnam, the Michigan Southern and Northern Indiana Railroad started work on a line from Lake Erie across southern Michigan.[39] While this railroad already had links with roads extending all the way to New York, they now wanted to establish connections with Chicago. In the meantime, a group of investors had obtained a charter from the Illinois legislature to build a railroad from the Illinois and Michigan Canal westward across the state to Rock Island, on the Mississippi River opposite Davenport, Iowa. Originally the Rock Island and La Salle Railroad Company, the corporate name was changed in early 1851 to the Chicago and Rock Island Railroad Company.

Around this same time, the Illinois legislature authorized the extension of the line all the way to Chicago.[40] But the Chicago and Rock Island promoters needed construction money and expertise, while the builders of the Michigan Southern and Northern Indiana needed access to Chicago. The solution was to combine forces. Henry Farnam became the contractor in charge of building the Chicago and Rock Island, while his business partner, Joseph E. Sheffield, raised the necessary capital. Eastern investors and engineers joined prominent men in Illinois and Iowa to form the railroad's government. Norman B. Judd, an influential Chicago lawyer, became the secretary and chief counsel, Farnam joined the board of directors, and John B. Jervis of Rome, New York, became the president. Jervis was one of the best-known civil engineers in the country, with a nearly forty-year-long record of engineering work on important canal, railroad, and aqueduct projects, including the Erie Canal, the Croton Aqueduct (which brought the first dependable supply of fresh water into New York City), and the Hudson River and the Michigan Southern and Northern Indiana Railroads.[41] With help from Jervis, Farnam coordinated the construction work that brought the Michigan Southern and Northern Indiana into Chicago, and the Chicago and Rock Island to the Mississippi.[42]

Construction of the Chicago and Rock Island line began in late 1851 and was completed in early 1854. On February 22, 1854, George Washington's birthday, a throng of spectators gathered in Rock Island to watch the first train pull up to the depot, 181 miles from its beginning in Chicago.[43] Henry Farnam addressed the crowd, saying: "Today we witness the nuptials of the Atlantic with the Father of Waters. Tomorrow the people of Rock Island can go to New York the entire distance by railroad, and within the space of forty-two hours."[44] Formal opening of the railroad was celebrated on June 5, 1854, when a special train left the Chicago station with celebrity guests aboard, including former U.S. president Millard Fillmore, Chicago mayor Isaac L. Milliken, the famous American historian George Bancroft, Catharine Maria Sedgwick, one of the most popular novelists of the day, and fifty newspaper editors. There was a banquet at Rock Island, after which the celebrities boarded steamboats chartered by the railroad to take them up the Mississippi to St. Paul and adjoining Fort Snelling and back again to Rock Island. Millard Fillmore declared the excursion an enterprise for which "history had no parallel, and such as no prince could possibly undertake."[45] Catharine Maria Sedgwick marveled at the continuous railroad connections between the East Coast and the Mississippi (her home was in Massachusetts) and extolled them as "the last link in the chain that binds, in *union* and brotherhood, the states from the Atlantic to the Pacific."[46] According to the railroad's principal historian, the celebrity tour and its attendant publicity made the Chicago and Rock Island "the best-known railroad west of the Alleghenies."[47]

Connecting New York with the Mississippi River was an achievement of which the promoters of the Chicago and Rock Island could be proud, but it was not their ultimate goal. They wanted to extend their rails across the Mississippi and had already made plans to do so. On January 17, 1853, the Illinois legislature granted the same promoters a charter for the Railroad Bridge Company and authorized it "to build, maintain and use a railroad bridge over the Mississippi river, or that portion within the jurisdiction of the state of Illinois at or near Rock Island." The company was authorized to connect the bridge "with any railroad, either in the states of Illinois or Iowa, terminating at or near said point," provided only that the bridge would not "materially obstruct or interfere with the free navigation of said river."[48] On February 5 of the same year, the Iowa legislature incorporated the Mississippi and Missouri Railroad Company and authorized it to lay rails across Iowa from the eastern line of the state at Davenport to the western line at Council Bluffs, and to construct and use all bridges necessary to complete that statewide span.[49] Between the Illinois and the Iowa railroads lay an island and a great river that had never been crossed by a railroad bridge—and beyond that a continent of broad plains, towering mountains, long valleys, and sandy deserts leading all the way to the Pacific Ocean.

The dream that a great transcontinental railroad would one day cross the Mississippi and link the Atlantic and Pacific coasts of North America was neither new nor novel in the early 1850s, but it was becoming more urgent and, in the minds of both businessmen and politicians, increasingly inevitable. Americans both North and South endorsed the idea. The proposed line was generally called the Pacific railroad, in recognition of its ultimate destination, although its supporters were unable to agree where the railroad should be built or how it should be paid for. As early as 1845, a New York–based merchant and promoter named Asa Whitney had proposed a route that would lead from the western shore of Lake Michigan across the Great Plains to South Pass in the Rocky Mountains, where it would divide into two branches, one that would connect with San Francisco Bay and the other with the Columbia River. Whitney had petitioned Congress for a massive land grant that would enable him to build a railroad along this route, but political opposition—and charges that he was only trying to enrich himself—killed the idea.[50]

In the South, Jefferson Davis of Mississippi also supported the construction of a Pacific railroad, although his favored route lay along the 32nd parallel of north latitude.[51] Davis believed that the best route would commence at some point on the southern Mississippi, most likely Memphis or New Orleans, and that it would proceed through San Antonio and El Paso in Texas, cross southern New Mexico, and finally emerge on the Pacific coast in southern California. He believed that it should be built by the federal government, for it would provide dependable routes for the transport of the U.S. Army troops that were then defending large sections of the territory recently acquired from Mexico against Indian attacks.[52] After he became secretary of war in early 1853, Davis sent reconnaissance parties west to survey four separate routes. One crossed the northern Great Plains from St. Paul to Puget Sound; a second began at St. Louis and ended at San Francisco; a third ran across Oklahoma into Los Angeles; a fourth followed Davis's favorite route across Texas to San Diego.

When the survey reports were all turned in, they did not show a clear preference for any of the four routes, but Davis still believed that the southern line would eventually be adopted. He was, of course, an ardent southerner, and a champion of slavery. He knew that if slavery in the United States was to expand, it would have to do so toward the west and the south, and a railroad across the land acquired in the Mexican War would bring new settlers to a hot and sultry land where agriculture could thrive, as it had in the Old South.[53] As slaveholders moved into this land, they would organize territories and then states that would help the existing slaveholding states resist northern cries that no more slave states should be admitted to the Union.

In 1853, in order to make sure there would be a good railroad route through the Southwest, the pro-southern President Franklin Pierce sent James Gadsden of South Carolina to Mexico City to purchase additional land from President Antonio López de Santa Anna. Santa Anna was at first reluctant to part with more of his national territory—Mexico had already lost two-fifths of its land to the United States—but the promise of a cash payment if he did and the threat of another war if he didn't persuaded him to reconsider. Signed in late 1853 and ratified in June of 1854, the new treaty between the two countries called for the payment of $10 million to Mexico and the transfer to the United States of additional land in the Mesilla Valley and south of the Gila River.[54] Encompassing close to thirty thousand square miles of land, the so-called Gadsden Purchase was clearly adequate to facilitate the construction of the southern crossing that Davis favored.[55]

But there were other men in other parts of the country who had different ideas. Among these were the financiers and engineers who were furiously building railroads across the upper Middle West, traversing Illinois from north to south and east to west, bringing their iron rails, locomotives, and railroad cars from the eastern seaboard up to the edge of the Mississippi River at a point far north of Jefferson Davis's favored southern crossing. Among these were the builders of the Chicago and Rock Island and the Mississippi and Missouri Railroads. These men not only nurtured dreams of crossing the Mississippi. They also harbored the seeds of a legal and political controversy of monumental proportions. The political controversy would be aired in the legislative halls of the states and the nation, and the legal controversy would be tried before a judge and jury in a Chicago courtroom, where Abraham Lincoln would be called on to participate.

THREE

His Peculiar Ambition

〜

A braham Lincoln did not become a lawyer until he was twenty-eight years old, but his interest in pursuing a legal career began many years before that.[1] In his native Kentucky, his father was troubled by the unsettled condition of the titles to the land he was farming. As Lincoln later recalled, the land laws then were "mysterious relics of feudalism, and titles got into such an almighty mess with these pettifoggin' encumbrances turnin' up at every fresh tradin' with the land, and no one knowin' how to get rid of 'em."[2] Thomas Lincoln's trouble with his land titles was one of the reasons he packed his family up when Abraham was seven years old and took them across the Ohio River into Indiana. Lincoln biographer Michael Burlingame has speculated that the senior Lincoln's troubled land titles may have stimulated his son's interest in law and surveying, both pursuits he followed in his later life.[3]

When he was a teenage boy living on his father's farm at Little Pigeon Creek in Spencer County, Indiana, Lincoln liked to attend trials held before the local justice of the peace and often walked to neighboring towns to watch the legal proceedings there. He attended one murder trial in the town of Boonville, seat of neighboring Warrick County, in which the defense attorney made a particularly effective closing argument. When, years later, that same attorney visited Lincoln in the White House, Lincoln remembered the closing argument he heard as a boy, saying that if he could have made as good a speech his "soul would have been satisfied." From that time forward, as one of his Indiana neighbors later said, "he formed a fixed determination to study the law and make that his profession."[4]

When Lincoln began his political career in Illinois in 1832, he issued a public statement in which he described his goals. "Every man is said to have his peculiar ambition," he wrote. "Whether it be true or not, I can say for one that I have no other so great as that of being truly esteemed of my fellow men, by rendering myself worthy of their esteem."[5] Earning the "esteem" of his fellow men was an admirable ambition for a young man from a poor farming background with only the barest rudiments of a formal education to help him better his condition in life. But how could he achieve it, and what benefit would he derive from it once it was achieved?

He sought initially to win the "esteem" of his fellow men by running for a seat in the Illinois legislature. Achieving elective office and helping other elected officials make laws for his community and state was certainly one way of earning "esteem," and if the laws were good and he conducted himself honorably while helping to make them, he could rightfully feel that he was worthy of the "esteem" he earned. Legislative service, however, was not a full-time occupation, or one he could count on to put food on his table. The Illinois legislature met for only a few weeks each year, and during Lincoln's first term the pay was a modest three dollars for each day of actual attendance, and four dollars for later terms. He had to find an occupation that would enable him to earn a living at the same time that he was pursuing his political career. Musing in later years about his choice of occupation, Lincoln said that he could have become a blacksmith or a lawyer.[6] He could also have been a grocer, an assistant postmaster, a surveyor (all occupations he followed for short periods), or a carpenter and farmer like his father (80 percent of the population of Illinois was then engaged in farming).

Given Lincoln's interest in politics, however, it is not surprising that he chose to become a lawyer. Men who seek public office often pursue legal careers before they enter the political arena. Most legislators (on the state and federal levels), and most presidents of the United States, have begun their professional careers as lawyers. John Adams and Thomas Jefferson were political adversaries in the formative years of the United States, yet both were lawyers in their early lives, as were James Monroe, John Quincy Adams, Andrew Jackson, Martin Van Buren, John Tyler, James K. Polk, Millard Fillmore, Franklin Pierce, and James Buchanan. Only four of the first fifteen presidents were not lawyers. George Washington and James Madison were planters, while William Henry Harrison and Zachary Taylor were professional military officers. (Although Madison was one of the most brilliant legal minds of his time, he never actually became a lawyer).[7] Andrew Jackson was a military hero, but he was a lawyer by profession and even served for a time as a judge. And the great political leaders of Abraham Lincoln's early life—Daniel Webster, John C. Calhoun, and Henry Clay—were all lawyers. By choosing a legal career, Lincoln was following in well-marked footsteps. He could combine politics and law—or law and politics—and with these two occupations pursue his goal of winning the "esteem" of his fellow men.

Lincoln did not become a lawyer until *after* he first ran for public office, but it is not hard to explain why he reversed this usual order. He was virtually penniless when he first came to Illinois, ill clothed, poorly educated, and unsophisticated. But he was a likable young man with an engaging personality, a natural, spontaneous sense of humor, and a gift for public speaking. When he evidenced an interest in running for the Illinois legislature, he found good support among his neighbors and friends in New Salem, the Sangamon County village in which he had made his home. Though his first campaign for the legislature, in 1832, was unsuccessful, his second, in 1834, resulted in his election. But becoming a lawyer requires a long period of purposeful study. Lincoln pursued that study—although it was interrupted from time to time by the necessity of taking jobs that would give him the wherewithal to continue his study—so he did not finally become a practicing lawyer until March 1837.[8]

After he became president, Lincoln told a deputy attorney general in Washington that he was "*a mast-fed* lawyer."[9] It was a backwoodsy way of saying that he was self-educated ("mast" is the accumulation of acorns and other nuts that pigs live on when they roam the forests). Lincoln's "mast," however, consisted of law books that he was able to borrow from neighbors and friends. He read Blackstone's *Commentaries on the Laws of England* (the bible of American legal studies in that time) and Chitty's *Pleadings*, an essential guide to legal procedure. It is probable that he also read Story's *Equity Jurisprudence* and Kent's *Commentaries on American Law*, treatises that, with Blackstone and Chitty, were considered indispensable guides to American law.[10] He often walked from New Salem into nearby Springfield to borrow books from John Todd Stuart, a prominent Springfield lawyer he met while serving in the Black Hawk War.[11] He held the books in front of him as he returned home, reading them as he went, and when he got there he continued to read them, often in the shade of a white oak tree.[12] His neighbors thought it odd to see a young man with practically no formal education spending so much time with books. When a neighbor who had employed him to work as a surveyor saw the young man sitting barefoot on top of a woodpile with his head in a book, he asked, "Abe, what are you studying?" "Law," Abe replied. "Great God Almighty," the man said as he walked away.[13]

In Illinois in the 1830s, choosing a career in the law was an honorable goal, and not one that many young men would scoff at. Much of the work of lawyers was performed in courthouses, and even in country villages courthouses were important places. They were the headquarters of local government, forums in which the public's official business was administered in view of all who cared to see. If men and women wanted to know how the law affected their own lives, they could make their way to the courthouse in the center of the nearest town and find a seat on one of the benches provided for spectators. They could watch the lawyers assemble inside the rail (or bar) that separated them and the audience, listen to the judge rap his gavel for order, and watch the drama of real life unfold before them. There were crimes to be tried, and criminals to be punished. There were neighbors' quarrels to be aired, and property disputes to be settled; debts to be proved and collected; slanderous attacks on honor and reputation to be avenged (or assuaged); domestic squabbles to be aired. It was not surprising that courts attracted so much interest in Lincoln's time, or that a man like Lincoln, who enjoyed the attention that was focused on him when he spoke in public, should seek a place in them. The courts were theaters of a sort; the judge and the lawyers and the witnesses were the actors onstage, the spectators the audience.

Lincoln knew, of course, that many people had a low opinion of lawyers—or at least *professed* to have a low opinion of them. Lawyers had always been ridiculed for their real (or supposed) deviousness and their underhanded dealings with clients and the general public. In notes for a lecture he prepared later in his life, Lincoln observed that there was "a vague popular belief that lawyers are necessarily dishonest." But he thought the impression was "vague, because when we consider to what extent confidence, and honors are reposed in, and conferred upon lawyers by the people, it appears improbable that their impression of dishonesty, is very distinct and vivid."[14] Lincoln was an honest man—honest to his core—and he had no intention of changing his ways after he became a lawyer.

Shortly after he was admitted to the bar, Lincoln joined a partnership in Springfield with John Todd Stuart, who had lent him books when he was studying law. Stuart was less than two years older than Lincoln, but he was already a veteran lawyer and an experienced politician. He spent much of 1838 campaigning against Stephen A. Douglas for a seat in Congress (Stuart won by a narrow margin) while Lincoln tended to the firm's legal business in Springfield.[15] In 1841, Stuart and Lincoln ended their partnership on amicable terms and Lincoln became the junior partner to Stephen T. Logan, a former judge who was nine years his senior and widely considered the best all-round lawyer in Sangamon County, if not in the state.[16] This partnership continued until 1844, when Logan decided to bring his son into his office in place of Lincoln and Lincoln formed his third and final partnership with William H. (Billy) Herndon, a young man who had read law with Lincoln and Logan and just been admitted to the bar. The partnership of Lincoln and Herndon continued until Lincoln went to Washington as president in 1861. In that time, Herndon and Lincoln handled more than 3,200 cases.[17] In the total of nearly twenty-five years that Lincoln practiced law, he took part in more than 5,200 cases and participated in nearly 500 nonlitigation activities.[18]

Yet even with such a busy schedule, Lincoln still found the time and energy to explore other fields. From his boyhood days, he read the Bible avidly, spent long hours devouring biographies of famous men, and savored poetry.[19] His oldest son, Robert Todd Lincoln, later remembered that he hardly ever saw his father "without a book in his hand."[20] In addition to his reading, Lincoln exercised his mind by studying Euclidian geometry. When he was traveling, he carried a book of Euclid with him so he could spend idle moments studying the exercises until, as Billy Herndon later remembered, "he could with ease demonstrate all the propositions in the six books."[21] Logic was always one of his strong suits, both in his legal practice and in politics, and he was determined to maintain, even strengthen it.

And he avidly studied the law applicable to his cases. Hiram Beckwith, a lawyer who often saw Lincoln, thought that "few, if any, practitioners were better, if as well, grounded in the elementary principles of the law. His knowledge of these, as well as the very reason for them, was so well mastered that he seemed to apply them to individual 'cases' as if by intuition." Beckwith believed that a mere "case lawyer" would have had "little chance" with Lincoln.[22]

Lincoln's ability to master difficult legal principles was often demonstrated in the Illinois Supreme Court, where in the course of his career he and his partners handled more than four hundred cases.[23] Because effective appeals require careful research in legal precedents and strong, logical arguments, attorneys throughout the state sought Lincoln's services when they had cases they wanted to appeal to the Illinois Supreme Court. Lincoln handled the appeals of more than two hundred cases that had been conducted by other lawyers at the trial court level, a fact that, in legal historian Mark Steiner's estimation, showed that he was a "lawyer's lawyer."[24] When Lincoln was preparing a case for argument in the supreme court, he often absented himself from other work for as long as a week or two. During that time, he would typically be found in his office or in the library of the supreme court hard at work.[25]

Lincoln was also attorney of record in several cases that were appealed to the United States Supreme Court. In four cases he did not present the oral arguments, but in one he personally argued the case before Chief Justice Roger Taney and the associate justices.[26] This was in March 1849, when Lincoln was serving his first and only term as a member of the U.S. House of Representatives. Herndon once heard Lincoln argue a particular case in the Illinois Supreme Court. It was, he says, "argued extremely well—it was logical— eloquent. In making his argument he referred to the history of the law, a useless part as I then thought, but know better now. After the speech was through and Lincoln had come into the law library room where the lawyers tell stories and prepare their cases I said, 'Lincoln, why did you go so far back in the history of the law as applicable to this case' & to which he instantly replied, 'I dare not trust this case on presumptions that this court knows all things. I argued the case on the presumption that the court did not know anything,' and in this he was right for our supreme court at that time did not know everything. Lincoln gained this very case by that very history he was so careful to state fully."[27]

Lincoln's work as a *nisi prius* (trial) lawyer gave him a reputation among the common people of Illinois. He was effective in the trial courtroom, where he could engage in legal arguments with opposing counsel, examine friendly witnesses, cross-examine unfriendly witnesses, and, at the end of a trial, address the jury. Leonard Swett, an attorney who appeared in many trials both with and against Lincoln, had abundant opportunity to watch him in action. "As he entered the Trial," Swett said, "where most lawyers object, he would say he 'reckoned' it would be fair to let this in or that and sometimes, where his adversary could not quite prove what Lincoln Knew to be the truth he would say he 'reckoned' it would be fair to admit the truth to be so & so[.] [W]hen he did object to the Court after he heard his objection answered he would [then] say 'Well I reckon I must be wrong.['] Now about the time he had practiced this ¾ through the case if his adversary didn[']t understand him he would wake up in a few minutes finding that he had [secured] the Greeks too late and woke up to find himself beat. . . . Any man who took Lincoln for a simple minded man would very soon wake [up] with his back in a ditch."[28]

In the trial courtroom, Lincoln was, as Henry Clay Whitney, a lawyer who often tried cases with him, later remembered, "entirely calm, unexcited, imperturbable; you could not discern by his manner that he had the slightest tinge either of trepidation or enthusiasm, but he remained inflexible and stoical to the last."[29] Whitney once tried an important railroad case with Lincoln. While listening to the arguments of the opposing lawyer, Whitney began to get alarmed and spoke to Lincoln. Lincoln remained "inflexibly calm and serene, and merely remarked: 'All that is very easily answered,' and when his time came, he blew away what seemed to me as almost an unanswerable argument as easily as a beer-drinker blows off the froth from his foaming tankard."[30]

Much of Lincoln's trial work was performed in Illinois's Eighth Judicial Circuit, a sprawling expanse of prairie that stretched from Sangamon County clear to the Indiana border. Samuel Treat, later a United States district judge, presided over the circuit until 1848; thereafter David Davis of Bloomington (whom Lincoln later appointed to the United States Supreme Court) was the presiding judge. The courts of the Eighth Judicial Circuit, like the other circuit courts of Illinois, were courts of general jurisdiction in both criminal and civil cases.[31] In them, most of the important legal disputes in the state were brought to trial and resolved. Whitney left revealing recollections of life on the Eighth Judicial Circuit late in Lincoln's tenure on it. The county seats were located at "small and primitive villages," Whitney said, and the business of the court was "meager and uninteresting." But when the judge and the company of lawyers who traveled with him were in town, there was a sense of excitement among the people. Whitney remembered that "the local belles came in to see and be seen" and that the tavern in the center of the town was "replete with bustle, business, energy, hilarity, novelty, irony, sarcasm, excitement and eloquence."[32] Because newspapers were scarce in country villages, the courthouse doubled as a kind of news center, where eyewitness reports of interesting events were exchanged, gossip circulated, and funny stories were told and retold. Lincoln was a gifted storyteller, with a seemingly endless supply of amusing yarns that people loved to hear. He told some of his stories in court—where even the judge enjoyed his efforts to enliven otherwise desultory proceedings—but most in the tavern, where the lawyers gathered after the court's business for the day was concluded.

The lawyers who traveled the Eighth Judicial Circuit commonly slept two in a bed, and there were as many as three or four beds in each room. At mealtime, "the Judge, lawyers, suitors, jurors, witnesses, court officers, and prisoners out on bail, all ate together and carried on a running conversation all along the line of a long dining-room." When one court session was through, the judge and all the lawyers "would tumble into a farmer's wagon, or a carryall, or a succession of buggies, and trundle off across the prairie, to another court; stopping by the way at a farm-house for a chance dinner."[33]

Before the late 1850s, when railroad travel became possible through much of Illinois, the lawyers made their way from town to town in buggies or stagecoaches, or on horseback. The roads were hot and dusty in the summer and muddy when it rained. Lincoln traveled the Eighth Judicial Circuit twice a year, first in the spring and then in the fall. The distance was considerable: more than four hundred miles before 1853 and more than two hundred thereafter.[34] Many lawyers covered only part of the circuit, preferring to stay close to home and declining to follow the judge when his duties carried him farther away. Lincoln, Swett, and Judge Davis were resolute in traveling the entire circuit. If they were within reasonable traveling distance of their homes, the judge and the other attorneys would typically go home to visit their wives and families on Sundays. Lincoln usually spent his Sundays at the country tavern and only went home at the end of the circuit or term of the court.[35]

Lincoln derived many benefits from his circuit court work. It brought him into contact with scores of lawyers who shared his interest in the cause of justice, in the effective presentation of arguments, and in the great political causes then stirring in Illinois and the nation. In county after county, he formed personal and legal friendships that endured over the years and, in time, matured into political alliances. He honed his debating skills in the county courts, trying hundreds of cases of varying types and seriousness, both civil and criminal. He learned how to communicate effectively with juries, to speak to them in words that would convince them that he was on the side of truth and justice and that his clients should prevail because *justice should prevail.*[36]

Many of the cases that Lincoln tried on the Eighth Judicial Circuit were modest disputes between people of modest means—what one commentator has dismissed as "grubby" cases.[37] As Whitney remembered, they often centered on "who was the owner of a litter of pigs, or which party was to blame for the loss of a flock of sheep, by foot rot; or whether some irascible spirit was justified in avowing that his enemy had committed perjury." Yet Lincoln "gave as earnest attention to such matters, as later, he gave to affairs of state."[38] The ownership of pigs, and liability for the loss of a flock of sheep, were legal questions and, for Lincoln, matters of substance. They were as important in the lives of ordinary people as clear title to landed estates, or incomes from bonds and debentures, in the lives of the rich and privileged.

As Lincoln's reputation grew, he began to get opportunities to leave the Eighth Circuit and go elsewhere to practice his profession—to places where more money could be made and, if possible, more fame and recognition could be won. Lincoln once received an invitation from a prominent Chicago attorney named Grant Goodrich to join his law practice in the northern city. He declined, explaining that "he would rather go around the Circuit ... than to sit down & die in Chicago."[39] He would have made a lot of money in Chicago, but his goal was never to make a lot of money. He did well enough in the country courts of central Illinois, doing his bit to see to it that rights were respected and wrongs remedied, and he enjoyed the work there.

Years later, it would become evident that Lincoln applied many of the rules that governed his legal practice to his political life. During the Civil War, he told Schuyler Colfax (then Speaker of the House of Representatives and later vice president of the United States) that he "habitually studied the opposite side of every disputed question, of every law case, of every political issue, more exhaustively, if possible, than his own side. He said that the result had been, that in all his long practice at the bar he had never once been surprised in court by the strength of the adversary's case—often finding it much weaker than he had feared."[40]

In his political life, Lincoln was often referred to as "Honest Abe." It was a good nickname for a politician who sought the confidence of voters and ultimately was rewarded with the highest office in their power to confer. In fact, however, the nickname was earned in Lincoln's early business life—his neighbors called him that when he was keeping store in New Salem—and it was burnished during his years as a lawyer.[41] Mrs. Lincoln once said that her husband was "almost a monomaniac on the subject of honesty,"[42] and those who knew how he practiced law testified to his devotion to factual truthfulness and integrity. Judge Thomas Drummond, who presided over the U.S. District Court in Illinois, said that Lincoln always tried his cases "fairly and honestly. He never intentionally misrepresented the evidence of a witness or the argument of an opponent. He met both squarely, and if he could not explain the one or answer the other, substantially admitted it. He never misstated the law, according to his own intelligent view of it."[43] And when Lincoln didn't know the answer to a particular legal question, he was willing to admit it.[44] Henry Clay Whitney recalled once asking him if, in an attachment suit, the service of the writ of attachment on the defendant had the force of a summons. "He cast his eyes up to the ceiling for nearly a minute," Whitney said, and then roguishly said: 'Damfino.'"[45]

Perhaps because of his honesty, evaluations of Lincoln's legal ability varied over the years, depending on the men who were judging him and their personal knowledge of his practice. Judge Drummond admitted that Lincoln's speaking voice was "by no means pleasant, and, indeed, when excited, in its shrill tones, sometimes almost disagreeable." He thought that Lincoln lacked the "personal graces of the orator" and did not outwardly seem to have "superiority of intellect" or "quickness of perception." But Drummond believed that Lincoln's "mind was so vigorous, his comprehension so exact and clear, and his judgment so sure, that he easily mastered the intricacies of his profession."[46] Isaac N. Arnold, a prominent Chicago lawyer who tried some cases (and argued some appeals) with Lincoln, thought that Lincoln "was, upon the whole, the strongest jury law-yer in the state. He had the ability to perceive with almost intuitive quickness the decisive point in the case. In the examination and cross-examination of a witness he had no equal. He could compel a witness to tell the truth when he meant to lie, and if a witness lied he rarely escaped exposure under Lincoln's cross-examination."[47]

David Davis, who presided over more of Lincoln's trials than any other judge, left conflicting assessments of Lincoln's legal ability. In a eulogy he delivered to a bar association in Indianapolis after Lincoln's assassination, Davis described Lincoln's mind as "logical and direct." "In all the elements that constituted a lawyer," Davis said then, "he had few equals."[48] In an interview with Billy Herndon two years later, however, Davis was more critical. He affirmed then that Lincoln was "eminently just," that he "felt for the poor," and that he was "conscientious."[49] But he thought that Lincoln had "no manag-ing faculty nor organizing power" and that "a child could conform to the simple and technical rules, the means and the modes of getting at justice, better than he."[50]

Herndon also left conflicting opinions of his partner. He thought that Lincoln "knew nothing of the rules of evidence, of pleading, or practice, as laid down in the text-books, and seemed to care noth-ing about them." But "he had a keen sense of justice, and struggled for it, throwing aside forms, methods, and rules, until it appeared pure as a ray of light flashing through a fog-bank."[51] Interestingly, Herndon said that Lincoln "was greatest in my opinion as a lawyer in the Supreme Court of Illinois." Appellate arguments are generally considered more demanding than jury trials; they demand a more confident command of legal authorities and a stronger application of logic. When a case is on appeal, it has already been lost in the trial court, and the attorneys advancing the appeal are arguing that the trial judge made some legal error in the proceedings. Herndon, however, believed that Lincoln was effective in the Illinois Supreme Court because he had the time to carefully prepare his cases and present his arguments to the justices.[52]

In 1859, a juror in a case that Lincoln lost at the trial level (the case was ultimately reversed on appeal) put his impressions of

Lincoln in print. "Lincoln tries a suit well," the juror said. "By his genial spirit he keeps the Court, the jury and the opposite counsel in good humor, and sometimes by a comical remark, or a clever joke, upsets the dignity of the Court. He never makes a big fight over a small or immaterial point, but frankly admits much, though never enough to damage his case. In this, he differs much from little lawyers, who adhere with unyielding pertinacity to trifles, and make their greatest efforts at nothing."[53] "Lincoln is not a *great* lawyer," the juror continued, "though he is a *good* one."[54]

Lincoln's own assessment of his legal abilities was characteristically modest. In his notes for a law lecture he said: "I am not an accomplished lawyer. I find quite as much material for a lecture in those points wherein I have failed, as in those wherein I have been moderately successful."[55] But Lincoln's modesty in speaking of his legal abilities, as in so much of the rest of his life, concealed a vast reservoir of confidence. He did believe in his ability to try cases as well, perhaps, as any other attorney in central Illinois—his success with juries attested to that. He did believe in his ability to argue cases in the Supreme Court of Illinois—the number of Supreme Court cases other attorneys referred to him attested to that. And he did believe in his ability to present effective arguments in the court of public opinion, in his home state and ultimately in the United States. His election to the presidency in 1861 attested to that.

At the end of 1860 and in the early days of 1861, Lincoln, his wife, and their children made preparations to move to Washington, D.C., where he was to enter on his new duties as president. He rented out his family house, gathered his personal possessions together (they were never very extensive), and made a last visit to the plain upstairs office he and Herndon shared in Springfield. After going over the office books and giving Herndon some instructions about cases they had that were still pending, he stretched himself out on the old sofa that occupied one wall of the room. He lay for some moments, looking at the ceiling, then spoke. "Billy, how long have we been together?"

"Over sixteen years," Herndon answered.

"We've never had a cross word during all that time, have we?"

"No," Herndon answered, "we have not."

Lincoln then mused about the early years of their partnership. He told Herndon about some of the lawyers who had sought to gain entrance into Lincoln's law practice, edging out Herndon, but he had resisted all of them. "I never saw him in a more cheerful mood," Herndon remembered years later.

Then Lincoln made what Herndon called a "strange request." He asked that the signboard that hung on rusty hinges at the base of the stairs leading up to their office remain in place after he was gone. "Let it hang there undisturbed," he said. "Give our clients to understand that the election of a President makes no change in the firm of Lincoln and Herndon. If I live I'm coming back some time, and then we'll go right on practicing law as if nothing had ever happened."[56]

Soon after, Lincoln left for Washington, while Herndon remained in Springfield. In the White House, Lincoln grew from a politician into a statesman. He became the commander in chief of the military forces of the nation during the most terrible war known in its history. He became the "great emancipator" of the slaves. He delivered speeches that are still considered the greatest public utterances ever made in American history. Ultimately, when an assassin's bullet entered his brain, he became a martyr. He returned to Illinois in a coffin, but his friends and colleagues in Springfield remembered what he had been before he left: a lawyer who wanted to return to practice law in the firm of Lincoln and Herndon.

FOUR

The First Bridge over the First River

≋

I t is hard to imagine a time when there were no bridges over the
Mississippi River. Great steel and stone and concrete structures
now span the waterway from north to south, providing smooth
and easy passage for pedestrians, bicyclists, automobiles, trucks, railroads, aqueducts, pipelines, electric cables, and virtually anything
else that human beings in the modern age need to move from one
place to another. Bridges are an essential feature of life in a civilized
society, but they are hardly new, or unique to civilization. If they were
not made by nature itself—a broken tree limb fallen across a stream
or stones scattered in a river—they were fashioned by early man out
of tree trunks or planks, dragged to the nearest bank of a stream
that had to be crossed and thrown across the water to the other side.
The greatest bridge builders of early times, the Romans, built their
spans of arched stone according to designs that would endure for
centuries, even millennia. Other bridges were made out of combinations of masonry and wood that lasted until they had to be replaced
with more durable materials. Bridges were built by the Native Americans according to their own time-honored designs. When the first
Europeans came to America, they constructed bridges that resem-
bled Old World models but were adapted to New World conditions.
They were structures capable of standing up to wet climates, severe
winters, and searing summers, but also resistant to the ever-present
danger of fires.

One of the first bridges in colonial America was built across the
Neponset River in Massachusetts in 1634 by a man named Israel

Stoughton.[1] Another bridge followed in 1654, built by Richard Thurley over the Newbury River between the towns of Rowley and Newbury. Having constructed the bridge with his own resources, Thurley
was authorized by the General Court of Massachusetts to collect tolls
from all who passed over the span.[2]

Other bridges soon followed along the Atlantic seaboard from
New England south through New York and Pennsylvania, across
streams that emptied into Chesapeake Bay, across rivers that flowed
down from the Appalachians to the ocean. It would, however, be a
long while before any attempts were made to build bridges across
rivers west of those mountains.

Bridge technology had made great strides by the time the Railroad Bridge Company began work on the Rock Island Bridge in
1853. Still, the challenges the company faced were not altogether
different from those of earlier builders—with one notable excep-
tion. There were natural obstacles, of course: the river itself, the
banks on either side, the often treacherous flow of the water between
them, the thick ice that clogged the northern rivers in the coldest
months of the year, the low water levels that in dry seasons made the
rivers virtually impassable, and the dangerous rocks and sandbars
that lurked here and there beneath the waters. There were legal
obstacles, too: authorizations that had to be obtained from legislative bodies at the state and national levels, property that had to be
acquired, lawsuits that had to be anticipated and defended against.
A third obstacle was of a different kind, for there was a powerful
public official in Washington who did not want the bridge across
the Mississippi to be built, or if it had to be built, did not want it to
be built at Rock Island. He was the strong-willed U.S. secretary of
war, Jefferson Davis, who claimed authority over Rock Island and
was determined to exercise it.

Rock Island is situated in the Upper Mississippi at a place where
the river suspends its north-south course and follows a generally
east-to-west course for a distance of about forty miles.[3] It lies a short
distance above the mouth of the Rock River, a substantial stream
that rises in southeast Wisconsin and flows for about three hundred
miles through Wisconsin and northern Illinois before joining the

Mississippi. The island measures about two and a half miles from east to west and three-quarters of a mile from north to south. Its land area of a thousand acres is underlain with limestone and in historic times was heavily wooded. As the crow flies, the island is not quite 200 miles west of Chicago and 286 miles northeast of St. Louis. When steamboats still plied the river, the distance from St. Louis was measured in "river miles" at exactly 347.[4]

The main channel of the Mississippi marks the northern edge of Rock Island, flowing in an archlike course from the eastern to the western end of the island. In the early days of steamboating, the treacherous Rock Island Rapids extended for about fourteen miles above the island, roiling the great waterway with winding currents and treacherous chains of rocks that challenged the best of the river pilots. The island itself belongs to Illinois, while the opposite side of the river is Iowa (a U.S. territory before December 28, 1846, and a state thereafter). Before the bridge was built, the river at Rock Island was about 1,400 feet wide and, at low water, six to eight feet deep.[5] It was, in fact, the narrowest point on the river for a hundred miles in either direction. The banks on either side were rock-bound and elevated well above the usual flood levels of the river.[6] On the south side of the island, a narrower stream (sometimes called the back or south channel but more formally known as Sylvan Slough) separates the island from the Illinois mainland. The land slopes on both sides of the river to bluffs that rise high above the water and command fine views of the river channel and its banks.

From the middle of the eighteenth century, the Sauk and Meskwaki (Fox) Indians maintained a village called Saukenuk a short distance south of the island near the mouth of the Rock River. Black Hawk, the Sauk leader who led a portion of his people in the short-lived Black Hawk War of 1832, left an evocative description of Rock Island:

This was the best one on the Mississippi, and had long been the resort of our young people during the summer. It was our garden, like the white people have near their big villages, which supplied us with strawberries, blackberries, gooseberries, plums, apples and nuts of different kinds. Being situated at the foot of the rapids its waters supplied us with the finest fish. In my early life I spent many happy days on this island. A good spirit had charge of it, which lived in a cave in the rocks immediately under the place where the fort now stands. This guardian spirit has often been seen by our people. It was white, with large wings like a swan's, but ten times larger. We were particular not to make much noise in that part of the island which it inhabited, for fear of disturbing it. But the noise of the fort has since driven it away, and no doubt a bad spirit has taken its place.[7]

The fort that Black Hawk referred to was Fort Armstrong, a large quadrangle of hewn logs that crowned a thirty-foot limestone cliff at the western tip of Rock Island. In 1829, a government agent at the fort ordered the Indians in the region to relocate to the Iowa side of the river because whites wanted to occupy the Illinois shore. Legal title to the land was tangled by a bitterly disputed treaty with the Indians. When Black Hawk stubbornly refused to give up his home-land, a short but bloody "war" broke out. Fort Armstrong became the headquarters of the army operations during the five-month-long conflict, although the fighting ranged over northern Illinois and into southwestern Wisconsin.[8] White casualties numbered about seventy-seven, but Indian deaths were estimated as high as six hundred. Black Hawk was ultimately captured and his followers sent across the river.

Before the fighting ended, some later-famous names were associated with the Black Hawk War. General Winfield Scott, who was to serve as Lincoln's general in chief at the outset of the Civil War, went to Fort Armstrong to take command of the troops. Colonel Zachary Taylor, elected president of the United States on the Whig ticket that Lincoln supported in 1848, was a commander in the area; and Second Lieutenant Jefferson Davis, a recent West Point graduate then serving under Taylor, was charged with the duty of capturing Black Hawk and taking him on a Mississippi riverboat to Jefferson Barracks near St. Louis.[9]

Lincoln also had a brief role in the Black Hawk War, for he was one of sixty-eight men from the village of New Salem who responded to Illinois governor John Reynolds's call for militiamen to join the fight against Black Hawk.[10] Officially mustered into service at Fort Armstrong, the twenty-three-year-old Lincoln was surprised when his fellow volunteers elected him captain of their company. It was his first electoral victory, and in later years he said it gave him "more pleasure than any I have had since."[11] Lincoln saw no combat, although he and his men discovered some casualties of the war: dead bodies that had been scalped, decapitated, and mutilated by the Indians.[12] His military service ended in July 1832, when he was honorably discharged.[13]

Lincoln was proud of his service, though in later years he joked about it, saying "I had a good many bloody struggles with the musquetoes; and, although I never fainted from loss of blood, I can truly say I was often very hungry."[14] Lincoln also made some valuable friendships during the conflict. It was there that he met several lawyers who were later active in Whig Party politics.[15] John Todd Stuart was the most prominent of the group. He was the polished Springfield attorney who lent Lincoln the law books he used in his early legal studies and, in 1837, became his first law partner.[16]

The year after Lincoln left Fort Armstrong, an assistant army surgeon named John Emerson was assigned there from his home in St. Louis. A Missouri slave Emerson had purchased in St. Louis also accompanied him to Fort Armstrong, where he worked as a valet for the surgeon and three other officers.[17] Illinois was forbidden by the Northwest Ordinance to permit slavery within its borders, so, in theory if not in practice, Emerson's slave, who later became known as Dred Scott, was a free man.[18] From Fort Armstrong, Dr. Emerson took Scott to Fort Snelling, which stood on land—then part of the Wisconsin Territory—acquired as part of the Louisiana Purchase. Slavery there was forbidden by federal law (in the Missouri Compromise of 1820, Congress had forbidden slavery in all U.S. territories north of 36° 30', the southern border of Missouri).[19] But Dred Scott later returned with his master to Missouri, where, in 1846, he filed a lawsuit to secure his freedom on the ground that he had lived as a free man at both Rock Island and Fort Snelling. Scott's lawsuit culminated nine years later in the United States Supreme Court's 1857 decision in *Dred Scott v. Sandford*, in which Chief Justice Roger Taney denied Scott's bid for freedom and declared that when the Constitution was adopted, persons of African descent were deemed to be so far inferior that they "had no rights which the white man was bound to respect."[20] Lincoln was outraged by the *Dred Scott* decision, which became one of the principal issues in his campaign for the Senate against Stephen A. Douglas in 1858. Though he lost the senatorial election that year, the outrage that he expressed in his debates with Douglas raised his political profile to a national level and did much to help him win the presidency two years later.[21]

Years before the Supreme Court's decision in *Dred Scott v. Sandford*, the federal government had decided that it no longer needed to protect the area around Rock Island from Indian attack and ordered the army to leave Fort Armstrong. The troops withdrew in 1836, Dr. Emerson and Dred Scott going with them. Not long after the army withdrawal, a town began forming on the mainland southwest of Rock Island. First called Stephenson, it was known as Rock Island City, or just Rock Island, after 1841. In 1848, Secretary of War William L. Marcy wrote Secretary of the Treasury Robert J. Walker that the land Fort Armstrong had occupied "is no longer required for military purposes, and it is therefore hereby relinquished, and placed at the disposal of the department which has charge of the public lands."[22] Then, on August 4, 1852, President Millard Fillmore signed a federal law that granted rights-of-way to companies that wanted to build railroads on public lands. These were granted to "all rail and plank road, or Macadamized turnpike companies, that are now or that may be chartered within ten years hereafter." The rights-of-way went "over and through any of the public lands of the United States, over which any rail or plank road or Macadamized turnpikes are or may be authorized by an act of the legislature of the respective States in which public lands may be situated," but only if the public lands were unsurveyed and "held for private entry and sale." Lands that were already being used, or reserved for government use, would not be included.[23]

The law was clearly an effort by Congress to avoid taking a stand on its own constitutional power to subsidize the building of railroads.

Congress said, in effect, that it would offer its aid to the construction of rail and other roads, but only when the state legislatures first acted to create corporations and authorize them to build the roads. Not surprisingly, the Illinois legislature was happy to cooperate with the congressional direction. On January 17, 1853, it incorporated the Railroad Bridge Company and gave it power to build a railroad bridge over the Mississippi River at or near Rock Island, provided it did not "materially obstruct" the free navigation of the river.[24] The state legislation went on to authorize the Railroad Bridge Company to connect the bridge with any railroad in the states of Illinois or Iowa terminating at or near the same point.[25]

Congress's qualms about directly aiding railroad construction had their roots in the constitutional doctrine of enumerated powers. Article I, section 8, of the Constitution sets forth a list of powers that are granted to Congress (called "enumerated powers"), and the Tenth Amendment specifically provides that the "powers not delegated to the United States by the Constitution, nor prohibited by it to the States, are reserved to the States respectively, or to the people." All constitutional scholars agree that the doctrine of enumerated powers limits what Congress can properly do, though there has always been a difference of opinion about how the doctrine should be applied. Alexander Hamilton and Thomas Jefferson quarreled over the issue in the earliest days of the republic, and their quarrels have been kept alive in subsequent generations. In 1819, the great Chief Justice John Marshall stated that the federal government "is acknowledged by all, to be one of enumerated powers," and the principle "that it can exercise only the powers granted to it...is now universally admitted."[26] But Marshall did not believe that the absence of a specific enumerated power strictly foreclosed federal action, because the list of enumerated powers in Article I, section 8, includes the power "to make all laws which shall be necessary and proper for carrying into execution" other federal powers. Under this clause (called the Necessary and Proper Clause) Marshall said that "the sound construction of the Constitution must allow to the national legislature that discretion with respect to the means by which the powers it confers are to be carried into execution which will enable that body to perform the high duties assigned to it in the manner most beneficial to the people."[27]

The issue arose in 1819 in the landmark case of *McCulloch v. Maryland*, in which the Supreme Court upheld the constitutionality of the Bank of the United States. The bank had been chartered by Congress despite the absence of any power to create a bank in Article I, section 8's list of enumerated powers. But the enumerated powers did include the power to tax and spend, to borrow money, to regulate commerce, to declare and conduct war, and to raise and support armies and navies. In the view of Marshall and the other justices of the Supreme Court (the decision in *McCulloch* was unanimous), the Bank of the United States was a legitimate means by which Congress could exercise its other enumerated powers. "Let the end be legitimate," Marshall said, "let it be within the scope of the Constitution, and all means which are appropriate, which are plainly adapted to that end, which are not prohibited, but consistent with the letter and spirit of the Constitution, are constitutional."[28]

Of course, the Constitution's list of enumerated powers did not include a power to build railroads, or even to *authorize* or *aid* the building of railroads. It did, however, include powers to regulate commerce among the several states, to establish post roads, to raise and support armies, and to provide and maintain a navy. Under John Marshall's broad interpretation of the Necessary and Proper Clause, it could be argued that granting rights-of-way for railroads, or even aiding in the financing of railroads, was a valid exercise of congressional power over post roads and the armies and navies of the nation, and for regulating interstate commerce. If roads are necessary and proper to facilitate the delivery of the U.S. mail, they are equally necessary and proper to facilitate the movement of military forces and the equipment necessary to support them. Railroads can contribute as much to the regulation of interstate commerce as equestrian or wagon roads, and nobody seriously argued that a railroad was not a form of a "road" for purposes of the Constitution.

The constitutional issues played a part in an important series of Supreme Court decisions announced before and during the construction of the Rock Island Bridge. In 1847, the legislature of

Virginia authorized the Wheeling and Belmont Bridge Company, a Virginia corporation, to build a large bridge across the main channel of the Ohio River from Wheeling in Virginia (now West Virginia) to an island in the middle of the river. Another smaller span, called the Bridgeport Bridge, had been built in the 1830s across the "back channel" that separated the island from the Ohio mainland and was still standing. The large bridge—called the Wheeling and Belmont Bridge—was a suspension bridge that, together with the smaller span, was intended to connect two stretches of the National Road, an important highway that began in Maryland and would eventually extend through Ohio, Indiana, and Illinois to Missouri. It was designed for foot and wagon traffic, not railroad cars, although it was believed that if rails were laid across it horses could safely pull individual cars from one end to the other. At its highest point, the bed of the bridge rose ninety-three and a half feet above the low water level of the river.[29] Completed in 1849, the Wheeling Bridge was the first bridge to carry land traffic over a navigable western waterway. It was a notable engineering accomplishment and immediately recognized as the forerunner of similar bridges that would in the future be built for railroad use.[30]

Steamboat interests upriver in Pittsburgh were outraged by the Wheeling Bridge. They complained that it was an obstacle to navigation on the river, for at high water levels steamboats with very high chimneys could not pass under it without striking the bridge bed. They also argued that it would seriously harm their very profitable shipping business (Pittsburgh was then a major entrepôt for trans-shipments between the Northeast and the West). Their arguments persuaded the State of Pennsylvania to bring suit in the U.S. Supreme Court to have the bridge abated as a public nuisance. Edwin M. Stanton, a prominent Pittsburgh attorney who was to become Lincoln's secretary of war during the Civil War, was Pennsylvania's principal attorney in the suit.

On February 6, 1852, after preliminary orders establishing jurisdiction and appointing a commissioner to gather evidence, the Supreme Court announced its decision in *Pennsylvania v. Wheeling and Belmont Bridge Company*. Justice John McLean, who was later to preside over the Chicago trial in which Lincoln argued the legality of the Rock Island Bridge, spoke for the Court's majority, announcing that the bridge was an obstruction to navigation because it was not high enough to permit steamboats to pass under it without damaging their chimneys.[31] He said that the bridge would have to be raised to a height of 111 feet above the low water or, failing that, would have to be torn down.[32] Chief Justice Roger Taney of Maryland and Associate Justice Peter Daniel of Virginia both dissented from the decision. Taney believed that the inconvenience to river commerce caused by the bridge was "small and occasional,"[33] while Daniel thought that the railroads had an "obvious superiority" over steamboats in meeting the transportation needs of the public.[34] Stunned by the High Court's decision, the owners of the Wheeling Bridge appealed to both the Virginia legislature and Congress for relief. After some confusion, Congress responded with legislation declaring both the Wheeling and the Bridgeport Bridges "lawful structures in their present position and elevation" and requiring all boats on the river to regulate their use "so as not to interfere with the elevation and construction of said bridges."[35]

Then, on May 17, 1854, the Wheeling Bridge blew down in a terrific windstorm.[36] When the bridge owners rebuilt it to the same specifications, the Pennsylvania interests sought a new Supreme Court order requiring that it be torn down. This time the Court decided that it did not have to be abated. Speaking for the majority on April 21, 1856, Justice Samuel Nelson of New York said that the bridge was still "an obstruction in fact," but "not so in the contemplation of law." Congress's legislation meant that the bridge now existed under "the concurrent powers" of both the state of Virginia, which had authorized its construction, and the United States, which had declared it legal.[37] The bridge could stand.

The situations of the Wheeling Bridge and the proposed Rock Island Bridge were strikingly similar. Like the Wheeling span, the Rock Island structure was designed to cross a great river at a place where an island stood in the channel. The bridge would traverse the main channel of the river, while the back channel (in Rock Island's case the slough) would be crossed by a smaller structure. In both places, the islands facilitated the river spans, because they narrowed the channels that the bridges had to cross. Construction of the Rock Island Bridge had been authorized by both the Illinois and the Iowa legislatures, while the Wheeling Bridge had been authorized by that of Virginia. Significantly, the applicable legislation had required that both bridges respect navigation rights. (The Virginia legislation provided that if the Wheeling Bridge obstructed "the navigation of the Ohio River in the usual manner by such steamboats and other crafts as are now commonly accustomed to navigate the same," the obstruction had to be removed or remedied as a "public nuisance.")[38] The Illinois legislation did not define the word "materially," though it was clear that it had significance. An *obstruction* alone was not enough. The obstruction had to be *material*.

Federal legislation had granted state-chartered railroads rights of way over public lands, and the Railroad Bridge Company had reason to believe that Rock Island was part of the public land, for Secretary of War Marcy had relinquished it. To make sure, however, the company applied to Secretary of War Jefferson Davis, who had authority over all military lands in the country, for his authorization. John A. Dix, a prominent New York politician and investor who had become president of the Iowa-chartered Mississippi and Missouri Railroad, made the first contact with Davis in September 1853.[39] Davis replied that he had no authority to grant rights-of-way; only Congress could do that. When John O. Sargent, an attorney for the bridge company, claimed that Congress's act of August 4, 1852, had been sufficient to grant the company the rights-of-way it needed,[40] Davis vigorously disagreed. He said that Rock Island was well suited for a federal arsenal or armory (none was then planned); failing that, it might be divided into town lots and sold. On March 14, 1854, Davis gave Dix a firm answer: he would not grant any right-of-way over the island.[41] Aware that the construction work on Rock Island had already started, Davis ordered that it be halted.[42] When the contractors ignored his order, he sent the U.S. Marshal for Illinois to the island to eject all "trespassers." Major E. B. Sibley, who accompanied the marshal to the island, reported back to the War Department that the roadbed for the railroad across the island was almost finished and that the company had excavated several acres of land to a depth of two to three feet.[43]

Aware that trouble was brewing on Rock Island, Congressman John Cook of Iowa went to the War Department in Washington and asked for copies of the order ejecting "trespassers." He spoke personally with Secretary Davis, who refused to give him any copies. Referring to the planned bridge, Davis said he would "order the first pier removed that may be placed in the channel, as an obstruction to navigation." Cook reported to an Iowa newspaper that Davis wanted "to put a stop to the work on the Island, thinking thereby to cut off the only chance to build the bridge." "I think you will agree with me," Cook said, "that the order of the War Department was 'intended to obstruct the grading of the railroad across the island,' and to prevent 'the erection of a Railroad Bridge at this point.'"[44] The congressman said that a bill had been introduced in the Senate to give the bridge company the right-of-way across the island, but it had been defeated by Davis. "Now, Sir," the congressman added, "a person not fully posted up might ask the question, 'Why should Jeff. Davis oppose the bridging of the Mississippi at Rock Island?' I answer—because he is opposed to the progress of a Northern railroad to the Pacific."[45]

Cook's assertion was supported by some good evidence. In a letter written as recently as December 7, 1853, Davis had expressed his desire for a southern railroad to the Pacific, stating that "if we had a good railroad and other roads making it convenient to go through Texas into Mexico, and through New Mexico into Southern California, our people with their servants [slaves], their horses and their cows would gradually pass westward over fertile lands into mining districts, and in the latter, especially the advantage of their associated labor [slaves] would impress itself upon others about them and the prejudice which now shuts us out of that country would yield to the persuasion of personal interest. This border once established from East to West, future acquisitions to the South would insure [sic] to our benefit, thus the equality might be regained and preserved which is incumbent [?] to a fair construction of the Constitution and the fulfillment of the great purpose for which our Union was established."[46]

After Davis's encounter with Congressman Cook, he asked U.S. Attorney General Caleb Cushing to issue an opinion on the controversy. Cushing was a Democrat from Massachusetts who sympathized with the southerners in Franklin Pierce's cabinet (the *New York Herald* dubbed him "a Boston man, with Texas principles"),[47] and he promptly set to work on the issue. On August 21, 1854, Cushing issued his opinion agreeing with Davis that Rock Island was still a military reservation and that existing laws did not grant a right of way through it.[48] Nevertheless, construction work still continued on the island.

On September 1, 1854, crowds gathered at Rock Island for a ceremony celebrating the beginning of work on the bridge piers. John Warner, the contractor in charge of the masonry work, took a large group of citizens into the river on his steamboat *Lightfoot* to witness the laying of the first stone for the first pier.[49] The *American Railroad Journal* reported on the "baptism of the *first* stone of the *first* pier of the *first* railroad bridge across the *first* of rivers—'the Father of Waters!'"[50] But that same railroad-friendly publication reported just eight days later that the War Department was trying to prevent the bridge's construction. It referred to the Pierce administration's recent purchase of the Gadsden Territory as "a worthless strip of Mexican Territory for a *Southern* route to the Pacific" and suggested that this created "a private interest adverse to any bridging of the Mississippi, unless coincident with the 'Gadsden' route."[51]

Davis wrote Franklin Pierce a long letter on October 20, informing the president that the marshal had been unable to eject the construction company, advising him that Attorney General Cushing had agreed that the railroad had no right of way across the island, and urging that "the matter be placed in charge of the proper law officers with instructions to resist the pretensions set up, and if necessary to obtain the decision of the highest judicial authority upon them."[52] Was another Supreme Court confrontation like that involving the Wheeling Bridge in the offing?

The matter was referred to Thomas Hoyne, Pierce's United States attorney for Illinois, who visited Rock Island and in November filed suit in the U.S. District Court in Springfield seeking an injunction to halt the bridge construction. Hoyne's bill of complaint alleged that, if the construction was allowed to proceed, "great and permanent injury" would be done to the "navigation of the Mississippi river, a common highway declared forever free to all of the inhabitants of the said Northwestern Territory and citizens of the United States." Further, the bridge would "inflict great and irreparable mischiefs upon the commerce of the section of the country, and a proportionate damage to the eligibility of Rock Island as a site for military purposes."[53] The initial hearing came up on January 3, 1855, before District Judge Thomas Drummond. The U.S. government was represented by Hoyne and a Peoria-based lawyer named Julius Manning. The railroad was represented by Norman B. Judd, Joseph Knox, and Norman H. Purple. The importance of the case was immediately recognized, and Judge Drummond referred it to his senior colleague, Supreme Court Justice John McLean, to be heard at a special term of the U.S. Circuit Court in Washington.[54]

If Jefferson Davis had expected McLean to show the same hostility to the Rock Island Bridge he had earlier showed to the Wheeling Bridge, he was disappointed. The justice was, after all, a member of a collegial court and bound to respect its precedents, including the final decision in *Pennsylvania v. Wheeling and Belmont Bridge Company* allowing the Ohio River span to stand. McLean carefully reviewed the history of Rock Island, Fort Armstrong, and the proposed bridge across the Mississippi. He found that Rock Island had been reserved for military purposes in 1825 but abandoned as a military post in 1836. "The abandonment," he said "was as complete as its reservation had been."[55] The Illinois legislature had authorized the Railroad Bridge Company to build a railroad and a bridge across Rock Island, but only if they did not "materially obstruct or interfere" with the free navigation of the river. The evidence was conflicting, but McLean believed that the railroad and the bridge would "add greatly to the value of the island."[56]

But was the bridge a "material obstruction" to traffic on the river?" McLean noted that many witnesses had been examined on both sides of the question, "and while those called by the plaintiffs say the bridge will, in a great degree, destroy the commerce of the river, those called by the defendants think it will be no material obstruction." The plaintiffs wanted McLean to halt the construction of the bridge. The justice did not think that would be justified. "Having considered this great case," he wrote, "in regard to the legal principles involved under the Federal and State Governments, the magnitude of the enterprise, the interest of the public in the road and in the commerce of the Mississippi river, I am brought to the conclusion that the complainants are not entitled to the relief asked; and, therefore, the motion for an injunction is overruled.[57] Nevertheless, he issued a warning: "If any injury should result to boats from any want of attention by the bridge company, or the structure of the draw, they being managed with reasonable care, an action at law may be resorted to, as in other cases of wrong."[58]

The message was clear enough. McLean would not order the bridge construction to stop; he would not issue an injunction, as he had once done in the Wheeling Bridge case. But if the bridge caused injuries or damages, a lawsuit might follow.

FIVE

A Collision of Interests

D espite the legal obstacles that were put in its way, construction of the Rock Island Bridge proceeded. Benjamin B. Brayton was the chief engineer of the project,[1] though he had the advice of Henry Farnam to back him up.[2] Brayton had worked some twenty years as a civil engineer in and around New York, where he was an assistant engineer on the Erie and Chenango Canals (the Chenango connected the Erie Canal to the Susquehanna River) and on the Hudson River Railroad. He lived with his family in Davenport while he discharged his duties as resident engineer of the Rock Island Bridge.[3] Two contractors carried out the actual construction work. John Warner and Company erected the stone abutments and piers, while the firm of Stone and Boomer built and raised the timber spans.[4] Warner was a German-born master mason who lived in Iowa.[5] Stone and Boomer owned the patent rights to the Howe truss, which was widely used in the construction of bridges in the Middle West.[6] They worked out of Chicago, where they had lots adjoining the Union Car Works.

Construction of the Rock Island Bridge was often regarded as a single undertaking, but it was in reality three related projects.[7] The first was the erection of a bridge across the slough that separated the Illinois mainland from Rock Island. This consisted of three spans of 150 feet each, which, with their connections and approaches, totaled 474 feet.[8] Since the slough was not a navigable stream, this bridge did not have to allow for the passage of steamboats. The second was the construction of the railroad across Rock Island from the bridge

over the slough to the river's edge. The third was the construction
of the great bridge itself.

The bridge that crossed the river was a timber span composed
of Howe trusses to which timber arches were added for additional
strength. The span was 1,581 feet long and rested on six stone piers
that rose 37 feet above the low water level of the river. Three fixed
spans, each 250 feet long, were on the Iowa side of the river, and
two were on the Illinois side. Between the fixed spans, a draw span
286 feet wide revolved on a turntable supported by twenty bearing
wheels. The turntable was supported by a stone pier (called the "long
pier") 32 feet wide and 350 feet long. When in the open position,
the draw had two openings, one on the Illinois side measuring 116
feet across and the other on the Iowa side measuring 110 feet.[9] The
river's regular steamboat channel ran through the opening on the
Illinois side. The draw was designed to remain open at all times
unless a train was approaching.[10] A single railroad track extended
the full length of the bridge. The piers that supported the timber
span were built by first placing wooden coffer dams in the bed of
the river, then pumping the water out with Archimedes screws and
erecting the stone piers in them.[11] The bridge timbers were covered
with two coats of white lead paint so approaching steamboats could
see them clearly—particularly at night. Lights were mounted on
either end of the long pier: a green lantern suspended from a pole
on the downstream end and a white light on the upper end. A small
house was built on the upstream end of the long pier and furnished
with beds that would accommodate the bridge superintendent and
watchmen who would staff the bridge at all hours of the day and
night. A smaller building on the downstream end provided space in
which the men could sleep in hot weather.[12]

The construction work began on July 16, 1853, and was finished
just over two years and eight months later. On April 1, 1856, a locomotive crept over the Rock Island abutment and onto the bridge in
a test run arranged by Farnam and John F. Tracy, superintendent
of the Rock Island Railroad. Farnam and Tracy watched the locomotive closely and, after it had returned to Rock Island, carefully
checked the bridge and its trusses to determine how they had borne

up under its weight.[13] They were, by all accounts, pleased with what they saw, but the official opening was not made until Monday, April 21. On that date, a locomotive named the *Des Moines* crossed from Rock Island to Davenport, where it was "welcomed by the huzzas of those who had assembled there to witness the event."[14] The following day, three locomotives drawing passenger cars crossed the bridge to a welcoming crowd.[15] A band of about fifty Sauk and Fox Indians was camped on the Iowa side of the river, watching the event.[16] The *Rock Island Argus* reported that church bells in Rock Island and Davenport "rang out their joyous notes in honor of the achievement, and cheer upon cheer went up from the crowds along the line."[17] The *Davenport Gazette* exulted that "the last link is now forged in the chain that connects Iowa and the great west with the states of the Atlantic Seaboard. The iron band that will span our hemisphere has been welded at Davenport; one mighty barrier has been overcome; the Missouri is yet to be crossed and then the locomotive will speed onward to the Pacific."[18]

The construction of the Rock Island Bridge had not gone unnoticed in Chicago, where businessmen were delighted with the quick and dependable transportation it promised across the Mississippi. The Great Lakes were now linked by rails with the most important river in the country, and that river was tied by rails not only to Chicago but, through it, to Boston, New York, Philadelphia, and Baltimore. At the same time, however, the bridge had also been watched closely by steamboat owners and operators on the river who regarded it as a threat to their dominance of the western waterways. Since steamboats first came to the Mississippi and its tributaries, their business had grown steadily. Now, with the opening of the first bridge across the great river, that growth was threatened.

New Orleans, of course, was a great steamboat center, but so was St. Louis, and because the Missouri city was located on the Upper Mississippi, its business was most directly imperiled by the new bridge. The St. Louis waterfront was so crowded with steamboats in 1856 that a watchman reported that he was able to walk along the shore for twenty city blocks, going from deck to deck and never once touching land.[19] The waterfront then was lined with warehouses, machine shops, construction sheds, wood lots, taverns, inns, and stores, all of which partook in some way in the prosperity that the steamboats brought to the city.

Immigrants, most from Germany and Ireland, had flocked to St. Louis in the late 1840s and early 1850s, brought there by steamboats from the Ohio.[20] In the 1850 census, St. Louis became the first city west of the Mississippi to rank among the ten largest in the country. It became the eighth-largest city in 1860, with a population of 160,733, while Chicago lagged 50,000 behind.[21] But it was clear to observers that Chicago was growing faster than St. Louis, and that it would continue to grow faster because of its rail links with the East and the promise of connections with the vast western country beyond the Mississippi.

Even before the Rock Island Bridge was opened, commercial interests in St. Louis had begun to grumble. In January 1853, the St. Louis *Missouri Republican* told its readers that the bridge at Rock Island should "open the eyes of our citizens to what is going on elsewhere, to divert trade from us." The bridge was part of an ongoing plan to link the East and the West by rails, and after the span was opened, the railroad would "take up its race westward." The *Republican* admired the "spirit of enterprise which can engage in such noble works," but it warned that the bridge was "likely in its construction to form an obstruction to the free navigation of the Mississippi." Regardless of where a bridge over the river was built, the newspaper said, "this consideration must always be kept in view.... The free navigation of the Mississippi is solemnly guaranteed, and every Legislature will, if it acts with ordinary prudence, provide against any obstruction to such navigation."[22]

Jefferson Davis's efforts to block construction of the bridge at Rock Island had favored the steamboat interests, not because the Mississippian himself favored steamboats over railroads, but because he favored a southern route over a northern line for the Pacific railroad. The injunction that the Franklin Pierce administration sought against the bridge had the same aim, and most likely the same purpose—for Pierce's purchase of the Gadsden Territory had clearly indicated his preference for a southern to a northern railroad.[23]

While St. Louis was one of the busiest steamboat ports on the Mississippi, Cincinnati had since the 1830s maintained its position as the leading shipbuilding center on all of the western rivers. The streams that fed into the Ohio were lined with forests that provided good timber for shipbuilding: oak for the construction of hulls, and poplar for decks and cabins. Jacob Sampson Hurd was an Ohioan in his late thirties when he made preparations for the construction of a large steamboat at Cincinnati in 1855.[24] Born in New Hampshire in 1816 and brought to Ohio's Scioto County while still a boy, Hurd had married there and for several years worked in the iron furnaces of the Hanging Rock region east of Cincinnati.[25] He had been involved in the steamboat business for about a decade before he and two other Ohio River men, Joseph W. Smith and Alexander W. Kidwell, commissioned the Marine Railway and Dry Dock Company and the Niles Works, both of Cincinnati, to build a new boat in July 1855.[26] Marine Railway was one of Cincinnati's premier boat-building yards. Niles was a foundry and machine company that built steam engines.

The boat the two companies were asked to create was a first-class steamboat capable of carrying large numbers of passengers and cargo over both the Ohio and the Mississippi. It was to be 230 feet long, with a 35-foot beam and a 6-foot hold, and powered by two sidewheels, each 38 feet in diameter. It was to have four boilers, 38 inches in diameter and 26 feet long, and two engines with 21-inch cylinders and 7-foot strokes. The main cabin would be equipped with fifty staterooms, each with its own wardrobe, closet, and wash-stand. Hot water would be piped to the saloon where guests gathered for meals, and cold water to the outhouses. Two iron chimneys would rise 46 feet above the hurricane deck. An officers' dining saloon would crown the texas, or very top deck of the boat. When finished, the boat would have a capacity of 700 tons and, unladen, draw only 26 inches of water. The outside would be decorated with colorful landscapes painted on the paddle boxes. In all, the cost was estimated at $40,000. Launched in September, it was not finally completed until early November 1855, when it set out on its maiden voyage. Hurd was the captain, Smith the clerk, and Kidwell the engineer.[27] Joseph McCammant of Cincinnati was hired as the pilot.[28]

The new boat was named *Effie Afton*, in honor of the author of a book of stories and poems that was published in Boston the previous year.[29] The author's given name was Sarah Elizabeth Harper, and she was born in New Hampshire in 1829, the daughter of a country physician who also had a career in politics (Joseph M. Harper was a member of the U.S. House of Representatives from 1831 to 1835 and briefly served as acting governor of New Hampshire in 1831).[30] Some time before the Civil War, she traveled to Texas, where she met and married a man named Jacques Eugene Monmouth. While still a young woman, she showed a talent for writing fiction and poetry, contributing to magazines such as *Waverly* and the *Boston Cultivator* under folksy pseudonyms such as Lil Lindon and Effie Afton. Effie Afton was the name she used for her most popular work, *Eventide*, in 1854.[31]

The *Effie Afton* was licensed on November 22, 1855, by the surveyor of customs in Cincinnati and enrolled the same day as a vessel "to carry on the coasting trade."[32] It then left Cincinnati for the nearby town of Lawrenceburg, Indiana, where it took on two thousand barrels of flour.[33] It returned to Cincinnati eight days later and loaded another large cargo destined for Wheeling. Proceeding from Wheeling to Pittsburgh, it carried 425 tons of freight and traveled at an average speed of ten miles per hour, all the while drawing only four feet of water, a remarkably shallow draft for such a heavy load. Returning downriver, the boat covered the 115 miles that separated Portsmouth, Ohio, from Cincinnati, in seven and a half hours, stopping twice along the route. As Elwin Page, a close historian of the *Effie Afton*, has written, "she was indeed a smart boat."[34]

Like St. Louis, Cincinnati had a busy waterfront in *Effie Afton*'s time. A local newspaper noted the arrival of no fewer than ten steamboats on a single day in November 1855. But there was ominous news along the banks. Four boats had recently fallen victim to accidents along the river, and wrecking operations were under way for five boats that had been sunk or burned. Steamboating was a great business, but it was also dangerous.[35]

With its crew very much aware of these recent accidents, *Effie Afton*'s next trip was all the way down the Ohio and Mississippi to

New Orleans. On the way, the boat reached Louisville in seven days, carrying forty-six cabin passengers, thirty-seven deck passengers, and 110 tons of freight. Page says that it was "hailed as the fastest side-wheeler of her draft on the Ohio and the Mississippi. Besides that," he added, "she was already proving profitable."[36]

Hurd and his partners now began to prepare for a trip from Cincinnati to St. Paul, Minnesota Territory. It would be an important trip for both the *Afton* and its captain, for neither had been on the Upper Mississippi before, neither had visited St. Louis, and neither had ventured as far north as Rock Island.[37] The boat left Cincinnati on April 28, 1856, accompanied by two other steamboats, the *Great West* and the *J. B. Carson*.[38] It performed admirably on the trip from Cincinnati to St. Louis, but when it arrived at the Missouri city there was a mechanical problem. One of the passengers later reported that the *Afton* had to put in for two or three hours of repairs in St. Louis. He said that there was "something the matter with the escape pipe."[39] Joseph McCammant had no piloting experience on the Mississippi above St. Louis, so it was necessary to take on a new pilot for the passage north of that city. Nathaniel W. Parker, a St. Louis–based pilot with more than twenty years' experience on the Upper Mississippi, was the man chosen for the job. Samuel McBride was hired as his assistant. Parker alone was promised a thousand dollars for taking the *Afton* up to St. Paul and back to St. Louis, a single run that was expected to take two weeks.[40] Parker, McBride, and McCammant were all aboard as the boat headed north from St. Louis.

The *Effie Afton* arrived at Rock Island on the morning of May 5, 1856. Aboard were livestock, machinery, farm implements, and groceries weighing in the aggregate more than 350 tons. Two hundred people were also on board: seventy-five cabin passengers, seventy-five deck passengers, and fifty crew members.[41] The Rock Island Bridge had been open just over two weeks. Hurd found a good number of boats that were tied up at the Rock Island docks about half a mile below the bridge; looking through the span, he could see other boats tied up above the crossing. The *J. B. Carson* was one of the other boats on the Rock Island side. The cause of the delay was a high wind that was whipping across the river. That, combined with high water and swift currents, persuaded the pilots that it would be wise to wait until the wind died down. Hurd later said that he thought there were as many as nine or ten boats waiting at Rock Island during the day, and as many as three or four may have arrived during the night.[42]

The following morning was quiet, for the wind had died down. As dawn broke over the river, three of the steamboats waiting at the Rock Island docks fired up their engines, moved out into the river, and passed through the open draw of the Rock Island Bridge, apparently without incident.[43] At about 6:30 a.m., the *J. B. Carson* also moved out, followed almost immediately by the *Effie Afton*. To leave the dock, it was necessary for the *Afton* first to back up and then turn toward the draw. A steam ferry called the *John Wilson* was then crossing the river. As the *Afton* backed up, it collided with the *Wilson*, damaging the *Afton*'s guard and breaking seven of its guard chains (iron rods that helped to support the guards and paddle wheels and prevent them from sagging).[44] The *Afton* was apparently unconcerned about any damage it had inflicted on the *Wilson*, for it did not stop or slow down but continued on its way.

The *Afton* was a faster boat than the *J. B. Carson*, even loaded with passengers and cargo. Though the *Carson* had started ahead of the *Afton*, the *Afton* decided to make a race for the bridge draw. Speed was one of the distinguishing features of the *Afton*; in fact, it was an attribute that was highly valued on all of the steamboats, for faster boats could deliver their cargoes and passengers more quickly than other craft and thus get a leg up on future business. Captain Hurd and his pilots (McBride and Parker were both on duty that morning) must have known that the assembled river boats, and many persons ashore, were watching them as they moved out and thought that they could make an impression.[45] The distance between the Rock Island docks and the bridge was less than a mile, but the *Afton* quickly gained on the *Carson*, passing it on the left (Iowa) side of the channel. Its speed was so great that it had no trouble leaving the *Carson* in its wake.

The *Afton*'s object was the Illinois side of the long pier. To enter the draw, it had to come around the *Carson* on the Iowa side, then steer for the opening on the Illinois side. All seemed to be going well until it was about halfway through the draw, when it began to sway from side to side. It struck one of the piers with an impact that was felt all over the boat (which pier was struck first would be a matter of dispute in the trial). In the pilot house, bells were rung, signaling to the engineers that power to the larboard (left) wheel was to be shut off. The wheel stopped, then started again, then stopped a second time. With the sound of hissing steam blaring in the morning air and bells ringing frantically, the boat then swung to the right, where it collided with the short pier. It seemed to stop there for a time, then swung farther to the right. As it did this, the upper decks and chimneys collided with the superstructure of the fixed span that adjoined the draw on the Illinois side. This shattered the upper cabins, broke the chimneys loose from their supports, and overturned stoves on the decks (it was a cold morning and the stoves were all red hot).[46]

Fires erupted. As the boat careened to its larboard side, water began to flow over its guards. The crew worked to extinguish the fires while frantic passengers began to climb off the boat and onto the bridge. The *J. B. Carson* came up close to rescue some of the passengers, and for a time the two hulls were lashed together. At first it seemed that all the fires on the *Afton* had been put out. Then a bigger and more aggressive fire flared up. The flames grew so intense that the *Carson* cut its lines to the *Afton* and began to back out of the draw. The timbers of the bridge itself were now on fire.

When and how the fires started, and how long they continued to burn, were issues that were to be settled later. But burn they did—for minutes or perhaps an hour or longer. The result was the complete destruction of the *Effie Afton* and its cargo and the similar destruction of the first fixed bridge span on the Illinois side of the draw. The timbers there burned ferociously and ultimately tumbled into the river on top of the wreckage of the *Afton*.

All of the passengers were able to escape without loss of life. It was not so with the horses and cattle aboard. Some managed to jump over the rails and swim to shore; others, not so fortunate, were burned or drowned in the river. The river current quickly grasped the remains of both the boat and the fallen bridge span and carried them downstream, where they lodged on a sandbar not far from the Rock Island waterfront.

Excited crowds flocked to the shores on both sides of the river as the disaster unfolded. Passengers and crews of boats that were waiting to make their passage through the bridge surveyed the scene in dismay. Some were able to climb up on the bridge, keeping their distance from the flames, and look down on the boats below them. The overwhelming reaction was, of course, horror. It was a disaster, a great loss of property, and a setback both for river and railroad transportation at Rock Island.

But not all who watched the events of May 6, 1856, were unhappy. The *Rock Island Argus* reported exultation among some of the witnesses to the collision and fire, writing that when the span of the bridge fell "the steamboats lying at both cities, and those on the river, all sounded their loudest whistle." Some supposed that the whistle signaled "joy that the obstruction to navigation had been partially removed," while others thought it was "to warn those on the river to look out for the floating wreck." The *Argus* reported a rumor that the accident was "intentional and done for the purpose of burning the bridge," but it did not think the rumor was "entitled to the slightest credit."[47] A few days after the collision, the *Argus* reported that the steamboat *Hamburg* had been seen going upriver flying a flag with the inscription: "Mississippi Bridge Destroyed, Let All Rejoice." "However much the river men's interest may clash with those of the railroad," the *Argus* commented, "this seems to be going it a 'leetle to [sic] strong.'"[48]

Six days after the *Effie Afton* struck the Rock Island Bridge, the *St. Louis Intelligencer* revealed the Missouri city's keen interest in the events at Rock Island. In an article cast in the form of an affidavit signed by "citizens of the Mississippi valley, and passengers on board the steamer *James Lyon*," the St. Louis paper condemned the bridge as an obstruction to navigation and urged "all interested in the free navigation of the Upper Mississippi river, to give public expression to their grievances." Those who signed the affidavit called on the St. Louis Chamber of Commerce and the river city's insurance underwriters to take steps to prevent future encroachments on the river.[49] The *Rock Island Argus*, which generally supported the steamboat interests against the railroads, agreed, writing that "there can be no doubt that the bridge, constructed in the manner it is, materially obstructs the navigation of the river, but whether the interests affected have any remedy is more than we can tell."[50]

Opponents of the Rock Island Bridge had tried in the past to stop its construction, and they had failed. Now they would see if they could force it to be torn down. If they could not do that directly, perhaps they could do it indirectly by demonstrating that lawsuits would be filed whenever a steamboat collided with the bridge. Money speaks a language all its own. The *Effie Afton* was a valuable steamboat, and its cargo was even more valuable. But all had been lost because of the bridge. Perhaps a lawsuit would force the bridge owners to make good on the damages they had caused and convince them that the Rock Island Bridge should never have been built in the first place.

SIX

The Suit Is Filed

~≈~

S ince his return from his one congressional term in Washington in 1849, Lincoln had gone "to the practice of the law with greater earnestness than ever before" and by 1854, his legal work "had almost superseded the thought of politics in his mind."[1]

Almost—but not quite, for it was in 1854 that Stephen Douglas, acting in his capacity as U.S. senator from Illinois and chairman of the Senate Committee on Territories, shepherded the Kansas-Nebraska Act through Congress. This remarkable piece of legislation, signed by President Pierce on May 30, 1854, repealed the Missouri Compromise of 1820 and opened the territories of Kansas and Nebraska to slavery, but only if settlers in the territories voted for it.[2] Douglas called this concession to voters "popular sovereignty" (he borrowed the term from Lewis Cass, the Democrats' candidate for president in 1848). He knew, of course, that all of the voters would be white men, for neither blacks nor women then held the franchise. Like Lewis Cass and Franklin Pierce, Douglas was a Democrat with presidential ambitions, and he believed that this law would win him political support in the South. Lincoln, however, was a Whig with strong anti-slavery (although not abolitionist) sentiments, and he found the Kansas-Nebraska Act outrageous. In his own words, it "aroused him as he had never been before."[3]

The Missouri Compromise had quieted the national argument about slavery for a generation, excluding the peculiar institution from all lands north of 36° 30' north latitude. Kansas-Nebraska abolished the exclusion and, in the process, reignited the national argument over slavery. In Lincoln's mind, Kansas-Nebraska represented an aggressive thrust by pro-slavery forces into a part of the country they had never been in before. It offended not only his notions of national unity but also his concept of racial justice. "If slavery is not wrong," he told a newspaper editor, "nothing is wrong. I can not remember when I did not so think, and feel."[4] Kansas-Nebraska's rekindling of the slavery argument pulled Lincoln back into the political arena with a force he could not resist. He responded to requests for speeches, and he put his name up for election to the Illinois legislature. In a speech he gave in Springfield on October 4, 1854, and repeated in Peoria on October 16, Lincoln articulated his opposition to Douglas's doctrine of popular sovereignty in words that would be remembered in history. He carefully researched the speech in the state library, much as he would have prepared an argument to be made before the Illinois Supreme Court.[5] When delivered, his speech was a cogent review of the history of slavery in the United States, a powerful indictment of the Kansas-Nebraska Act, and a frontal attack on Douglas's professed neutrality on the issue of slavery—a neutrality he condemned as moral indifference. "This *declared* indifference, but as I must think, covert *real* zeal for the spread of slavery, I can not but hate," he said. "I hate it because of the monstrous injustice of slavery itself. I hate it because it deprives our republican example of its just influence in the world—enables the enemies of free institutions, with plausibility, to taunt us as hypocrites—causes the real friends of freedom to doubt our sincerity, and especially because it forces so many really good men amongst ourselves into an open war with the very fundamental principles of civil liberty—criticizing the Declaration of Independence, and insisting that there is no right principle of action but *self-interest*."[6]

On election day, November 7, 1854, Lincoln was elected to the legislature along with a majority of anti-Nebraska men, some Whigs and some Democrats. He had begun to think about running for election to the United States Senate against the incumbent James Shields, a pro-Nebraska Democrat whose term was expiring in 1855. While Thomas Hoyne, Franklin Pierce's U.S. district attorney in Illinois, was preparing his petition for an injunction against the Rock Island Bridge, Lincoln was writing letters seeking support in his bid for election to the Senate. Because a member of the legislature was ineligible for election to the Senate, Lincoln declined to accept his legislative seat and instead concentrated on lining up support for his senatorial bid. He went into the legislative voting on February 8, 1855, with a commanding lead of forty-five votes to forty-one for Shields and five for the anti-Nebraska Democrat, Lyman Trumbull.[7] Only fifty votes were required for election. As the balloting continued, however, it became evident that Governor Joel Matteson, a wealthy Democrat whose position on Nebraska was as equivocal as his personal ethics, was working behind the scenes to siphon votes away from both Lincoln and Trumbull, and Matteson was coming perilously close to election. Determined that the anti-Nebraska cause should prevail, Lincoln threw his support to Trumbull, who was elected on the tenth ballot.[8]

One of the anti-Nebraska Democrats who was adamant in his refusal to support Lincoln throughout the voting was Norman B. Judd, the powerful Chicago lawyer who two years later would invite Lincoln to join him in the *Effie Afton* trial. Lincoln was deeply troubled when his early lead in the voting did not result in his victory and anti-Nebraska Democrats like Judd refused to support him. Illinois congressman Elihu B. Washburne later wrote that "no event in Mr. Lincoln's entire political career brought to him so much disappointment and chagrin as his defeat for United States Senator in 1855."[9] Lincoln consoled himself with the knowledge that he had acted out of principal rather than personal interest. His goal was to strike a strong blow against Kansas-Nebraska and its author, Stephen Douglas, and he could not "let the whole political result go to ruin, on a point merely personal to myself."[10] Later asked if he harbored any enmity against Norman Judd because of his failure to support him, Lincoln said: "I can't harbor enmity to any one; it's not in my nature."[11]

Lincoln's political interests extended through the summer, as the anti-Nebraska forces were preparing to form a new political party. But he also spent much of his time on his law practice. He was attending court in Chicago in July about the time that he was asked to join the defense team of the John H. Manny Company of

Rockford, Illinois, a manufacturer of reaping machines. Manny had been sued in Chicago's U.S. Circuit Court by the powerful Cyrus H. McCormick for alleged infringement of his reaper patents. Lincoln had a reputation in Illinois not only as an effective courtroom advocate but also as a lawyer with a particular interest in things mechanical. Grant Goodrich, a Chicago lawyer who had worked with him in previous patent cases, wrote that Lincoln "had a great deal of Mechanical genius, could understand readily the principles & mechanical action of machinery, & had the power, in his clear, simple illustrations & Style to make the jury comprehend them."[12] The Manny Company gave Lincoln a $1,000 retainer, probably to make sure he didn't agree to work for McCormick.[13] When Justice McLean announced that the trial of *McCormick v. Manny* would be moved to Cincinnati, where he lived, Lincoln prepared to go to the Ohio city. But Manny's lead lawyer, George H. Harding of Philadelphia, and his associate, Peter H. Watson of Washington, were not enthusiastic about Lincoln's participation in Cincinnati. They regarded him as an unsophisticated backwoodsman who would not make a good impression in the "Queen City of the West." Inste\ad, they hired Edwin M. Stanton, the prominent Pittsburgh-based attorney who had sued to bring down the Wheeling Bridge, to prepare the case for trial. But they neglected to tell Lincoln. McCormick was represented by Edward M. Dickerson of New York and Reverdy Johnson of Baltimore, the latter one of the most eminent appellate lawyers in the country.

Lincoln prepared for the Manny trial during July and most of August 1855. He visited the Manny factory in Rockford, researched the law applicable to the case, and prepared an argument to be delivered in Cincinnati. But it wasn't until he reached the Ohio city on September 20 that he learned that he was not to participate in the trial. When he presented a brief he had prepared for the case, the other lawyers accepted it without looking at it, and eventually returned it unread. When McLean hosted a dinner for the lawyers at his home just outside Cincinnati, Lincoln was not invited. In the words of Robert Henry Parkinson, a lawyer who later gathered information about Lincoln's trip to Cincinnati, he "was throughout treated by the other counsel with marked discourtesy, sidetracked from the participation which had been assigned him, excluded from consultations as well as argument, and shown less respect than probably befell any other of those in attendance." According to Parkinson, Stanton was the principal instigator of the discourtesy shown to Lincoln.[14]

Lincoln remained in Cincinnati during the trial, although he did not enjoy himself. When he said good-bye to the woman in whose home he had stayed, he thanked her for inviting him to return but said he never expected to be in Cincinnati again. "I have nothing against the city, but things have so happened here as to make it undesirable for me ever to return here."[15] He went back to Springfield resolved to improve his legal skills; he was determined to study the law harder than he ever had before, so he would never again be regarded as an unworthy colleague of lawyers like Edwin Stanton or Reverdy Johnson.[16]

As fate would have it, less than half a decade later, President Lincoln was to name Edwin Stanton to his cabinet as secretary of war, at once giving testimony to Stanton's ability and Lincoln's own refusal to hold grudges. And when Stanton was later reminded of the discourtesy he had shown Lincoln in Cincinnati, he remembered it with regret, saying, "What a mistake I made about that man when I met him in Cincinnati."[17] McLean went on to decide the case of *McCormick v. Manny* against McCormick and, on appeal to the U.S. Supreme Court, his decision was upheld.[18] After Lincoln returned to Springfield, Manny's lawyers sent him a check for the fee he would have received had he participated in the Cincinnati trial. He returned it with the explanation that he had not earned it. But they sent it back to him again, and he finally accepted the money, along with the valuable lessons the Cincinnati experience had taught him.[19]

During the last months of 1855 and the first months of 1856, Lincoln was traveling with Judge Davis and other lawyers on the Eighth Circuit, appearing in the U.S. courts, arguing cases in the Illinois Supreme Court. At the same time, however, he was concerning himself with the anti-Nebraska cause, which was assuming greater importance as a political issue both inside Illinois and outside. Men who shared his conviction that slavery should not be allowed to spread into the western territories were coalescing to form a new political party. Lincoln was hesitant about joining the new party—he was an "Old Line Whig" and dedicated to Whig principles. But the new party, now called the Republicans, had announced that it would hold a presidential nominating convention in mid-June 1856 at Philadelphia. Although Lincoln was chosen as a delegate to the convention, he declined to go, instead sending a representative in his place. Still, he paid close attention to the event and frequently expressed his opinion as news of the convention made its way back to Springfield.

The convention in Philadelphia would be the first ever for the Republican Party, and its nominees for president and vice president would be the first Republicans ever to face the voters in a nationwide election. Potential candidates for its presidential nomination included Governor Salmon P. Chase of Ohio, Speaker of the U.S. House of Representatives Nathaniel P. Banks of Massachusetts, Senator William Henry Seward of New York, and John C. Frémont, the charismatic western explorer and former U.S. senator from California. Lincoln believed that these men were too radical on the slavery issue to win the support of many of the old Whigs. He favored a candidate with more moderate views, one who would keep the old Whigs from flocking to the Democratic candidate, James Buchanan of Pennsylvania. "The man to effect that object is Judge McLean," he wrote in June 1856.[20]

John McLean had long made it known that he was interested in serving as president. He was opposed to slavery and defended the power of Congress to prohibit its spread into the territories, although he was insistent that whatever Congress did should conform to constitutional rules.[21] Lincoln's friend Orville H. Browning, a Whig lawyer from Quincy, Illinois, shared Lincoln's views about the Supreme Court justice: "McLean, in my opinion, would be stronger in this state than anyone whose name has been suggested. We have many, very many, tender footed whigs, who are frightened by ugly names, that could not be carried for Freemont [sic], but who would readily unite with us upon McLean."[22]

But McLean was not a young man—he was seventy-one years old

in 1856, while Frémont was just forty-three. When the delegates met at Philadelphia, McLean received 196 votes to Frémont's 359 on the first ballot, and the nomination ultimately went to Frémont.[23] Lincoln was not pleased (he never felt optimistic about "the Path-finder's" chances of winning the election), but he was pleasantly surprised by the news that he himself had received 110 votes in the vice presidential balloting.[24] William L. Dayton of New Jersey ultimately received the vice presidential nod, but Lincoln received some unexpected (and unsolicited) recognition in the early voting. He realized then, if he had not before, that his voice was being heard, not just in Illinois but also outside the state.

L incoln's opposition to the Kansas-Nebraska Act in 1854, his unsuccessful bid for election to the Senate early in 1855, and his abortive trip to Cincinnati to participate in the Manny trial later in the same year all took place against the backdrop of continuing activities at Rock Island. Work on the bridge continued unabated through 1854 and 1855, undeterred by the efforts of Jefferson Davis and Attorney General Caleb Cushing to stop it with an injunction. When the first trains crossed over the span in April 1856, and the *Effie Afton* crashed into it early in May, the stage was set for the great trial that was soon to come.

The *Effie Afton* was covered by insurance when it crashed into the Rock Island Bridge, but the amount was reported to be only $15,000, far less than the value of the vessel, to say nothing of the cargo, and the only risk the insurance covered was fire. It was of some help to Jacob Hurd and the two other men who owned the boat, and it gave the insurers the right to authorize salvage teams to go to the wreck and see what they could recover. The salvagers found that the boat itself was a total loss but that much of the cargo was still in good condition. At the same time, the Railroad Bridge Company began to rebuild the span. The stone piers had not been damaged by the fire, so only the timber trusses on the Illinois side of the turntable pier had to be replaced. The reconstruction proceeded at a good pace during the summer of 1856 and was completed early in September.

Cost of the work was reported to be $12,000. The first trains passed over the rebuilt span on September 8, only four months and two days after the bridge was damaged.

Lincoln spent much of the summer of 1856 campaigning for Frémont and other Republican candidates. He delivered more than fifty speeches in Illinois and neighboring states attacking the Democratic candidacy of James Buchanan and the Know-Nothing candidacy of former president Millard Fillmore.[25] A northern man with southern sympathies, Buchanan supported Stephen Douglas's call for "popular sovereignty" in the territories. The Know-Nothings (formally styled the American Party) were opposed to immigrants and Catholics and favored all sorts of laws that would limit their participation in the civic life of the nation. Lincoln hated slavery and Buchanan's toleration of it, but he was also opposed to Know-Nothingism. "I am not a Know-Nothing," he wrote to his old friend Joshua Speed. "That is certain. How could I be? How can any one who abhors the oppression of negroes, be in favor of degrading classes of white people? Our progress in degeneracy appears to me to be pretty rapid. As a nation, we began by declaring that 'all men are created equal.' We now practically read it 'all men are created equal, except negroes.' When the Know-Nothings get control, it will read 'all men are created equal, except negroes and foreigners, and catholics.' When it comes to this I should prefer emigrating to some country where they make no pretence of loving liberty—to Russia, for instance, where despotism can be taken pure, and without the base alloy of hypocrisy [sic]."[26]

Lincoln was not surprised when, on election day, Buchanan carried Illinois with 44 percent of the vote to Frémont's 40 percent and Fillmore's 16 percent. Nor was he unprepared to learn that Buchanan did even better in the nation as a whole, winning 45 percent of the popular vote to Frémont's 33 percent and Fillmore's 21 percent. But he was encouraged by the victory of the Republican candidate for governor of Illinois, William H. Bissell. Lincoln believed that the election of 1856 was, above all, a victory for equal rights. In a speech delivered at a Republican banquet in Chicago on December 10, 1856, he referred to Buchanan's assertion that in the election of 1856 the people had "asserted the constitutional equality of each and all of the States of the Union as States." Lincoln rejected the idea that "all States are equal" or that "all citizens as citizens are equal" in favor of what he called "the good old 'central ideas' of the Republic" and "the broader, better declaration" that "all *men* are created equal."[27]

While Lincoln was reviewing the 1856 presidential election and pondering its significance for the future, Jacob Hurd and his partners were preparing a lawsuit. It is likely that they contemplated some kind of legal action from the date of the *Effie Afton*'s collision with the Rock Island Bridge. The monetary loss they suffered was enormous, and they could hardly be expected to endure it without seeking compensation from some party or parties. The bridge owners were a logical target for their judicial wrath. But where should they file their suit? Hurd and his partners were citizens of Ohio, and the Railroad Bridge Company was incorporated in Illinois, so they could rely on diversity jurisdiction in their choice of courts. Article III, section 2, of the U.S. Constitution gives federal courts jurisdiction over cases "between citizens of different states." Congress had provided by statute that the U.S. Circuit Courts had jurisdiction (concurrently with state courts) of civil suits between citizens of different states when the amount in controversy was more than $500.[28] The loss suffered by the owners of the *Effie Afton* was estimated to be in excess of $50,000, perhaps as much as $750,000, so the boat owners easily met the requirements for filing suit in the U.S. Circuit Court in the Northern District of Illinois.

Whether Hurd and his partners first sought legal help in Illinois or on their home turf in Ohio is not clear, but they soon assembled a formidable team of lawyers from both states. Hezekiah M. Wead of Peoria was their lead attorney in Illinois. Born in Vermont in 1810, he had moved to Illinois in 1840, where he achieved a reputation as one of the best "river lawyers" in the state.[29] An ardent Democrat in a state dominated by Democrats (Lincoln's Whigs were in a distinct minority in Illinois), he had been a member of the convention called to revise the state constitution in 1847 and served from 1852 to 1855 as judge of Illinois's Sixteenth Circuit. Wead's law practice earned him the respect of his courtroom opponents, while his judicial service entitled him to be addressed (even in the heated give-and-take of trials) as "Judge Wead." Corydon Beckwith was thirteen years younger than Wead, also a native of Vermont, and a lawyer who had achieved a considerable reputation after moving to Illinois in 1853. Practicing in Chicago, his reputation for legal scholarship was so good that in 1864 he was appointed to a brief term on the Illinois Supreme Court.[30] Timothy D. Lincoln (commonly called T. D. Lincoln) was the Ohio-based member of the plaintiffs' legal team. A native of Massachusetts, Lincoln had moved to Cincinnati in 1841, where he achieved a good reputation as an admiralty, insurance, and patent lawyer.[31] He was, so far as the evidence shows, unrelated to Abraham Lincoln.[32]

The case of *Jacob S. Hurd, Joseph W. Smith, and Alexander W. Kidwell v. The Railroad Bridge Company* was begun in October 1856, when Wead filed opening papers with the clerk of the U.S. District Court for the Northern District of Illinois in Chicago.[33] In a declaration filed in November, Wead alleged that the Mississippi River was "a public navigable stream" and that all citizens of the United States had the right to navigate it "free from any interference or obstruction whatever." He declared that Hurd, Smith, and Kidwell were the owners of the *Effie Afton*, a steamboat duly licensed and enrolled under the laws of the United States, and that the boat was built "at great expense" and "particularly fitted" for a trip on the Upper Mississippi between St. Louis and St. Paul. The defendant had "wrongfully and injuriously" caused a railroad bridge to be constructed across the river at Rock Island. The piers of the bridge were set at "such angles to the natural current of the river" that they constituted a "permanent obstruction in the course of said river" and materially prevented the "safe navigation of steamboats in ascending and descending the river at that point." On May 6, 1856, while the *Effie Afton* was being navigated "with due care and skill," it was "forcibly driven by the current and eddies caused by said piers" against one of the piers, so that "a large portion of the cabin was torn off," the steamboat was "set on fire by the upsetting of the stoves," and it was "wholly consumed with her machinery and cargo." The losses occasioned by the collision were enormous, for the value of the steamboat was alleged to be $75,000, the owners' personal property on board was stated to be worth $200,000 (the value of steamboat cargos often exceeded the value of the boats that carried them), and the freight being carried was valued at another $150,000. The declaration went on to say that the collision had caused the owners to lose another $500,000 in future profits, as well as the $5,000 they had paid the crew for the trip from St. Louis to St. Paul. The total of the losses was now claimed to be an astounding $930,000. A summons was served on Henry Farnam, the Bridge Company president, on September 18. On January 6, 1857, Chicago attorney Norman B. Judd filed the defendant's plea denying that it was guilty of the "grievances" alleged in the declaration and denying liability for the claimed losses.[34]

If Hurd and his partners were well represented by the lawyers who signed on to their case, they were also supported by the steamboat interests in St. Louis. On December 16, 1856, boat owners and businessmen met in the Merchants' Exchange in St. Louis and appointed a committee "to take measures to remove the railroad bridge from the Mississippi river" at Rock Island.[35] A committee of steamboat captains and pilots was authorized to go to Rock Island, survey the scene of the *Effie Afton* disaster, and produce a report that could be used in the legal proceedings in Chicago.[36]

After visiting Rock Island, the committee reported that the bridge was "a great and serious obstacle to navigation." The Railroad Bridge Company had not lived up to its own state charter, which required it to build a bridge that did not "materially" interfere with the free navigation of the river. To make matters worse, the company had never obtained a charter from Iowa permitting it to build on the Iowa portion of the river.[37] (This was wrong, for the Mississippi and Missouri Railroad had obtained permission to build and use a bridge across the Iowa half of the river when it was chartered by the Iowa legislature in 1853, and it was working closely with the Railroad Bridge Company to erect and use the Rock Island Bridge).[38]

Then, on February 11, 1857, the Chicago Board of Trade convened a meeting to discuss the bridge, and the meeting was attended by a delegation from the St. Louis Chamber of Commerce that had traveled to Chicago to present arguments against the span. One of the most prominent members of the delegation was Josiah W. Bissell, an energetic engineer who had just designed a suspension bridge for construction across the Mississippi at St. Louis. Bissell's design had won him plaudits in St. Louis, but investors there rejected it because of its exorbitant cost (estimated at $1.5 million).[39] Bissell had brought a map to Chicago that showed the long pier of the Rock Island Bridge occupying the center of the main channel of the river at Rock Island. He told the Chicagoans that the Rock Island Bridge had caused tremendous losses to lumbermen and to St. Louis planing mills because of the inability of boats to carry their work through the bridge. He asserted that the St. Louis Chamber of Commerce was not opposed to bridges across the Mississippi so long as they were built "in such a manner as not to injure navigation on the river." In response to a question, Bissell revealed that a second lawsuit was being prepared for filing against the Rock Island Bridge. This suit, he said, would be "brought by the St. Louis Chamber."[40] The Board of Trade responded by unanimously passing a resolution stating that railroads had "to a great extent superseded water communication, by opening up shorter and more active routes of transporting commodities from and to remote sections of the country." Bridges were "of great service and benefit to the country generally," though they should be built so that they preserved the "navigable value" of all streams. The navigable value of streams was preserved when navigation was "not destroyed thereby, or prejudiced beyond what is actually necessary for the permanent construction of such bridges."[41]

Early on, it was clear that newspapers friendly to the steamboat interests had begun a print campaign against the Rock Island Bridge. The St. Louis press, of course, was opposed to the structure because it imperiled the economic interests of their city (two thirds of the produce once carried to St. Louis from eastern Iowa by steamboats was already being shipped to Chicago by rail).[42] But other journals (chiefly pro-Democratic papers) in other cities soon joined the chorus. After the Chicago Board of Trade met with the St. Louis Chamber of Commerce, the St. Louis *Missouri Republican* (despite its name, a pro-Democratic newspaper) published a long editorial on the bridge question. The *Republican* claimed that it had "no objection to a bridge across the river at the point in question," provided the bridge was built so as to "occasion no detriment to any other interest." It claimed that the Rock Island site presented "superior advantages for the erection of requisite towers for a suspension bridge" and asserted that, if such a bridge was built high enough above the river, "there would be no conflict" between the railroad and the river interests. The *Republican* denied reports circulating in Chicago that St. Louis interests were financing Jacob Hurd's suit against the Railroad Bridge Company, but it left no doubt that those interests sympathized with the suit. "Beyond a doubt, the *Effie Afton* should be paid for by the railroad company," the *Republican* said. "We have no reason to apprehend that the courts will not decide that it shall be paid for. As little do we doubt that they will command the removal of the Rock Island bridge as a nuisance."[43]

The *Illinois State Register,* the pro-Democratic newspaper in Springfield, reported in March that the Rock Island Bridge was "very seriously obstructing the navigation of the river, and by every principle of law and equity should be made to pay for all damage done in consequence of the obstructions." The *Rock Island Argus* (despite its proximity to the new railroad bridge still firmly supportive of the steamboats) printed several stories about boats and rafts that had had trouble passing under the bridge. Some had merely been delayed, the *Argus* said, while others had scraped up against the long pier. Apparently none had suffered damage comparable to that of the *Effie Afton*.[44] The *Galena Courier* reported in April that almost every steamboat on the upper Mississippi was displaying in its grand saloon the map that Josiah Bissell had drawn showing the long pier of the Rock Island Bridge smack in the center of the main channel of the river. It was a warning of the peril that faced all who contemplated passing that spot, and a not so subtle reminder to the traveling public of the solidarity of the steamboat interests in opposing it. The *Courier* reported that millions of dollars of losses were being caused by the bridge every year, and it assured its readers that "the thing" would be "condemned as a nuisance, and ordered to be taken down."[45]

The St. Louis Chamber's denials that it had anything to do with Jacob Hurd's suit against the Railroad Bridge suffered a setback when the *St. Louis Democrat* reported on a meeting held in the Merchants' Exchange on April 16. A committee that the chamber had appointed "to have the Rock Island bridge removed" reported that $16,000 would be needed to prosecute the lawsuit and that assurances had been received from Pittsburgh, Cincinnati, Memphis, and cities and towns along the Upper Mississippi that the sum "would be very easily made up." A resolution was adopted instructing the committee to bring an additional suit in the U.S. District Court in Illinois against the Bridge Company and, if necessary, to take an appeal to the U.S. Supreme Court. The committee was further authorized "to do all things which in their opinion may be necessary, legally, to effect the object contemplated by this chamber."[46]

On June 17, the *Argus* published a long editorial under the heading of "Railroads vs. Navigation," boldly asserting that "the whole country is rife with alarm concerning the gigantic monopoly of the railroad interest." The western rivers generated an annual commerce worth some $400,000,000, the *Argus* said, which, combined with the commerce of the Great Lakes amounted to a grand total of $700,000,000. But "the iron rail" was seeking to divert it all "into new and unnatural channels" by obstructing the rivers with "bridges at every objectionable point." "Shall the river interest then longer submit to be taxed for the maintenance of this towering nuisance?" the *Argus* asked. "To pay tribute to this overshadowing monopoly? To be stricken down upon the door steps of its own dwelling? To lower its flag to this insolent stranger, and to humiliate itself to this usurper of its inalienable and constitutional rights? No! is the deep, strong, indignant response, which comes up from the ten thousand craft, which, crippled and insulted, swarm from end to end and from side to side of the great basin of the Mississippi."[47]

The *Argus*'s questions were excited and clearly exaggerated. But they were proof, if any was needed, that the Rock Island Bridge had inflamed passions, that the trial that was soon to determine its fate would be a bitter one, and that the decision it rendered would be consequential.

SEVEN

Preparing the Ground

≈

W hile the steamboat interests in St. Louis were marshaling their forces against the bridge, the bridge owners were preparing their defense. From the start, their lead attorney was Norman B. Judd of Chicago. Judd was the logical man to resist the *Effie Afton* suit, for he had been one of the incorporators of the Railroad Bridge Company in 1853 and was now its secretary; he had been a director of the Chicago and Rock Island Railroad Company at least since 1854; and he had led the successful defense of the bridge against the efforts of Jefferson Davis, Thomas Hoyne, and Caleb Cushing to persuade Judge McLean to order it torn down in 1855.[1] A short, stout man, with a full beard and a rosy complexion topped by a thin layer of silky hair, Judd had come to Chicago in 1836 from his native New York and quickly launched himself on a busy political and legal career. He drafted Chicago's first city charter in 1837 and served as its first city attorney in 1838. He was the attorney for Cook County in 1839 and a city alderman in 1842. From 1844 on, he was a member of the Illinois State Senate.[2] Because he was a Democrat, Judd had little political contact with Lincoln before 1856, though the men did legal business with each other as early as the 1840s.[3]

Judd was joined on the defense team by Joseph Knox of Rock Island. Born in Massachusetts in 1805, Knox had come to Rock Island in 1837 and built a reputation as a skillful lawyer and civic leader. He had been one of the principal speakers at the ceremonies celebrating the laying of the cornerstone for the bridge on

September 1, 1854, and he had been part of Judd's defense of the bridge against Davis, Cushing, and Hoyne in 1855.[4]

Lincoln did not join the defense team until more than a year after the *Effie Afton*'s collision and more than six months after Hurd and his partners began their lawsuit. During that time, scores of witnesses had been interviewed and more than a thousand pages of written depositions had been taken.[5] Lincoln was in Chicago in early July 1857 for the July term of the U.S. Circuit Court, and on Tuesday, July 7, he was asked to become a part of the bridge's defense team, presumably by Norman Judd. By his own statement, Judd had the chief burden of preparing the case for trial and thus was in a good position to know when he needed help.[6]

Years later, it was claimed that Judd asked Lincoln to join the bridge defense team because Joseph Knox had told him that it would take "a strong, popular man to handle the case." Judd is supposed to have told Knox and Henry Farnam, while they were enjoying after-dinner cigars in Chicago's Tremont House hotel, that "there is only one man in this country who can take this case and win it, and that is Abraham Lincoln." "And who is Abraham Lincoln?" Farnam asked. "A young lawyer from Sangamon County," replied Judd, "one of the best men to state a case forcibly and convincingly that I ever heard, and his personality will appeal to any judge or jury hereabouts. I heard him first at the waterways convention here in Chicago back in 1847, when we were after President Polk's scalp for vetoing as unconstitutional the bill which Congress had passed for the improvement of rivers and the construction of harbors in our Lake Michigan." Farnam is then supposed to have said, "Let's get him up here tomorrow and discuss the matter."[7]

Aside from the undeniable facts that Judd knew Lincoln and admired his courtroom ability, and that they had both participated in the Chicago waterways convention of 1847, there is little reason to believe there was any such conversation between Judd, Knox, and Farnam. The first account of the conversation did not see print until the 1920s, when it was published without any attribution.[8] Further, details of the alleged conversation raise tantalizing questions as to the reliability of the story. Why would Judd describe Lincoln as "a young lawyer" when Lincoln was actually six years older than Judd? (Lincoln was then forty-eight and Judd forty-two.) And why would Henry Farnam in 1857 have asked Judd who Abraham Lincoln was? Lincoln had served in Congress from Illinois from 1847 to 1849; he had come within a whisker of being elected U.S. senator from Illinois in 1855; he had handled an important and high-profile tax case for the Illinois Central Railroad between 1853 and 1856; and he had received 110 votes for the vice presidential nomination of the Republican Party in Philadelphia in 1856. When Judd tapped him to join the bridge defense team, Lincoln had a reputation that extended beyond Illinois. (When the pro-steamboat *Rock Island Argus* first told its readers that Lincoln had joined the defense team for the bridge, it described him as "Hon. A. Lincoln—This distinguished lawyer.")[9] And Judd certainly did not believe that Lincoln was indispensable to victory in the upcoming trial, for he himself was a skillful courtroom advocate and had every intention of exercising principal control over the case, as the trial itself would soon demonstrate. Judd was no doubt glad to have Lincoln join him and Knox, but as part of a team, not as the "only man in this country who can take this case and win it."

More important, perhaps, in Judd's decision to ask Lincoln to join him in the *Effie Afton* trial was the personal trust the two men had already established between them. That trust is evidenced by a transaction they entered into on the eve of the trial. Around the middle of August, Lincoln received his large fee of $4,800 for representing the Illinois Central in the McLean County tax case.[10] After giving Billy Herndon his half, Lincoln combined the remaining $2,400 with another $100 and lent $2,500 to Judd. Judd wanted to invest in land in Council Bluffs, Iowa, where he believed the projected transcontinental railroad (long talked about but not yet approved) would begin its history-making route to the Pacific Coast. He needed cash to invest. Lincoln had no interest in speculative schemes, but he did like to lend money out on interest. On or about September 1, 1857, he lent Judd $2,500 in return for a promissory note bearing interest of 10 percent per annum, principal and interest all payable September 1, 1859.[11] Of course, the loan had no direct relationship to the *Effie Afton* trial, though it did indicate that the two men were not strangers, either personally or financially.

The trial of *Hurd et al. v. The Railroad Bridge Company* was to be held in the Chicago courtroom of the U.S. Circuit Court. Both of Chicago's federal courts (circuit and district) met in 1857 in a large, three-story frame structure that stood at the southeast corner of Lake and Clark Streets and bore the curious name of the Saloon Building. Built in 1836, it had served a variety of official and unofficial functions in its twenty-plus years of civic life. In January 1837, it was the site of a meeting called to plan preliminary action for procuring a Chicago city charter. In 1839, it was the building in which Stephen Douglas made his first speech in Chicago; in the same year, it was the site of a debate between Douglas and Lincoln's first law partner, John Todd Stuart, when they campaigned against each other for a seat in the U.S. House of Representatives.[12] It also served for several years as the first Chicago city hall and, for much of that time, housed the U.S. Post Office. John Wentworth, a prominent lawyer, newspaper editor, and politician who served both as a congressman and as a two-term mayor of Chicago, said that when the Saloon Building was first opened it "was the largest and most beautiful hall this side of Buffalo."[13] Judging from pictures, it is hard to imagine why Wentworth considered the Saloon Building so beautiful. Yes, it was large, it was tall, it had a certain symmetry, and it occupied a prominent site in Chicago, but in later years neighboring buildings towered over it, and its wooden walls and floors fell into a very unattractive disrepair. That it was regarded in the late 1830s as an ornament to Chicago may tell us something about the great distance (cultural as well as geographic) that separated the frontier city at the edge of Lake Michigan from the older and more cultivated cities east of the Appalachians.

In 1857, the ground floor of the Saloon Building was occupied by stores and the second floor by offices, while the spacious third floor was home to the courts.[14] The courtroom itself was about forty feet square, with a high ceiling. Half the space was set aside for the judges, clerks, and attorneys; the other half was occupied by long benches for the accommodation of the public. A large stove stood near the door.[15] The author of a history of Chicago published a half century after the Saloon Building was opened admitted that the building's name "would, to the casual reader, appear to connect it with a house of no very good repute," but he insisted that "such an impression would be erroneous. The word 'saloon' as applied to this edifice had a very different meaning from what it now has. Its use was synonymous with the French *salon*, which means literally a grand and spacious hall."[16]

When Lincoln was in Chicago, he customarily stayed at the Tremont House, an imposing, five-story hostelry that stood just a block east of the Saloon Building and provided convenient access to the courts for lawyers who were doing business there.

Lincoln's first appearance in the case of *Hurd et al. v. The Railroad Bridge Company* was made in the Saloon Building on July 9. It was the beginning of the U.S. Circuit Court's July term, and District Judge Thomas Drummond and Circuit Judge John McLean were both on the bench (federal statutes then permitted the district and circuit judges to preside alone or together in circuit court cases). When the case was called up for trial, Lincoln requested that the judges continue it until the following term, set to begin in December. He read an affidavit signed by Judd asserting that the defendants were not then prepared to go to trial and that the suit was "one of vast importance, involving in the particular case, between $150,000 and $200,000." Beyond that, the parties had treated the case in their preparations "very much with reference to the future maintenance of the bridge . . . over and across the Mississippi at Rock Island." Judd had devoted almost the whole of his time from the previous March to the preparation of the defense. He and his co-attorneys had received about 1,100 pages of depositions, and nearly 600 of those had not been opened before the first day of the current term.[17] Judd had not had sufficient time or opportunity to examine and digest "this mass of testimony" and could not do so without the "aid of assistant counsel." The testimony of several witnesses who were not then ready to appear was necessary to the trial. Lincoln then read another affidavit, this signed by himself, in which he said that he had been engaged as an attorney in the case only two days earlier. Since that time, he,

Judd, and another Chicago-based attorney named John M. Douglass had devoted most of their time to "the examination of said case." As it then stood, the case was not ready for trial.[18]

Hezekiah Wead then argued against the requested continuance. His side was ready to proceed, he said, and had been since the previous December. It was important to try the case now, for water in the river was low and many of the river men who would be called as witnesses could then come to court. During the rest of the year (except in the winter when the rivers were blocked by ice) they were too busy on the rivers to take time away from their work. Wead understood that the defendants did not want Judge Drummond to preside over the trial; they were "anxious," he said, to try the case before Judge McLean. Wead denied that anything was involved in the case but whether his clients were entitled to damages for the loss of their boat and its cargo. Judd's assertion that the case was also about "the future maintenance of the bridge" was "doubtless a very honest opinion," but Wead did not share it. "It has never entered into my mind," he said, that the suit was to "determine the existence of that bridge. I repeat, we have nothing to do with that."[19]

Lincoln then made an argument for continuance. "This case for the size of it is not a very old one," he said. "It is very rare that a case of the consequence of this is tried in a year from the time it is brought." He denied that his side wanted the case to be tried before Judge McLean and not Judge Drummond. "I am quite willing to try the case before Judge Drummond or before Judge Drummond and Judge McLean, as before either or both." (The law then permitted the judges themselves to determine which of them would preside, alone or together.)[20] Wead's contention that river men could not conveniently come to trial at another time of the year did not ring quite true with Lincoln. "I would suggest," he said, "while it is in my mind, that October is really less of a navigable month than July—that in all probability there is more steamboat navigation now than in October. I should at least think so from the little recollection I have on this subject, since I was on a flat boat many years ago. I should think that as a rule the rivers are lower in October than in July and will probably be lower in the coming October than in this coming month. This, however, I say I don't know much about."[21]

Lincoln's willingness to have the case tried before either Judge McLean or Judge Drummond was, if nothing else, evidence of his courtroom tact. Why should he or his colleagues express a preference for one of the two jurists when doing so might offend the other? McLean was, of course, the more eminent of the two, and the senior in both age and judicial service, for he was seventy-two years old and in his twenty-eighth year as an associate justice of the United States Supreme Court. Drummond, in contrast, was forty-seven and had served as a U.S. district judge for only seven years. Both men, however, were well-respected judges, and both could be expected to conduct a fair trial.

John McLean had been born in New Jersey in 1785, although he moved with his family to Virginia in 1789, to Kentucky in 1790, and to Ohio in 1796. He worked on his family's farm until he was sixteen and, like Lincoln, was largely self-educated. But he was an intelligent man with a driving ambition that quickly set him apart from other Ohio farm boys. He published a newspaper before beginning the practice of law, then plunged into a long life of public service and political finagling, which included a term as head of the U.S. Land Office in Cincinnati from 1811 to 1812 and one as a member of the U.S. House of Representatives from 1813 to 1816. From 1816 to 1822, he was an associate justice of the Supreme Court of Ohio. He was thirty-eight years old when, in 1823, President James Monroe appointed him as U.S. postmaster general. Satisfied that McLean was a loyal supporter, John Quincy Adams kept him as postmaster general through his presidential term, but when Andrew Jackson assumed the presidency in 1829 McLean switched his loyalty from Adams to Old Hickory and was promptly rewarded with Jackson's first appointment to the United States Supreme Court. Supreme Court judges in those days spent more time presiding over trials in the circuits to which they were assigned than hearing appeals in Washington. McLean's Seventh Circuit first embraced the states of Ohio, Kentucky, and Tennessee, but after the judicial reorganization of 1837 it was redrawn to embrace Ohio, Indiana, Illinois, and Michigan.[22] He had to travel (in the early days by boat and stagecoach, in later years by rail) over his far-flung circuit, presiding over trials, alone or in conjunction with the U.S. district judges in the various districts.

McLean had a reputation as a hardworking, conscientious judge, and his views on the great legal issues facing the United States were for the most part mainstream. He wrote the majority opinion in the controversial case of *Pennsylvania v. Wheeling and Belmont Bridge Company* in 1852, in which the Supreme Court declared the suspension bridge over the Ohio River a nuisance and ordered it to be raised to a greater height or torn down.[23] Four years later, however, he refused to issue an injunction against the Rock Island Bridge, ruling that it did not constitute a nuisance as a matter of law, although a lawsuit for damages might one day be brought against its builders.[24] McLean was also a perpetual dabbler in presidential politics, making it known over the years that he would be available as a presidential candidate for the Anti-Masonic, Free Soil Democratic, Whig, and finally Republican parties. Lincoln thought enough of McLean in 1856 that he expressed his support of McLean as that year's Republican presidential nominee,[25] but the national convention chose Frémont. Lincoln continued to express political support for McLean right up through the early part of 1860, repeatedly saying that he was a good candidate for the presidential nomination, although his age (he was then seventy-five) militated against him in the eyes of many Republicans.[26]

McLean was a large man, with a large head (in later years mostly bald although framed by long, somewhat disheveled hair) and a handsome face. He was courteous to all who entered his courtroom, although more stiff and proper than amiable.[27] Salmon P. Chase, a prominent Ohio attorney and politician (he was to join Lincoln's presidential cabinet as secretary of the treasury in 1861 and win Lincoln's nomination to succeed Roger Taney as chief justice of the Supreme Court in 1864) knew McLean well, for both men made their homes in Cincinnati. Chase thought highly of McLean's intentions but not of his manner. "It is a thousand pities that a man of such real benevolence of heart as the Judge possesses," Chase once commented, "should not allow more of it to flow into his manners."[28]

McLean's most notable judicial opinion was the dissent he filed just a few months before the opening of the *Effie Afton* trial in the infamous case of *Dred Scott v. Sandford*. In his thirty-five-page dissent from the opinion of Chief Justice Roger Taney, McLean mounted a vigorous attack on slavery, arguing that Dred Scott should be recognized as a free man because he had been taken by his master to live on free soil. Slavery, in McLean's view, was a state institution and not protected by the federal constitution or laws.[29] Lincoln agreed with the views McLean expressed in *Dred Scott*,[30] but his impressions of the judge himself may not have been altogether positive. He had, of course, seen McLean in action in Illinois in cases in which he was an attorney. But when he went to Cincinnati in 1855 to take part in *McCormick v. Manny*, he had an opportunity to see the Supreme Court justice in a different light. Although Lincoln was rudely excluded by the other attorneys from participating in the Manny trial, he stayed long enough in the river city to get a good impression of McLean on the bench in a very important case. Henry Clay Whitney said that when Lincoln returned from his unpleasant experience in Cincinnati, he said, "Judge McLean is a man of considerable vigor of mind but no perception at all; if you was to point your finger at him and also a darning needle he would not Know which was the sharpest."[31]

Thomas Drummond was a judge everybody seemed to admire. Intelligent and well educated, he combined the work ethic of his native New England (he was born in Maine in 1809) with the legal professionalism of Philadelphia, where he studied law and began his legal career in 1833. He moved to Illinois in 1835, settling in the lead-rich mining town of Galena (at one time second only to Chicago among Illinois's most populous cities), where he practiced law and was elected to the Illinois House of Representatives. Walter Q. Gresham, a prominent lawyer, politician, and judge who knew Drummond very well in later years, said that "all things considered, Judge Drummond was the most perfect man I have ever known." William Howard Taft, who became acquainted with Drummond as a young man in Cincinnati and later served not only as president of the United States but also as chief justice of the Supreme Court, said that everybody who came in contact with Drummond "felt that he was of the material and timber which Supreme Court judges ought to have."[32] Lincoln knew Drummond well, for he represented clients in at least twenty-four cases in which Drummond presided, and after he became president he considered nominating him to the Supreme Court at least twice, although other considerations ultimately persuaded him to name different men.[33] Drummond began his service as judge of the U.S. District Court in 1850, presiding over courts in both Springfield and Chicago until 1855, when Congress divided Illinois into Northern and Southern Districts. Drummond thereafter served in the Northern District in Chicago while Judge Samuel Treat took up duties in the Southern District in Springfield.[34]

When Lincoln appeared before Judges Drummond and McLean to ask that the trial of *Hurd et al. v. The Railroad Bridge Company* be continued to a later date, both Wead and Judd had commented on the interesting (and very important) question of whether the case was only about seeking damages or had some larger implications. "We hope that we are quite aware that nothing more will be absolutely determined by the decision in this case," Lincoln told the judges. "That is we are quite aware, as we think, that the bridge will not be torn down, not be abated as a nuisance on any judgment in this case." But both parties had been "shaping their testimony in this case with reference to something more" than the mere issue of damages. "If this case should be half tried," Lincoln said, "or tried upon half the evidence that should be gone in, that would bear upon [the larger question], we should have another long law suit about this bridge, which if we get it fully tried, we may never have. Both parties do look upon it in that view. The examination of these 1,100 pages of testimony shows it."[35]

As he looked about the courtroom, Lincoln noticed a reporter who was busily taking down everything that was being said, including Lincoln's own remarks. "I don't know the gentleman," Lincoln said, "—he is a gentleman to all appearance—but I would risk a trifle that he is a St. Louis reporter, and of course Judge Wead does not know him. Of course he does not."

Judge McLean interrupted to say, "That is quite immaterial. The gentleman has a right to report."

"Of course," Lincoln replied, "and he may have come here on his own hook. It may be that Judge Wead don't know him at all." It was easy to detect a note of sarcasm in Lincoln's remarks, but the sarcasm was justified. He knew that the upcoming trial was being closely followed in St. Louis. Newspapers from the great river city did not usually send shorthand reporters to cover trials in Chicago, particularly if the only purpose of the trial was to determine whether steamboat owners from Cincinnati could collect damages for a boat that was destroyed more than three hundred miles north of St. Louis. "To keep inside the record by the affidavit," Lincoln continued, "it will be made to appear that the main question is the general obstruction of the navigation by this bridge."[36]

The reporter Lincoln referred to was Henry Binmore, a twenty-three-year-old, British-born journalist from St. Louis who had developed a unique method of taking shorthand notes. It enabled him to work quickly and efficiently, but since his notes were of his own invention, nobody else could read them.[37] He had been sent to Chicago to cover the *Effie Afton* trial for the St. Louis *Missouri Republican*, an influential newspaper that, like the steamboat interests in St. Louis, was strongly opposed to the Rock Island Bridge. If Binmore brought a degree of professionalism to his work, it was mixed with a heavy dose of anti-Chicago bias. He was by most accounts a peculiar man, variously condemned as "seedy," "a complete little fop and fool," and "hard to get along with."[38] He would eventually be fired by the *Missouri Republican* for unethical conduct, but then hired in 1858 by Stephen Douglas to report that year's debates between Douglas and Lincoln for the pro-Douglas *Chicago Times*. Years later, Robert R. Hitt, who reported the same Lincoln-Douglas debates for the *Chicago Press and Tribune*, asserted that Binmore was paid to cover the debates for the explicit purpose of misrepresenting Lincoln's remarks, making him "appear ignorant and uncouth beside Douglas."[39] Binmore's anti-Lincoln malice was not so evident in his coverage of the bridge trial in 1857, although his opposition to the Rock Island Bridge was an ever-present background to his reporting.

Hitt's own reports of the trial, printed in the *Chicago Press*, were not entirely unbiased either, for, as Hitt confided to his journal, Norman Judd paid him "a lot of money" for reporting the "bridge case."[40] If Henry Binmore was in the employ of the *Missouri Republican*, Robert R. Hitt was in the employ of Norman Judd and the railroad interests he represented.

Despite these obvious conflicts of interest, the newspaper reports of Binmore and Hitt were to become essential records of the trial. Because the official court records were destroyed in the great Chicago fire of 1871, the newspaper reports emerged as the only surviving records of the case. They enjoyed another distinction as well, for they were eventually to be recognized as one of only three verbatim transcripts of the oral testimony of courtroom witnesses in all of Lincoln's law practice.[41]

After the arguments on Lincoln's motion for a continuance were completed, Judge McLean made his ruling. The trial would be continued to a special term of the circuit court to begin in September. When the precise date of the commencement was set, Judge McLean would announce it.[42]

In early September, Henry Binmore wrote what he called a "summing up" of the *Effie Afton* story for the *Missouri Republican*. He had read some of the depositions taken in preparation for the trial and concluded that the steamboat owners would rely primarily on the testimony of river pilots to prove that the Rock Island Bridge was a "material obstruction" to navigation. The bridge owners, in contrast, would rely primarily on the testimony of engineers to prove that it was not. Betraying his pro-steamboat, anti-bridge bias, Binmore told his readers: "The case seems to depend, so far as agreement goes, upon whether the jury will be governed more by the plain and unvarnished facts of the case, or whether they will be 'befogged' by an accumulation of scientific illustrations." Binmore continued: "As a collateral question will, of course, come up, the effect of the bridge as a nuisance, including the question as to whether it is built in such a way as to cause eddies, cross-currents, and the piling of the water, &c., &c. Scientific men will of course differ hereupon, and the men who should know all about it, disagreeing, a jury of twelve men who *know nothing* about it will be called on to decide the scientific question."[43]

Lincoln remained in Chicago until July 18 and then went home to Springfield. He had some court cases to attend to, but none that occupied a lot of his time. He and Mrs. Lincoln were able to leave Illinois in late July for a two-week vacation, which took them to Niagara Falls and other points of interest in New York and Canada. He was back at work in Springfield by August 5. On August 17, he responded by letter to an invitation from Governor James Grimes of Iowa to give a political speech in Davenport. He told Grimes that he was engaged in the Rock Island Bridge case in Chicago, that it was scheduled to begin on September 8 (the date had since been announced by Judge McLean), and that it would probably last two or three weeks. He thought that "all hands" might come over to take a look at the bridge before the trial started, and told Grimes that if it was possible "to make it hit right," he could speak in Davenport.[44]

Some accounts of Lincoln's participation in the Rock Island Bridge case assert that he spent "months" in preparation for the trial, that he interviewed prospective witnesses, and that he took "numerous depositions for use upon the trial."[45] Some claim that he hired a steamboat (or steamboats) to take him through the draw of the bridge several times to test the boat's reaction to the currents and the piers.[46] Like the conversation with cigars between Judd, Knox, and Farnam in the Tremont House, these accounts raise more questions than they answer. They were not published until many years after the event, and it is generally agreed that, other things being equal, the passage of a long period of time between an event and the first account of it undermines its credibility. Further, the accounts were not attributed. Who was present when Lincoln hired the boat (or boats)? Who saw him use them to test the currents? We are not told. Lincoln himself said in open court that he did not come into the case until July 7, 1857, and that by that time more than a thousand pages of depositions had already been taken. How many more depositions had yet to be taken? It is clear from Lincoln's other activities between July 7 and the opening of the trial (barely two months in all) that he was busy with other cases and that he took some time to make a sight-seeing trip with Mrs. Lincoln. There is no reason to doubt that Lincoln prepared carefully for the trial; it was his nature to prepare carefully for important cases. He certainly researched the law, studied the depositions that had been taken before he joined the defense team, and discussed the issues that would arise in the trial with his co-counsel. It is stretching the facts, however, to say that he spent "months" getting ready, or that his preparation was "prodigious."

Some doubts have been expressed as to whether Lincoln visited the bridge before the trial.[47] Not long after he wrote Governor Grimes to say that he might be able to speak in Iowa if he and the other attorneys were able to come over and "take a look at the Bridge," the Rock Island Argus reported that Lincoln was "expected in Davenport in a few days, for the purpose of examining" the bridge.[48] Sometime in the 1930s, a valuation engineer for the Chicago and Rock Island Railroad announced that the railroad archives contained a letter-book copy of a letter purporting to have been written by Judd to Lincoln on September 4, 1857, acknowledging that Lincoln had in fact visited the bridge.[49] In the letter, Judd expressed the hope that Lincoln "suffered no ill effects" from his trip to Rock Island and his "inspection of the Mississippi river bridge last Tuesday [i.e., September 1]." The letter was dated at Chicago and addressed to Lincoln in Springfield, and it was not in Judd's own hand but in that of another, unidentified person.[50] Because Lincoln was already in Chicago when the letter was sent to Springfield, and because Judd normally wrote out his letters in his own handwriting, some questions have been raised about the authenticity of the letter. Why didn't Judd communicate with Lincoln personally, or at least send the letter to him in Chicago? Why didn't he write out the letter in his own hand?[51]

There is no doubt that Lincoln left Springfield for Chicago during the first week of September.[52] And there is good evidence that, just before or after his arrival in the lakeside city, he visited the Rock Island Bridge in conjunction with some of the other lawyers and engineers who were involved in the case. Benjamin B. Brayton, the engineer who had located the bridge, designed it, and supervised its construction, was on hand to help him inspect the span and answer his questions. Brayton's teenage son, Benjamin B. (Bud) Brayton Jr., was also there, and years later he recorded his recollection of what had happened during the visit.

Bud Brayton said that Lincoln did not seem to be satisfied by the explanations offered by the bridge engineers about the currents in the river. He approached Brayton and said, "Young man, are you employed on the bridge? If so will you go with me to the head of the draw pier and answer some questions?" Brayton readily complied. After a time, Lincoln said that he understood the situation. He thanked young Brayton, said good night, and rejoined the other men who had come with him to Rock Island. He then boarded the special Rock Island car that had brought him west from Chicago and returned to the lakeside city.[53]

Lincoln's departure from Springfield in the first week of September; his letter to Governor Grimes in which he expressed willingness to speak in Iowa (although there is no evidence that he did in fact do so); the newspaper report that he was expected in Davenport; Judd's letter acknowledging that Lincoln did in fact visit the Rock Island Bridge; Bud Brayton's later memories of Lincoln's appearance on the span; and the detailed knowledge that Lincoln revealed of the bridge during the trial: all of these point to the conclusion that Lincoln did in fact visit the bridge and did study its structure and its operation, although probably only in the company of other men who went there with him. It would have been highly out of character for him to go into such an important case without inspecting the object of the controversy, particularly when by simply taking a train from Chicago to Rock Island he could quite easily have done so.

Lincoln's preparations were now complete. The trial was about to begin.

EIGHT

A Very Serious Obstruction

≈

The U.S. Circuit Court for the Northern District of Illinois met on Tuesday morning, September 8, 1857, on the third floor of the Saloon Building in Chicago. Promptly at nine o'clock, Judge John McLean took his seat on the bench and rapped his gavel for order. Looking across the courtroom, the judge could see that the seats inside the bar were all occupied and that the spectators' benches were packed; not surprisingly, for Chicagoans knew that the trial the newspapers were already calling the *Effie Afton* case would have far-reaching consequences for the transportation future of the country. Adding to the crowd, the sheriff had brought prospective jurors to be examined and selected, men who eyed the lawyers with curiosity and listened somewhat nervously as the judge spoke.

The counsel table was lined with the attorneys who had come to do battle in the case: Hezekiah Wead of Peoria, T. D. Lincoln of Cincinnati, and Corydon Beckwith of Chicago for the plaintiffs, and Norman B. Judd of Chicago, Abraham Lincoln of Springfield, and Joseph Knox of Rock Island for the defendants. Henry Binmore of the St. Louis *Missouri Republican* was on hand with his shorthand pad, eager to transcribe the proceedings for his readers in the Missouri City, while Robert R. Hitt was ready to do the same for readers of the *Chicago Press*.[1] Another reporter (unnamed in the newspaper accounts) represented the *Chicago Tribune*. The Chicago and St. Louis reporters knew that when they filed their reports, newspapers in cities and towns throughout the country would reprint them, anxious to apprise their readers of the drama that was now unfolding in Judge McLean's courtroom.

According to Binmore's reports, John M. Douglass appeared with Judd, Knox, and Abraham Lincoln for the defendants, although there is no indication that he actively participated in examining witnesses or making arguments. Douglass was a lawyer of skill and some influence who had practiced for several years in Galena before moving to Chicago, where he became counsel (and eventually president) of the Illinois Central Railroad.[2] He may have acted as an assistant to Judd, Knox, and Lincoln, helping them schedule witnesses and access the depositions and other documents they would need during the trial. Lawyers who perform these functions in complicated trials often render valuable services, though their names appear infrequently in the records.

Judd was the first attorney to speak. He rose from his seat and, with the suavity that characterized his many courtroom appearances, asked Judge McLean to clarify a question relating to the use of depositions. So many of these out-of-court transcripts had been taken that some were already likening the case to *Jarndyce v. Jarndyce,* a trial described in Charles Dickens's *Bleak House* that dragged on for generations, impoverishing the litigants while it enriched the lawyers. Judd said that both sides would have "exceptions to considerable portions of the depositions," and he wanted to know if the exceptions should be taken up before the trial began. It was a reasonable question, and Judge McLean lost no time in answering it. The only objections that could be raised before the trial began would be "of a formal character," he said, "involving the regularity of giving notice of taking depositions, and the residence of parties, and so on. As to the materiality of evidence, that could only be ascertained during the progress of the case."[3]

The next question related to the selection of jurors. Congress had in its earliest statutes laid down some general rules for this but left broad discretion to the courts to flesh out the details. Jurors in federal courts were to have the same qualifications as jurors in the state courts of the federal district and, to the extent practicable, be selected in the same manner. When, from challenges or other reasons, there were not enough prospective jurors to make up a full jury panel, the judge could order the marshal to summon "talesmen" from among bystanders who were in the courtroom or close by and otherwise qualified to serve as jurors.[4]

The accustomed practice in the U.S. Circuit Court for Illinois was to call prospective jurors in groups of four, permitting first one side and then the other to examine them.[5] When the trial began only thirteen prospective jurors were present, and by the time of the court's adjournment at two o'clock only eight had been selected, so McLean ordered the marshal to summon talesmen.[6]

Each prospective juror was questioned about his place of residence, his occupation, his previous knowledge of the case, and his willingness to be impartial. All were, of course, white men, for women had no right to serve on juries in the middle of the nineteenth century, and anyone, male or female, who was not white was disqualified from jury service in Illinois and much of the rest of the country as well.[7] None of the prospective jurors had any personal interest in the Rock Island Railroad or the Railroad Bridge Company, although one explained that he operated a small "eating place" on the railroad between Chicago and Rock Island and that it drew most of its business from railroad traffic; he didn't think this would affect his ability to be impartial. Most but not all of the prospective jurors lived in Chicago. Two were from Peoria. One was from the town of Marengo, west of Chicago; another was from Macomb, in the west central part of the state. The operator of the "eating place" was from Sheffield, a coaling stop on the Chicago and Rock Island Railroad. One came from the Logan County town of Lincoln, named for Abraham Lincoln in 1853. Not surprisingly, all of the prospective jurors had read about the case in the newspapers, but most assured the judge that they had not formed any rigid opinions about it. The talesmen summoned by the marshal were brought into the courtroom at three o'clock and subjected to the same questioning as those who had gone before.[8]

The newspaper accounts did not specify which of the attorneys examined the jurors, so we do not know if Lincoln participated in this part of the trial. Nor was it altogether clear from the printed stories how many of the prospective jurors were challenged for cause and how many were challenged without any specification of cause (challenges of this sort are called peremptory). At least three of the prospective jurors admitted that they had formed opinions about the case that would be hard, perhaps even impossible, to change. They were excused by the judge. The plaintiffs issued peremptory challenges to at least three of the prospective jurors, and the defendants to at least one. One of the prospective jurors was found acceptable by both the plaintiffs and the defendant but sought to be excused because of the "necessities of his business." Judge McLean denied his request. The examination concluded by four o'clock, when twelve jurors were sworn. Their names as set forth in the *Chicago Press* were Isaac Underhill, Richard Vinecose, James Clark, Elisha D. Putnam, Isaac Dempsey, E. Rice, H. G. Otis, J. P. Warner, H. H. Husted, William P. Ross, C. D. Smith, and John Elting.[9] (The spelling of these names varied slightly in the *Missouri Republican* and the *Tribune*, bearing witness to the imperfections of the reporters who were transcribing the proceedings. Hitt was so imperfect that he repeatedly wrote the name of Abraham Lincoln as "Abram Lincoln").[10] None of the jurors were, so far as the evidence shows, notable individuals in their own right. But by taking their places in the jury box in Chicago's Saloon Building on September 8, 1857, all were destined to play a part in history.

As lead attorney for the plaintiffs, it fell to Judge Wead to make the first opening statement. A canny courtroom advocate with ample experience addressing juries, Wead was sometimes criticized for an excessively combative spirit, a quality that impressed his clients but struck impartial observers as unattractive.[11] His zeal, however, translated into strong and decisive words in the courtroom. "May it please the Court, and gentlemen of the jury," Wead began, "this is an action brought by the owners of the steamboat *Effie Afton*, to recover from the Bridge Company at Rock Island, the value of a steamboat, and a portion of her cargo, and such other damages caused by the destruction of her freight, as she may be entitled, under the law and the evidence, to recover."[12]

Wead reviewed the basic facts of the case: the circumstances leading up to the *Effie Afton*'s collision with the bridge on May 6, 1856,
and the losses that were suffered as a result of the collision and the
fire that followed. He told the jurors that the *Effie Afton* was an unusually long boat and that it was carrying an unusually heavy cargo at
the time of the collision. The water in the river was running high,
and it was windy. When the *Afton* first arrived at the bridge, it found
"several boats lying there." Some were detained in going up the river
and some in going down, on account of the difficulty in passing the
draw. The next morning, the *Afton* attempted to pass through the
draw, but it collided with the bridge, caught fire, and was destroyed.[13]

Wead told the jurors that the bridge was built at a point in the
river where there was an island, and the channel between the island
and the Iowa side of the river was "narrower than anywhere in that
neighborhood, or, as I am told, anywhere on the Mississippi River."
The water was thus "compressed into a very narrow channel." As it
flowed under the bridge, it struck the draw pier at an angle, creating
eddies and cross-currents. "Although the draw pier is one hundred
and sixteen feet in width," Wead said, "it does not admit a current
of one hundred and sixteen feet in width for boats to use in passing
up and down."

Judge McLean interrupted Wead to ask if that was "the exact
width of the draw." Judd hastened to supply the answer. "One hundred twenty feet is the width," he said. Wead admitted that that was
"somewhere about it." Knox then intervened. "It is one hundred
twenty feet at the top," the Rock Island lawyer said, "but the piers
are a little narrower at the bottom."[14]

Wead believed that the main issue in the trial would be whether
the angle at which the water currents approached the draw of the
bridge made it "hazardous." He said that this question could only
be answered by witnesses who had practical experience navigating the river, not by "experts" whose knowledge of navigation was
purely theoretical. Before the bridge was built, there was no
obstruction of the river, Wead said. "The river has always been
free, without difficulty of navigation there." (Here he was conveniently ignoring the treacherous natural obstructions lurking in

the Rock Island Rapids less than a quarter of a mile upstream.) Wead thought that a suspension bridge might be built without obstructing the navigation of the river, or a tunnel dug under the river channel. "With the question as to whether they may build a bridge, or whether that bridge shall be destroyed, we have nothing to do, but we have the right to insist that if they build a bridge they shall do it so as not to obstruct our lawful navigation of the river."[15]

As Wead resumed his seat, Judd rose to present the defendants' opening statement. "I have listened with some attention to the statement of the case on the other side," the Chicagoan told the jurors. That statement was "mistaken as to the facts." The *Effie Afton* decided not to go through the bridge on the first day it arrived at Rock Island because of the high wind that was blowing over the river, not because the bridge was obstructing navigation. Just a quarter of a mile above the bridge the Rock Island Rapids awaited boats, Judd said, and they were "such an obstruction as prevents useful navigation." Wead had failed to tell the jury about the *Afton*'s erratic movements on the morning of the collision. "The first thing she did was to run into the ferryboat *John Wilson*," Judd said. Then she tried to make a race to the bridge, quickly passing by another boat (the *J. B. Carson*) that had started out first. There was "a good channel" in the draw, Judd said, but in passing the *Carson* on the Davenport side the *Afton* entered an eddy. "As a necessary consequence she was out of the channel and in the wrong place, and the result of that was her bow ran across the entrance of the draw and struck the small pier on this side." The *Afton* got in a dangerous position—a "very dangerous position," Judd said—"by the negligence of the parties having the management of that boat."

Judd then made an accusation that was calculated to astonish the jurors. He told them that the small fires that broke out on the *Afton* at the time of the collision were successfully put out in five or ten minutes, but the great fire that consumed the boat and damaged the bridge did not begin for another hour or more. "How, how did it happen?" Judd asked. "I will tell you how it would happen. The boat had got where it would probably be lost. She had no insurance except as against fire, and some of them conceived the design that it was better to take 'half a loaf than no bread.' And so the boat burned, and I think we can show beyond all question that the burning was from design."[16]

If gasps of astonishment swept across the courtroom at this accusation, nobody would have asked why. Judd was accusing the steamboat owners of deliberately starting the fire that destroyed the *Afton* and brought down a section of the bridge. It was a shocking charge.

Judd was only warming to his case. He next referred to the concerted opposition to the bridge that had been organized in river cities such as Pittsburgh, St. Paul, and St. Louis. This opposition was "under the lead of the St. Louis Chamber of Commerce," Judd charged, "organized at a meeting held on the 16th December [1856]." T. D. Lincoln was offended by this charge. "You really do not state that?" the Cincinnatian asked Judd almost impulsively. Judd was not daunted. He said that he had a deposition showing that the lawsuit had to be "vigorously pursued, because a decision in this case might prevent their tearing down all the other bridges. I have read it." The influence of the St. Louis Chamber was so great that no pilot "dares to express his true opinion" about the cause of the collision, and opposition to the Rock Island Bridge had been "organizing from Pittsburgh to St. Louis." Judd said he had been at the bridge when he saw a boat approach and the captain order all of the passengers to get off and walk around the bridge because it was "dangerous"—but as soon as the passengers were off, the boat came "kiting up through the bridge." "Why do they do this?" Judd asked. "So that passengers may go and tell half the world what great danger they have been in from this bridge."

Judd next refuted Wead's assertion that the bridge had been built at the narrowest point of the river for the convenience of the railroad, disregarding the needs of the river navigation. He insisted that the span was "located by skillful engineers as being the most convenient point for the uses to which it was to be applied." Boats could "easily pass" through it, Judd said, adding that the *Effie Afton* could have successfully passed through it on the day of the collision "if she had been properly managed."

T. D. Lincoln then asked for leave to address the court. He said that, as far as he knew or believed, neither the Chamber of Commerce of St. Louis, nor any other combinations, had anything to do with this case. He insisted that he had never received compensation from anyone but the plaintiffs. He then showed the jurors "a rough sketch of a map" and spoke to them about it. Judd and Knox followed this up with what Henry Binmore called "a few desultory remarks" and the reporter for the *Tribune* called "more explanations."[17] So far as the newspaper accounts reveal, Abraham Lincoln did not take part in the opening statements. After cautioning the jury not to speak concerning the case among themselves or to anyone outside the courtroom, Judge McLean adjourned the court to the following morning.

Wead and his colleagues knew from the outset that if they were to prevail in their lawsuit against the Rock Island Bridge they would have to call on witnesses who were scattered widely through the river country. Some of the men who had experience on the Upper Mississippi, or who had personal knowledge of the *Effie Afton*'s disastrous collision with the bridge, hailed from such distant locations as Pittsburgh, while many others came from St. Louis, and a good number lived and did most of their business in the river towns of Ohio and Kentucky. The lawyers knew that it would be difficult, if not impossible, to bring all of those witnesses to Chicago to testify, so they began months before to take their depositions with the understanding that if the witnesses could not attend the trial, the attorneys would read their depositions to the jury. Testimony read to jurors from written depositions does not have the force and effect of testimony given on the witness stand, where the jurors can personally observe the witnesses' demeanor and judge whether they seem to be open and sincere in what they say or are hesitant or unsure. But written testimony is better than no testimony at all, so the lawyers in the *Afton* trial made abundant use of the depositions they had spent months gathering.

It is customary for attorneys in all jury trials to stand whenever they address the jury—it is a mark of respect for the men (and later the women, when they were admitted to juries) who hold their clients' futures in their hands. The newspaper accounts of the *Effie Afton* trial do not disclose whether T. D. Lincoln and the other lawyers who read depositions followed this practice, although it is reasonable to assume that they did.

The Cincinnatian was the first lawyer to read depositions to the jury. He started on Wednesday morning, the second day of the trial, reading depositions that established that the *Afton* was owned by Hurd, Kidwell, and Smith, and that it was licensed and enrolled by the United States surveyor of customs at Cincinnati on November 22, 1856.[18] He then continued with other more interesting transcripts.

One was that of James W. Connor, a steamboat pilot from New Albany, Indiana, who had been a pilot on the Ohio and Mississippi rivers for fifteen or sixteen years. Connor was asked how the erection of the Rock Island Bridge had "affected the navigation of the Mississippi River at the place," what "class of boats were in the habit of navigating it where the bridge crosses it," and whether steamboats could navigate the river there "with barges or crafts in tow."[19] These questions elicited a quick objection from Norman Judd, who reminded Judge McLean that the Bridge Company had been sued because of the loss of the steamboat *Effie Afton* and not because barges had difficulty passing through the draw of the bridge. Judd did not object to questions tending to show that the bridge had been built at an angle to the current of the river and that the angle had caused the loss of the *Afton*. "But when you ask 'Can boats navigate that draw with barges?' I say it is not competent, because you have not said you have been lost by such obstruction."[20] Responding, Wead and T. D. Lincoln argued that the questions were proper because they were included in the general allegations of the declaration, while Joseph Knox and Abraham Lincoln argued that they were not.[21] Because much of what was said during the trial was not reported verbatim in the newspaper accounts, we can only speculate what Abraham Lincoln said on this point. It is reasonable to assume, however, that his argument was persuasive, for after a long period of discussion and reflection Judge McLean sustained Judd's objection. The questions asked were too general, the judge ruled. The plaintiffs could not claim to recover for the *Afton*'s loss "because a boat having barges has not been able to pass the draw." They could only claim to recover because of the specific loss actually suffered.[22]

McLean's ruling permitted T. D. Lincoln to continue reading Connor's deposition, but without the objectionable questions. Connor's recorded testimony revealed that on May 11, 1857, he had been on board a steamboat named the *Tennessee Belle* that was coming down the river on a trip from Galena to St. Louis when he saw another vessel, a steamboat named the *Saracen*, approach the bridge. The *Saracen* headed for the draw and, as it was about to enter, collided with the long pier of the span. The impact broke some of the *Saracen*'s chain braces and "made her leak pretty badly." About ten minutes later, as Connor's own boat approached the draw of the bridge, it also collided with it. The *Tennessee Belle* "struck the short pier first," Connor said, "and then darted to the long pier, striking that. It tore off all the larboard guard on the larboard side—took off the knuckle streak, and on the starboard side carried off some thirty feet of her guard." The *Tennessee Belle* was detained at Rock Island for three weeks while it was repaired. The collisions of the *Saracen* and the *Tennessee Belle* convinced Connor that the angle at which the bridge had been built had the effect of throwing boats "against the pier as they tried to pass through the draw." It made the river current so strong that in high water it was "impossible for any ordinary boat to go through without having all the steam that can be got, and even more than the law allows them to carry."[23]

More steam, of course, provided the boats with greater power and speed, but at the risk of potentially disastrous boiler explosions. (Mark Twain's younger brother, Henry Clemens, was badly scalded when a boiler exploded on a steamboat he was working on below Memphis in 1858, and he died soon thereafter).[24] The maximum pressure permissible in steam boilers was prescribed by Congress and enforced by federal inspections.[25] Connor thought the need for extra steam made the Rock Island Bridge "very dangerous in this respect, as often the only alternative presented to heavy loaded boats is to break the law, by carrying an extra head of steam, or to abandon their trips, or at great expense unload and have it towed along the shore in barges."[26]

About a week after the *Tennessee Belle* accident, Connor saw another steamboat—this named the *Arizona*—strike the long pier at Rock Island and sink. He also saw the *Isaac Shelby* unload its cargo and have its freight hauled along the shore because of its inability to pass through the Rock Island draw. Connor admitted that he had gone through the draw only two times and that when he went up the river in his own boat he encountered no difficulty. It was only when he was coming down that his boat struck the pier. "The long pier acts like a funnel," Connor said, "drawing in more water to the draw than ought to go through such a space. . . . I consider it more dangerous than any other place on the Ohio or Mississippi Rivers."[27]

Connor's powerful indictment of the bridge was quickly followed by similar testimony. Robert Herdman, who lived in Allegheny County, Pennsylvania, was a river captain who had command of the steamboat *Arizona* when it collided with the Rock Island Bridge. "It was Sunday morning about six, or half past six," Herdman said, "and just at the entrance the current drove the boat on the head of the long pier. The boat striking the pier on the starboard guard and knuckle, knocking off about twenty-six foot of the guard and knocking the stern post out. She bounded off and went through. She commenced taking water fast, but we forced her as fast as possible, and she sunk at Rock Island." Herdman considered the bridge "a very serious obstruction and a very dangerous one."[28]

William Fuller of Cincinnati had been a river pilot for twenty-one years and a steamboat captain for three. His deposition revealed that he was in command of the steamboat *General Pike* when it collided with the Rock Island Bridge on June 7, 1857, sustaining damage that had to be repaired at St. Louis. Fuller described the water that collected at the long pier, creating eddies and currents, and said he had never known a boat attempting to pass through the bridge without a "high pressure of steam." Fuller thought the bridge was "a very serious obstruction to the navigation of the river." It is "so dangerous," he said, "that I would not venture through it a second time, though I had every prospect of a fine trip."[29]

12. Norman B. Judd was a prominent railroad attorney and corporate officer in Chicago before and after he invited Lincoln to join him in the defense of the Rock Island Bridge. Originally a political adversary of Lincoln, Judd became an important political ally after the *Effie Afton* trial.

13. Associate Justice John McLean of the U.S. Supreme Court presided over the *Effie Afton* trial as part of his circuit-riding duties. Although Lincoln supported McLean for the Republican presidential nomination in 1856, he had mixed feelings about the jurist, once saying: "Judge McLean is a man of considerable vigor of mind but no perception at all; if you was [*sic*] to point your finger at him and also a darning needle he would not Know which was the sharpest."

14. The *Effie Afton* trial took place on the top floor of Chicago's historic Saloon Building in September 1857. The oddly named structure ("saloon" was then synonymous with the French word "salon") served many functions over the years, including that of the Chicago city hall, U.S. post office, and early home of the federal courts in Chicago.

15. Subject of the infamous Supreme Court decision bearing his name, Dred Scott's trail intersected Lincoln's in ironic ways. He came to live at Rock Island, Illinois, as a slave (or servant) to an army surgeon the year after Lincoln served there as a volunteer in the Black Hawk War. His later claim to freedom was based in large part on his residence on the slave-free ground at Rock Island. The Supreme Court decision denying Scott's claim was announced only six months before Lincoln's participation in the *Effie Afton* trial in 1857. Lincoln's eloquent opposition to the *Dred Scott* decision, along with his high-profile participation in the *Effie Afton* trial, elevated his political reputation beyond the limits of Illinois and helped to pave his path to the presidency only four years later.

16. The Rock Island Bridge was modified in the 1860s by replacing the original, flat-topped Howe trusses with new trusses with curved or arched tops. Installed on the original piers with minimal interruptions to river and rail traffic, the new trusses accommodated the heavier locomotives and railroad cars that were then passing over the bridge.

17. In March 1868 a massive ice floe damaged the piers and the timber spans of the Rock Island Bridge so badly that trains could not pass over, and just a week later the bridge was hit by a wind that local newspapers called a tornado. Though the bridge was badly damaged, construction crews brought from Chicago were able to reopen it to railroad traffic only six weeks later.

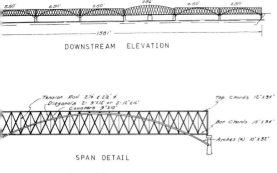

DOWNSTREAM ELEVATION

SPAN DETAIL

BRIDGE NO. 1 1853-1866

7. As opened in 1856, the Rock Island Bridge rested on eight stone piers, two that rested on the river banks and six that rose from its bed. Five stationary spans, two on the Illinois side and three on the Iowa side, were built of timbers on the patented Howe truss design, with curved arches added on each side for additional strength and stability. Between the stationary spans, a draw span rotated atop a long pier to permit steamboats to pass through the bridge. Technical drawing by William Riebe from the *Rock Island Digest*, 1982.

8. St. Louis was the throbbing center of steamboat traffic on the Upper Mississippi in 1855, the year before the steamboat *Effie Afton* crashed into the Rock Island Bridge. Steamboat owners and the St. Louis Chamber of Commerce provided financial and strategic support for the ensuing lawsuit against the bridge owners.

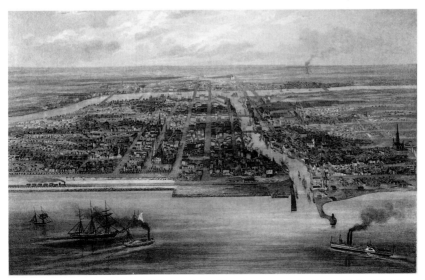

9. Chicago was a small but rapidly growing railroad center at the foot of Lake Michigan in 1856, the year the *Effie Afton* crashed into the Rock Island Bridge. Although smaller than St. Louis, the Illinois city was recognized as a menace to St. Louis's domination of transportation in the Middle West because of its rail connection with the Rock Island Bridge. The *Effie Afton* trial was officially titled *Hurd et al. v. The Railroad Bridge Company*, but it might as well have been *St. Louis v. Chicago*.

10. This photograph of the bridge was taken from high ground on the Iowa side of the river. It shows the long pier that supported the draw span, with the woods of Rock Island beyond and Rock Island City in the distance.

Steamer Morning Star on the Mississippi near Rock Island, Ill.

11. There is no known photograph of the steamboat *Effie Afton*. This photograph of the steamboat *Morning Star* on the Mississippi near Rock Island bears a good resemblance to the earlier boat.

1. Lincoln was photographed by Alexander Hesler in Chicago on February 28, 1857, a little more than six months before the beginning of the *Effie Afton* trial.

2. In 1837, Lieutenant Robert E. Lee of the U.S. Army Corps of Engineers was sent to the Upper Mississippi to make a survey and recommend methods to remove obstructions to navigation at St. Louis and in the Des Moines and Rock Island Rapids.

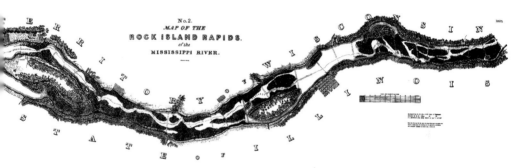

3. This map of the Rock Island Rapids was prepared by Lee with the assistance of Lieutenant Montgomery Meigs and a German mapmaker named Henry Kayser.

4. Like Lincoln, future Confederate president Jefferson Davis saw military service at Rock Island during the Black Hawk War of 1832. As U.S. secretary of war from 1853 to 1857, Davis fought to stop construction of the Rock Island Bridge, believing that a southern rather than a northern railroad crossing of the Mississippi would help to plant slavery in the Southwest. Davis's opposition to the bridge that Lincoln defended foreshadowed the opposition he would lead against Lincoln's efforts to save the Union during the Civil War.

5. The first railroad bridge to cross the Mississippi, the Rock Island Bridge opened for traffic between Rock Island, Illinois, and Davenport, Iowa, on April 22, 1856. This artist's view shows Davenport in the background. The draw span, in the lower right, rotated to allow steamboats to pass up and down the river. Barges, as shown in the foreground, could pass under the stationary spans. The steamboat *Effie Afton* crashed into the bridge on May 6, 1856, caught fire, and sunk, but not before it destroyed a part of the bridge.

6. Another artist's view shows a steamboat passing down the river from Rock Island. Indians, some of whom remained in the area after the Black Hawk War, watch. The Rock Island Bridge and Rock Island are in the background.

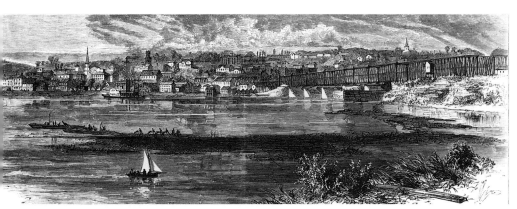

18. In 1872 the original Rock Island Bridge was replaced with an iron span located a short distance downriver. A two-level bridge with rails on the first level and a roadway for pedestrians, horses, wagons, and carriages on the second, it crossed the Mississippi between Rock Island, Illinois, and Davenport, Iowa, as its predecessor had. Jointly financed by the U.S. government and the Chicago, Rock Island and Pacific Railway Company, the new span was called the Government Bridge.

19. The 1872 Government Bridge was replaced in 1896 with a heavier and stronger steel structure that rested on the original 1872 piers. With twin tracks and two decks, the Government Bridge still stands today, spanning the river from Rock Island, Illinois, to Davenport, Iowa.

20. The Rock Island Bridge was built to permit trains of the Chicago and Rock Island Railroad to cross the Mississippi. Known as the Chicago, Rock Island and Pacific Railroad Company after August 1866, the railroad continued to use the original bridge and its successors at Rock Island until 1980, when it went out of business. This canceled stock certificate shows a typical Rock Island locomotive and tender of 1915.

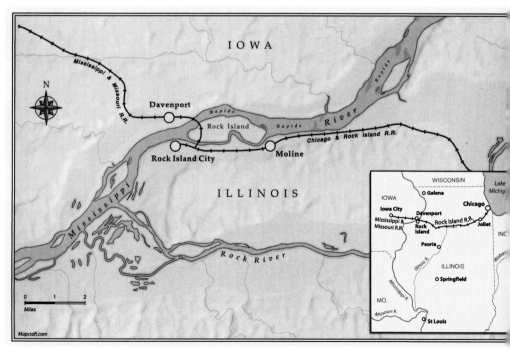

21. The scene of the disaster: the intersection of the river, the railroads, and the bridge.

Pleasant Devinney of St. Louis was captain of the steamboat *Grace Darling* when, on the day before the *Effie Afton* disaster, it made several unsuccessful attempts to pass through the draw of the bridge. Devinney was on hand the following day when the *Afton* crashed into the bridge and burned. "She went in as pretty as a boat could go," Devinney said, "and I thought she would succeed in getting through." He soon learned otherwise. "Her head passed the short pier. The cross-current from the long pier hit her on the larboard bow and threw her on the head of the short pier forward of her wheels." Soon the current "took her right down under the bridge and keeled her over until the water was over her larboard guard. She then took fire and was finally destroyed." Devinney was sure that the bridge was "a very serious obstruction." In fact, he "never knew anything equal to it."[30]

The third day of the trial, Thursday, September 10, opened with yet more depositions from the plaintiffs' attorneys. The witnesses were unanimous in declaring the bridge a serious obstacle to navigation of the river, though they offered different opinions as to how the obstacle might be removed. John Grammar of Cape Girardeau, Missouri, a veteran pilot on the Upper Mississippi, thought the solution might be to replace the existing drawbridge with a suspension bridge.[31] (Was Grammar aware of the furor that the steamboat interests on the Ohio River had directed against the suspension bridge at Wheeling, Virginia, only a few years before?). Thomas Parker, a steamboat pilot who had passed the location of the Rock Island Bridge on an average of twenty times a year over a period of sixteen years, thought that the only way to avoid the obstruction was to "remove it."[32] George McClintock of Pittsburgh, captain of the steamboat *Henry Graff*, which was thrown against the long pier at Rock Island when it attempted to pass through the bridge on April 21, 1856, and later sank at Rock Island City, thought the draw span should be widened (the draw "should be as wide as the other spans," he said) and the piers should be set "straight with the current."[33] (Of course, such "modifications" could be accomplished only by demolishing the existing bridge and building a new one.)

Tales of the grief that steamboats encountered at Rock Island continued. George McLean of Beaver County, Pennsylvania, was captain of the steamboat *Argonaut* when it came through the Rock Island Bridge on the day after the *Afton* was lost, striking the long pier and sustaining minor damage. He gave live testimony in which he blamed the angling piers of the bridge for the mishap.[34] Frank T. Batcheler of Cincinnati, commander of the *W. L. Maclay*, a steamboat that was badly damaged when it came through the Rock Island Bridge on May 2, 1856, was another live witness. He thought it was "very difficult to enter the draw straight." "There is a great danger of swinging," Batcheler added, "and then there is no time nor space to catch her up."[35]

Bilbe Sheppard of Bellevue, Iowa, a millwright who was a passenger on the *Afton* on the day she was lost, gave live testimony in which he vividly described the *Afton*'s collision with the bridge. "As the boat went into the draw," Sheppard said, "I felt a jar as though the stern had struck the center pier. The whole boat had got in beyond the end of the long pier. I saw the bow then springing toward the center pier, to the right. They stopped the wheel I think on the right hand side, on the starboard side. The boat then straightened up, but came more against the current, and commenced swinging round toward the small pier." Sheppard thought it was "but a short time" between the collision with the bridge and the burning of the *Afton*. "It did not exceed half an hour," he said.[36]

Cephas B. Gall, a river pilot with twenty years of experience who was a witness to the damage suffered by the *Henry Graff* and the *W. L. Maclay*, gave a deposition in which he declared that it was "generally necessary to have all the steam that the law allows to get through the draw,"[37] while Peter Hall of Davenport, a river pilot who had been acquainted with the Mississippi at Rock Island since 1836, gave live testimony in which he emphatically declared the bridge "an obstruction to navigation."[38]

The newspaper accounts of the trial, hastily transcribed and hurriedly rushed into print, left much of the give-and-take of the courtroom drama unreported. Binmore's reports for the *Missouri Republican* were more detailed than Hitt's for the *Chicago Press*, but neither transcribed every word that was said in the courtroom. Both were content from time to time to summarize points they considered marginally important and eliminate those they considered obvious, repetitious, or merely trivial.[39] Witnesses' names were often spelled differently in the two newspapers.

Some of the color and drama of the *Effie Afton* courtroom was remembered many years later by a Chicagoan who witnessed a good part of the trial and published a short recollection of it in the *Century Magazine* for February 1897.[40] Francis G. Saltonstall was a stock and bond broker who had been alerted to the proceeding by John F. Tracy, superintendent of the Chicago and Rock Island Railroad. "Our case will be heard in a day or two," Tracy told Saltonstall. "You had better look in; I think it will interest you." Inside the courtroom, Saltonstall noted that "much time was taken up by testimony and contentions between counsel; and as the participation of the St. Louis Chamber of Commerce was openly charged, great interest was manifested in the evidence and in the manner in which it was presented. As the character of the Mississippi River was described—the nature of its currents, their velocity at certain periods, the custom of navigators and pilots in allowance for drift, the depth of water at the 'draw' of the bridge, the direction of the piers in relation to the channel, and many other points involving mechanics and engineering being drawn out—the spectators showed their sympathies unmistakably."[41]

When Saltonstall recalled the trial in later years, it was natural that he should note Abraham Lincoln's presence in the courtroom and completely overlook that of T. D. Lincoln. Abraham Lincoln had by that time attained the status of a national hero, and it was understandable that men who had known him, or merely seen or heard him in person, would delight in recounting their memories of him. Saltonstall remembered that during the *Afton* trial, Lincoln "seemed to have committed all the facts and figures to memory, and often corrected evidence so effectively as to cause a ripple of mirth in the audience." The courtroom in the Saloon Building was "crowded day after day."

"During a tedious examination by one of the opposing counsel," Saltonstall said, "Mr. Lincoln rose from his chair, and walking wearily about—this seemed to be his habit—at last came down the aisle between the long benches toward the end of the room; and seeing a vacant space on the end of the bench which projected some distance beyond the stove, came over and sat down." Saltonstall continued: "Having entered the room an hour before, I sat on the end, but, as Mr. Lincoln approached, moved back to give him room. As he sat down he picked up a bit of wood, and began to chip it with his knife, seeming absorbed, however, in the testimony under consideration. Some time passed, when Lincoln suddenly rose, and walking rapidly toward the bar, energetically contested the testimony, and demanded the production of the original notes as to measurements, showing wide differences. Considerable stir was occasioned in the room by this incident, and it evidently made a deep impression as to his comprehension, vigilance, and remembrance of the details of the testimony."[42]

Particulars of Lincoln's conduct during the trial may have been hazy when Saltonstall recorded his recollections (an attorney who interrupts the testimony of a witness being questioned by another attorney to correct his facts is at least stretching the rules of courtroom decorum), but his memory of Lincoln's whittling rang true. Whittling was in fact one of Lincoln's favorite pastimes. He neither smoked nor drank nor swore, so if this was a vice—or just a rather messy habit—it was forgivable.[43]

NINE

A Chorus of Protests

$\approx$

J oseph McCammant of Cincinnati was one of the most important witnesses in the trial, for he was the chief pilot of the *Effie Afton* on the Ohio and Lower Mississippi Rivers, although he did not have charge of the boat after it headed north from St. Louis. McCammant had been a river pilot between St. Louis and New Orleans for about twenty years before the *Afton* met its grief at Rock Island. When the boat reached St. Louis, however, Nathaniel Parker, a pilot experienced in navigation on the Upper Mississippi, was employed to take it north to St. Paul. McCammant's testimony included a long description of the *Afton's* collision with the bridge. "I was standing in the pilot house during the whole time that she struck," he testified. "The striking was caused by the force and the direction of the current, and the cross-currents that are created by the long pier." The jolt was felt the length of the vessel, upsetting stoves throughout the cabins, cook house, barber shop, and bakery. "It was not over ten minutes or at most fifteen, after she struck before she was burning all over. . . . Boats on the Western waters are all built very light and dry, and there is a good deal of paint and varnish on them, which makes them burn almost like shavings." McCammant said that he was "personally observant of the conduct of all the officers of the *Afton*," and there was "no want of care and skill on their part in attempting to pass the draw."[1]

David Brickel and Henry White of Pittsburgh offered strong support for McCammant's testimony. Brickel was the captain of the *J. B. Carson*, the steamboat the *Afton* passed in its rush to enter the draw of the Rock Island Bridge on May 6, 1856. In his judgment, the *Afton* was "carefully navigated."[2] White had been a pilot on the Upper Mississippi for twenty years and had passed the point where the Rock Island Bridge crossed the river an average of eighteen times a year. He was the pilot of the steamboat *Lucie May* when it struck the long pier at Rock Island on April 6, 1857, suffering damage that cost a thousand dollars to repair. White believed that the bridge was "an obstruction" and that "any pier bridge would be an obstruction, if built at that point." But the force of his condemnation of the bridge was weakened when he revealed that he had made nine trips from St. Louis to St. Paul on the steamboat *Minnesota Belle*, that he had passed through the Rock Island Bridge on all of those trips, and that "no accidents ha[d] happened to any of the boats except the *Lucie May*."[3]

Nathaniel Parker, the pilot in charge of the *Afton* when it struck the bridge, did not testify until the second week of the trial, but when he did so he added some compelling detail to the plaintiffs' case. "I was at the wheel when the *Effie Afton* was lost," Parker told the jurors. "I have been a pilot for the past twenty-two years between St. Louis and Galena and St. Paul." When Parker got to Rock Island on May 5, 1856, "there were ten or eleven boats laying above and below the bridge." Parker and his assistant pilot, Samuel McBride, were both in the pilot house when the *Afton* set out for the draw of the bridge on May 6. "We first struck the right hand pier," Parker said. "We came in fair with the current. I think her larboard wheel got in the eddy of the long pier and that made her strike first." Parker said it was more difficult to take a side-wheel boat through the bridge than a stern-wheeler. "I did all that I could to safely navigate that boat, and so far as I know, the engineers were at their posts; everything, so far as I know, went on skillfully and properly."

Parker was asked if he had attended the St. Louis Chamber of Commerce's meeting of December 16, 1856—the meeting at which plans were discussed for a consolidated attack on the Rock Island Bridge. He answered that he "was at a meeting in St. Louis to make a survey of the bridge and rapids. It was in January last." A series of heated questions and objections followed. "Was not a part of the object of that meeting a prosecution of this suit?" Parker was then asked. "Perhaps it was," he answered, "but the primary object was to bring a suit to abate the bridge as a nuisance."[4]

Thomas Taylor of St. Louis, whose deposition was read to the jury on the fourth day of the trial, was the oldest pilot in terms of service then working on the Upper Mississippi, having passed the point where the Rock Island Bridge was erected at least five hundred times. Taylor testified that the bridge was "a *very* serious obstruction" to navigation, and he assured the jury that the reputation of Nathaniel Parker as a river pilot "cannot be surpassed."[5]

The plaintiffs' attorneys offered a series of witnesses who testified to the value of the *Effie Afton* and the property on board at the time of its loss. John G. Isham, a steamboat furnisher from Cincinnati, testified that the boat was worth at least $50,000. "I don't think I would have taken $80,000 for her, had she been mine," Isham added. "Her equipment was as perfect as I ever saw."[6] Daniel Weaver, a pilot from Cincinnati who had piloted the *Afton* on several of its early trips, thought the boat was worth between $50,000 and $65,000. "She was a first-class boat for freight and passengers," Weaver said, "very light draft and easy to handle; a good boat for any stage of water."[7] Benjamin P. Hoomes, first clerk of the *Afton*, testified that the boat had fifty staterooms and that the property on board was worth at least $100,000. To support his claim, he produced a long list of items that were carried on the boat, with values stated for each.[8]

At one point, T. D. Lincoln offered the testimony of nine witnesses to show that the Rock Island Bridge had raised the costs of insurance for boats traveling on the Upper Mississippi. The defense attorneys vigorously objected to this testimony, and when McLean sustained their objection, T. D. Lincoln withdrew his offer.[9]

Orrin Smith was one of the most interesting of all the witnesses called by the plaintiffs. He had been involved in navigation of the Mississippi River for thirty-three years, and for seven or eight of those years he had been president of the Galena Packet Line, a fleet of commercial packet ships that regularly ran between Rock Island, Galena, and St. Paul. He had passed the site of the Rock Island Bridge many times and had a good knowledge of conditions there. Smith said that the difficulties of passing through the Rock Island Bridge would have been "very much lessened" if the bridge had not been constructed in swift water. To explain this point, he reviewed some of the difficulties that boats experienced when they came down the river. First, they had to negotiate the treacherous Rock Island Rapids that occupied some eighteen miles of the river above the bridge. Once the rapids were passed, they had to "run down hill" until they got "pretty close to the pier" of the Rock Island Bridge. "My impression has been that many of the accidents have been from a want of knowledge as to how far to get down before turning the boat," Smith said. "We have a couple of boats passing twice each week day—one each up and down and they have gone through with comparatively little trouble. They are small boats, however." (Smith's reference to "comparatively little trouble" cannot have pleased the plaintiffs' attorneys.) Smith added that some of his boats were "pretty large" and that he would consider it "somewhat hazardous if they had to pass through." But when asked if his packet line had taken its largest boats through the bridge, Smith answered, "Yes, sir, and we got them through this spring without serious accident."

Smith then offered a revealing bit of information that showed how boatmen on the Upper Mississippi were adjusting to the new bridge. They were not throwing up their hands in frustration and trusting in their lawyers to get the bridge torn down. They were adopting techniques that would enable them to navigate the river with a degree of safety. "The boats now run on the Mississippi in sections," Smith said, "one class to Keokuk, another to Rock Island, another to Galena, and another of an entirely different class to St. Paul." Smith spoke in some detail about the Rock Island Rapids and the chutes, or chains of rocks, that threatened steamboats there. "I have always considered these Rapids as a serious obstruction to navigation," he said, "I never heard that controverted." Smith then made some comments about the Rock Island Bridge itself: "I am not aware of any serious accidents to our boats in running through the draw; they may have injured their upper-works, but nothing more than is common in running a boat. I reside at Galena. The packets come in every day, and I see them.... Our boats have met with slight injuries, nothing more."[10]

James Boyd's testimony was more supportive of the plaintiffs' case than Smith's. He was a river captain who had been running boats on the western rivers since 1842. A former resident of Pittsburgh who had lived in St. Louis for about two years, Boyd had piloted his steamboat the *Ben Bolt* up the river to Rock Island in early May 1856 and tried several times to get it through the draw. When the boat sustained major damage, he gave up the attempt and brought the boat back to the Rock Island shore, then walked out on the bridge to study the water currents. He was on the span when the *Effie Afton* made its disastrous attempt to pass through the draw and saw it collide with the bridge. Boyd eventually sold the *Ben Bolt*, sustaining a considerable loss in doing so. He thought the bridge was a great danger to navigation on the river. "In my opinion," he said, "it is so dangerous that I should hate to build a boat to run in that trade; nor would I have sold the *Ben Bolt* at the great sacrifice I did, but for it."[11]

When Joseph Knox asked Boyd on cross-examination if he and the other steamboat captains blew their whistles when they saw the Rock Island Bridge was on fire, the plaintiffs objected. But McLean allowed the question. Boyd said he did not personally ring a bell or blow a whistle when the bridge took fire, "but when the bridge fell I blew one—a long and loud one. . . . So many were blowing and the bells were ringing so on the boats and in the town that I could not hear."[12]

More than a dozen of the plaintiff's witnesses were asked to estimate the speed of the river current as it passed through the draw of the bridge. It was an important part of the plaintiffs' case to show that the bridge had greatly increased the speed in the draw and thereby increased the difficulty that boats experienced in passing through it. Boats going upriver had to fight the increased speed, while boats coming down had to contend with the instability caused by the swiftly flowing waters. The witnesses, however, offered an almost bewildering array of estimates. George McClintock thought the current flowed through the draw at "about eight or ten miles an hour."[13] James W. Connor thought the water was flowing through the draw at twelve miles an hour on the day the *Tennessee Belle* struck the bridge.[14] Elias Owens, pilot of the *J. B. Carson* on the day the *Afton* was lost, set the speed at nine miles per hour, although he admitted that the speed varied at different stages of water.[15] Joseph M. Kelly, a bookkeeper from Covington County, Kentucky, who was aboard the *Afton* when it collided with the bridge, thought the current was running between twelve and fifteen miles per hour at the time of the *Afton*'s collision,[16] while Pliny A. Alford, a pilot from St. Louis, said "the current at high water is at least eight miles an hour, and in low water about five miles. It is most strong at high water."[17]

The jurors cannot have escaped the force of the almost unanimous chorus of protest that the steamboat captains, pilots, engineers, and crew members raised in opposition to the bridge. They all seemed to agree that the bridge was an obstruction to navigation—a serious, even dangerous, obstruction. If the jurors listened carefully to the chorus, however, they might have heard an occasional discordant note. For example, John Jacobs, a St. Louis–based river pilot who said he thought the obstruction caused by the Rock Island Bridge was "the greatest on the Western rivers," admitted that he had passed through the bridge forty or fifty times since it was built, and yet mentioned no difficulties when doing so.[18] William White, a Galena-based river pilot who called the bridge "a very material obstruction to navigation," admitted that he had passed through the draw a total of ten times—seven times in 1856 and three times in 1857—and that he "got on without injuring my boats materially."[19] George Krautz, the second engineer on the *Effie Afton*, who testified to the *Afton*'s disastrous collision with the Rock Island Bridge, admitted that he saw three other boats pass through the draw of the same bridge before the *Afton*, and apparently without difficulty.[20] Jesse T. Hurd, Jacob Hurd's brother, himself an experienced steamboat captain, testified that the Rock Island Bridge was "a very serious place for a steamboat to pass," yet he admitted that he had been through the bridge three times, once on the steamboat *Granite State*, which struck one of the short piers and tore off about thirty-two feet of its guards, and twice on the steamboat *Galena*. "Nothing happened to the *Galena*," Hurd admitted. "We went through without material difficulty."[21] John Grammar, who testified to the accident suffered by his steamboat the *Lucie May*, admitted that he had passed through the bridge "a number of times," but the only accident he witnessed was that of the *Lucie May*.[22] Pliny Alford, whose experience on the Upper Mississippi went back to 1842, called the bridge "a decided obstruction" yet admitted that he had passed through the draw of the bridge about eight times and "never saw an accident."[23] Nathaniel Parker, the pilot in charge of the *Effie Afton* at the time of its disastrous collision with the bridge, told the jurors that he had passed through the bridge twice before he took the *Afton* in and about twelve times since, yet the only accident he testified about was that of the *Afton*.[24] If the very location and design of the Rock Island Bridge caused steamboats to collide with it, how could so many boats make it through without colliding? Were other factors at play—negligence, perhaps? Lack of navigational experience on the part of some of the pilots? Adverse weather conditions? Defects in the boats themselves?

When George Collins, the assistant engineer of the *Effie Afton*, was called to the stand on the seventh day of the trial, he testified that when the *Afton* set out for the Rock Island Bridge on the morning of May 6, its machinery was "in complete order—as complete as it could be." But Collins offered some testimony that seemed to contradict Nathaniel Parker's claim that the *Afton* did not strike the long pier of the bridge. "I think the boat struck the larboard pier," Collins said. "I know that by the jar of the boat."

A rustle of excitement ran through the courtroom when Collins was asked a potentially explosive question: "Have you ever been offered a sum of money to swear that this boat was burned up purposely, and if so, when, where and by whom?" "A man came to me a year ago this spring," Collins began, "while I was on the *Royal Arch*." Before he could continue with his answer, the defendant's attorneys interposed a vigorous objection. The question was improper, they said, unless it could be connected to one of the parties to the suit. It was immaterial if Collins was offered money for his testimony unless the plaintiffs could prove that the Railroad Bridge Company or any of its officers or attorneys were behind the offer. McLean sustained the objection over the plaintiffs' attorneys protest that they would "prove that this man was introduced to the witness by a man who had been connected with the railroad and the bridge." It was a weak protest, and a tenuous connection at best. In fact, the subject was never broached again.[25]

With Collins, the plaintiffs' attorneys rested their case in chief. They had presented an impressive body of evidence and called, either to the stand or by way of depositions, an even more impressive array of witnesses. There were more than eighty witnesses in all, each contributing in some way to the case the plaintiffs' attorneys were presenting to the jury. But where were the testimonies of Jacob Hurd, the captain of the *Effie Afton*, Alexander Kidwell, the chief engineer, and Joseph Smith, the chief clerk? Hurd, Kidwell, and Smith were, after all, the owners of the *Afton*. These three men knew a great deal about the boat and what had happened to it at the Rock Island Bridge. Yet they were never deposed, and they were never called to the stand in Judge McLean's Chicago courtroom to tell the jury what they knew. The explanation for their absence was, of course, that they were deemed to be incompetent witnesses under the law that then governed the production of evidence. In later years, a trial seeking to recover for damages sustained by a valuable steamboat would prominently feature the steamboat's owners as witnesses. Not so, however, in 1856, or for some years thereafter, for, as Simon Greenleaf, a professor of law at Harvard University, said in the 1850 edition of his *Treatise on the Law of Evidence*, "the general rule of the Common Law is, that a *party to the record*, in a civil suit, *cannot be a witness*, either for himself, or for a co-suitor in the cause." Greenleaf said that this rule was "founded not solely in the consideration of interest, but partly also in the general expediency of avoiding the multiplication of temptations to perjury."[26] In other words, parties to the case would be likely to lie, or at least exaggerate, and because of this they would not be permitted even to take the stand. In 1847, the United States Supreme Court specifically endorsed this rule in an opinion written by Justice Samuel Nelson of New York (and agreed to by Justice John McLean of Ohio).[27] So Hurd, Kidwell, and Smith did not take the stand in the *Effie Afton* case. They could not offer direct testimony, which might potentially have strengthened their suit. At the same time, however, they did not have to subject themselves to cross-examination, which might potentially have weakened it.[28]

* * *

Henry Binmore reviewed the developments of the first week of the trial in a special article for the St. Louis *Missouri Republican*. He thought his reporting had amounted to a "Herculean task" and told his readers that he had transcribed 96,280 words, which if stretched from end to end would extend for 1,872 yards, or more than a mile. He had already formed some opinions about the case and was not shy about expressing them. "The Rock Island Bridge being erected," Binmore declared, "became an obstruction to navigation. There can be no question of that. No bridge can be erected but on its piers and, if piers it has, it will more or less impede the free navigation of the waters." He thought the Bridge Company might have erected a suspension bridge, or made the draw wider, or placed the piers straighter, "or probably done a dozen things to decrease the risk of navigation.... To my mind it seems they ought to be liable because they have not taken care to avoid injuring the river and free intercourse upon it."[29]

The pro-bridge *Davenport Gazette* had a different impression. The *Gazette* commented sarcastically that there was "some very pretty swearing going on" in Judge McLean's Chicago courtroom. "One man swears that this bridge is a greater obstruction to navigation than the Falls at Louisville or the Mississippi Rapids! When we recollect that the Falls are not navigable on an average scarcely a month altogether the whole year, and that the Lower Rapids of this river are only really navigable for medium sized steamers at times of a high or good stage of water, and that to get around the one, millions of dollars have been expended to build a canal, and thousands to build a railroad around the other...it may be very safely surmised that there is no limit to the tip-top swearing now going on before the Chicago Court, among those opposed to this bridge." The *Gazette* noted one witness who said that he had been up the river as far as Rock Island only two times since the bridge was built yet still claimed that "it is more *chance* than certainty to get through the draw.... And yet," the *Gazette* continued, "there have been nearly eight hundred steamboat passages at the draw this season—and probably of the whole number not half a dozen boats, or a dozen at the utmost touched the piers even in the slightest manner! What remarkable *chance*, especially when the 'obstruction' is so dangerous! But we have only given these as specimens of the beautiful swearing having for its object the destruction of this magnificent bridge."[30]

Binmore acknowledged that much of the evidence in the case was technical and confusing and that to listen to it day after day was "a mad, sick and serious job. . . . I see around me of an afternoon one or two jurors who are 'nid, nod, noddin',' at times, and even the very worthy Judge who presides, occasionally shuts his eyes in an almost doze. My fellow reporters are getting sick of it, and I beg to inform you that I don't care how soon it is over."[31]

The *Illinois Daily Journal*, published in Springfield, ran a short article emphasizing the importance of the Chicago trial. The *Journal* was supportive of Abraham Lincoln and his policies, and supportive of the railroads as well. It said that the lawsuit brought against the Rock Island Bridge "touched so nearly the question at issue between the railroads and the navigable rivers" that "it assumes a most momentous legal and national bearing. In this view, the case is one of the most important that has ever engaged the attention of our courts."[32]

Though they viewed the trial from different angles, the St. Louis, Davenport, and Springfield papers all made perceptive observations about the trial then taking place in Chicago. Almost everybody recognized that it was one of the most consequential that had ever taken place in an American court. And it was not yet over. The plaintiffs had presented their case, but the defendants—aided by a plainspoken lawyer from Springfield with a remarkable memory and a keen sense of trial strategy—had yet to be heard.

TEN

The Bridge Itself on the Stand

≋

N orman Judd opened the case for the defense on Tuesday morning, September 15, the seventh day of the trial. The conclusion of Nathaniel Parker's lengthy testimony, followed by the much shorter testimony of George Collins, had occupied a good part of the morning session, and when Collins left the witness stand Judd was not ready to call his most important witnesses. He began instead by reading the deposition of William Phillips, a steamboat pilot from Portsmouth, Ohio, who had worked as steersman on the *Effie Afton* for five months in the spring of 1856.

Phillips reviewed some basic facts relating to the *Afton*: It was 230 feet long and had a beam of about 32 feet; at its widest point it measured about 40 feet from outside to outside; its wheels were 32 feet in diameter and 9 feet wide. Running upstream against a four-mile-per-hour current, it could attain a speed of about eight miles per hour; running downstream in the same current, it could do fifteen. Phillips thought the *Afton* was worth $50,000 but noted that the value of steamboats had risen "right smart" between the dates of the boat's launching and its destruction.[1]

When Judd reached the end of Phillips's deposition, he informed Judge McLean that his principal witness of the day was not ready to take the stand, and he asked for an adjournment until the afternoon session. Wead told McLean that he had seen "partial and incorrect reports" about the trial in some of the newspapers and asked McLean to caution the jury against reading them. McLean did so and then adjourned the trial to half past two o'clock.[2]

* * *

Judd opened the afternoon session by calling one of the most interesting witnesses of the entire trial to the stand. Seth Gurney was a fifty-one-year-old New Englander who lived in the wooden house on the upper end of the long pier of the Rock Island Bridge. His position was variously described as superintendent or caretaker, for it was his duty to operate the bridge turntable, close it when trains were about to cross the span, and keep it clear and open at all other times so boats and barges could freely pass through. Before beginning his duties at the bridge on April 19, 1856, Gurney had been employed making turntables for bridges and railroads. Before that he had been a millwright.[3]

Gurney was not on the bridge when the *Effie Afton* struck. "I got on to the long pier at about the time that the bridge fell," he said. But he was a witness to almost everything else that had happened at the bridge since he began his duties there. Following the *Effie Afton* disaster, the bridge was rather quickly repaired; by August 4, 1856, repairs were so far along that steamboats were once again confined to the draw space when passing through the bridge. Ice closed the river to navigation about November 29, but it opened again in the spring. "The twenty-fifth of March, I think," Gurney told Judd, "was the first boat that went through."

Gurney's principal value as a witness lay in the detailed written record he kept of all boats and barges that passed through the bridge from August 4, 1856, through September 10, 1857, and in the irascible, almost cantankerous manner with which he answered questions. Asked by Judd how many boats had passed in that period, Gurney answered, "According to my record, carefully kept, there have been 958 passages." "How many boats of that 958 have been injured?" Judd asked. "To the best of my knowledge," Gurney answered, "the number injured is seven."

Judd produced a model of the bridge that helped Gurney explain how the span was built and how the turntable operated. The seven boats that, according to Gurney's record, had mishaps while attempting to pass through the bridge were the *Lucie May*, which ran straight into the upper end of the turntable pier on April 6, 1857; the *Rescue*, which came up the river from Rock Island in a gale of wind and snow and struck the bridge on April 10, 1857; the *Tennessee Belle*, which collided with the short pier on May 11, 1857; the *Arizonia*, which entered the draw "very much sideways" from upriver on May 31, 1857, and broke its guard when it struck the bridge; the *General Pike*, which suffered some damage while coming downriver on June 7, 1857; the *Mansfield*, which came down the river on June 26, 1857, heading directly toward the long pier and struck it; and the *Ben Coursin*, which came down the river on September 7, 1857, towed by a tugboat, and struck the upper corner of the long pier.

The newspaper reports of Gurney's testimony suggest that he was a strong-minded witness with a touch of quirkiness and not at all intimidated by the attention that was being focused on him. He was determined to answer the questions put to him, and answer them in his own way. Several times he refused to give his recollections of the circumstances under which boats struck the draw pier, explaining that he had recorded that information in his record book. "It would be remarkable," he said, "that of a thousand boats I could remember all the circumstances of all the boats." When questioning him about one boat's contact with the bridge, Judd asked Gurney, "Have you a memorandum of it, made by yourself?" Gurney answered, "I have an account of it, made by myself at the time. Therefore, I did not charge my memory with the circumstances." When, during his cross-examination, one of the plaintiffs' lawyers asked Gurney a series of questions about the draw of the bridge, he snapped, "I say, are you not heating up a bit?" "No, not a bit," the attorney replied. "If I do we will blow off." To which Gurney retorted, "What is the use of telling you anything. I will tell the jury."[4]

If Gurney was a cantankerous witness, he was also an effective one, for he spoke with an air of authority mixed with a New Englander's frankness, and his handwritten record of the steamboats that had successfully passed through the bridge spoke volumes. It showed very clearly that in less than a year, almost one thousand boats had successfully passed through the bridge that the plaintiffs' lawyers were now calling a "material obstruction" to navigation of the river.

Gurney was followed to the stand by Daniel L. Harris, a Massachusetts-based civil engineer who had been engaged in bridge building for the previous ten years. Among other things, Harris was the owner of Howe's bridge plan (the plan that had been used to build the trusses at Rock Island) for three New England states. "I have built half the bridges erected in New England during the past ten years," Harris told the jurors. Harris saw the Rock Island Bridge for the first time soon after it was disabled but returned for another examination about May 27, 1857. "It was mere curiosity that led me to go," he said. "I went there to see and ascertain whether what I had been informed by newspapers and reports was true."

Harris's examination of the bridge persuaded him that it was located differently than he would have located it. "Still, in the place where it is," he said, "it could not be bettered. On the Rock Island side, the current, after entering the draw, passes on uniformly straight, so far as I could judge by looking at it; I saw nothing to indicate aught but that." He explained that, if the upper end of the pier faced straight into the river current, cross-currents would form on both sides of the pier. Because the pier was located at a slight angle, however, the current on the Illinois side was improved. In the end, Harris saw nothing at Rock Island that would adversely affect the navigation of a steamboat.[5]

Benjamin B. Brayton of Davenport, the engineer who located, designed, and supervised the building of the Rock Island Bridge, was the next witness. Recognizing Brayton's importance in the construction of the span, the *Missouri Republican* introduced its account of his testimony with a title reading, "The Bridge Itself on the Stand." This seemed to signal a turn in the testimony away from the travails of particular steamboats and toward a new focus on the span. The owners and pilots of the steamboats clearly wanted to bring the bridge down, although the only method now available to them was to blame it for the *Effie Afton*'s loss. Now the jury would learn the essential characteristics of the span, how it was built, and how it operated.

Brayton's testimony combined authority with some welcome modesty. "I was the engineer in the building of this bridge," he told the jurors. "I suppose I am responsible for it to a certain extent. I made the survey and location and then submitted it." Using diagrams, the engineer gave the precise dimensions of the piers and the openings between them, explaining that, because the piers sloped up slightly from their bases to their tops, the openings became wider as the water level rose. At low water, the river was 1,322 feet wide, but only 10.5 percent of the water surface was obstructed by the piers. When the water rose, only 8.5 percent of it was obstructed. Brayton testified about the rapids above the bridge, identifying the chains and the channels by the familiar names navigators had given them: Sycamore, Campbell's, Rock Island, Davenport's. He gave their dimensions and the speed of the water that flowed through them, and he explained the difficulties that steamboats encountered when they tried to navigate through them. The rapids were, it seemed, an even greater obstruction to navigation than the Rock Island Bridge.

On cross-examination, Brayton denied that he had had anything to do with the bridge after it was finished, although he admitted that he had taken a new position as engineer of the Mississippi and Missouri Railroad, an affiliate both of the Railroad Bridge Company and the Chicago and Rock Island Railroad. (If Brayton had had a present pecuniary interest in the bridge, he would be unable to offer any testimony, and the testimony he had given up to that point would have been stricken, for a rule of evidence similar to the one that made the owners of the *Effie Afton* incompetent witnesses would have applied to him. Witnesses with a pecuniary interest in the subject matter of a suit were also incompetent to testify in the suit.)[6] Also on cross-examination, Brayton admitted that he made a mistake when he originally located the long pier of the bridge. It was not in the exact center of the draw, he explained, so the opening on one side was five feet wider than on the other. The error was not discovered until the work was well along, and instead of starting all over with the construction of a new pier, it was decided to leave the pier in place and center the turntable to one side of it. This equalized the length of the spans atop the turntable pier, although the openings on either side were unequal. Brayton explained that at low water the opening on the Iowa side was 111 feet wide, while that on the Illinois side was 116 feet.

An important part of Brayton's testimony was devoted to an explanation of the tests he had conducted on the river currents using
floats. "Mr. E. H. Tracy assisted me in these tests," he said. Floats were
typically pieces of wood with attached rods that projected down into
the water from two to twelve feet.[7] Brayton estimated that he and
Tracy and the men working for them had "put out 500 to 800 floats"
and said that the floats helped them understand how the currents
flowed through the bridge openings. "On the Iowa side there is an
eddy," Brayton said, "but none on the Illinois side." Brayton had seen
between fifty and one hundred steamboats pass through the draw,
and he had run two hundred to three hundred floats by the same
point. His observations and tests had persuaded him that there were
no problems in the currents that passed through the Illinois side.
"The current below the bridge runs uniformly toward the Illinois
shore at Rock Island," he said.[8]

Brayton's testimony was followed by that of John B. Jervis, potentially one of the most powerful witnesses in the trial. Jervis's formidable reputation as a civil engineer was based on his nearly forty
years of canal, railroad, and aqueduct building in New York and
adjoining states.[9] He had been president of the Chicago and Rock
Island Railroad from late 1851 until 1854, but during that time he
managed the railroad's business and did not act as engineer on
either the railroad or the bridge construction.[10] Jervis had gone to
Rock Island in September 1856, and again in May 1857, to inspect
the bridge and observe its operations. "I got a man to throw blocks
into the current from the head of the pier," Jervis said. "I stood on
the bridge and observed that they passed directly through. . . . I did
not notice that they varied any towards the pier." Jervis thought that
the Rock Island draw was wide enough "for the ordinary purposes
of navigation" and that the bridge was placed "as well as it could be,
in view of all the circumstances." In fact, he said, "I do not see how
the draw could be better placed."[11]

William D. Gilbert followed Jervis to the stand. He had been a
railroad engineer for twenty-six years, for most of that time in New
York, but most recently in Wisconsin, where he was the engineer
of a railroad being built from the St. Croix River to Lake Superior.

Gilbert testified that he had made four passages through the draw of the Rock Island Bridge, two going up and two going down, and that he had paid close attention to the currents. He came down the river on May 17, 1857, on the steamboat *Arizonia*, which was damaged when it struck the bridge. He saw the *Arizonia*'s two pilots shortly after the accident and thought that they were intoxicated. One pilot in particular, Gilbert said, was so badly intoxicated "as to put me on my guard."[12] Gilbert's other trips were made on the Rock Island and Galena packets. "The long pier is clearly at an angle with the current," he said. "The effect is that a direct current is forced on the Illinois side. On the Iowa side it forms an eddy, represented by an angle to the short pier on the Iowa side. Had the pier been straight with the current, a cross-current would have been caused on both sides of the pier, which is now obviated, I think."[13]

Edward H. Tracy testified on Thursday morning, September 17, the ninth day of the trial. Tracy's background included work both as a mechanical and a civil engineer, and he had experience on the Chenango Canal, the Croton Aqueduct, and the Canandaigua Canal in Canada. He was now the chief engineer of the Des Moines River improvements in Iowa. He had helped to make the model of the Rock Island Bridge that was shown to the jury and used in explaining the span's structure and functions. "It is as near certain and accurate as we could make it," he said. "The scale is fifty feet to an inch." Working with Benjamin Brayton, Tracy had run floats in the water beneath the bridge to determine if there were any cross-currents. "The angling of the pier improves the Illinois side of the draw to the disadvantage of the Iowa side," Tracy said. "Placing the pier at an angle," he said, "improves the Illinois channel and makes the Iowa one worse."[14]

Roswell B. Mason did not take the stand until the late afternoon of Friday, September 18. A native of New York, Mason had been a civil engineer for more than thirty years, during the course of which he had worked on canals and railroads in New York, Pennsylvania, New Jersey, Connecticut, and Illinois. He had also been the principal engineer in the building of the great Illinois Central Railroad, then perhaps the single most extensive engineering project in the western states.[15] Like Brayton and Tracy, Mason was commonly addressed as "Colonel," more as a reflection of his status as a gentleman than as a military officer. Nobody in the courtroom when Mason began his testimony could have known that, thirteen years later, he would be elected mayor of Chicago and that he would be in that office when the great fire of 1871 swept through the city, causing hundreds of deaths and destroying, among other things, all of the official records of the trial they were now attending. If anyone could have foreseen that dire tragedy, interest in what Mason had to say would have been even more intense than it was on the tenth day of the *Effie Afton* trial.

Mason told the judge and the jury that he had been at the bridge when floats were put in the water some two thousand feet above the draw and allowed to float down in the current. All of them passed through except one, and as he watched them, he could not discover any cross-current. The angle of the pier differed from the straight flow of the river current by only seven degrees, Mason said, and he thought that a boat doing eight miles per hour would have no difficulty in passing safely through the draw. On cross-examination, he admitted that he "never knew of a bridge before this one that was not built, or intended to be built, straight with the current," but he did not think the angle of the Rock Island Bridge was a serious problem. "My impression is that the location of the Rock Island pier is as favorable for navigation as though it was straight with the stream."[16]

Patrick Gregg, who was called to testify on the same day as Edward Tracy, was a physician who had lived in Rock Island City for twenty-one years and was then serving as its mayor. Gregg's long residence at Rock Island had made him familiar with the river currents. He testified that the draw of the bridge stood "pretty near in a direct line" with the chute of the Rock Island Rapids, "where steamboats pass and have passed during the past twenty-one years." "The water passes through the draw piers straight and evenly as possible," Gregg said. "There is no cross-current. . . . I feel very confident the bridge is not any material obstruction."[17]

Fifty-three-year-old John Deere of Moline, who took the stand on Thursday, September 17, was one of the most interesting witnesses in the case, not because of the testimony he gave but because he was already on his way to becoming one of the most successful industrialists of the Middle West—in fact of the entire country. Deere had come to Illinois from his native Vermont while still a young man to practice his trade as a blacksmith. Learning how difficult it was for farmers to till the sticky clay of the western prairies with the crude cast-iron plows then commonly in use, he had invented a self-scouring plow with a curved blade made of polished steel. He sold ten of his plows in 1839, forty in 1840, and seventy-five in 1841.[18] By 1855, he was selling as many as ten thousand every year.

Deere's Moline residence was two and a half miles from the Rock Island Bridge, and it gave him a good view of the Rock Island Rapids. He had seen steamboats as they came through the rapids on their way to the Rock Island Bridge, and he had also seen some of the floats that were put out in the river to test the currents. Deere said that he "could not from the tests seen, discover any cross-current." Asked why some witnesses said that boats commonly "laid by" (i.e., stopped and waited) when they approached the river from the direction of the rapids, Deere answered, "I suppose the lying by spoken of was because of obstructions above the bridge and not because of any at the location of the bridge."[19]

Two more witnesses who were familiar with the river at Rock Island were called to describe the location where the bridge was built. David Barnes was a Rock Island lumberman who had been through the draw on boats fifteen to twenty times and testified that the current ran "straight through the draw."[20] Henry Decker was a Rock Island–based pilot who had worked on the Upper Mississippi for twelve years. He had been through the draw of the bridge some forty or fifty times with barges, and once on the *Resolute*, a stern-wheel steamer built for towing. "I have gone through the draw oftener than any other boat except the Galena packets," he said, adding that he "never saw any cross-current."[21]

The defendants' lawyers called several witnesses who had been present when the *Effie Afton* crashed into the bridge and had some startling information to impart. George D. Talcott of Minneapolis was a passenger on the *Afton* at the time of the disaster. He was standing next to Captain Hurd on the hurricane deck when the

Afton was in the draw and swinging around against the piers. One of the passengers asked why the boat was swinging, and Hurd said that it was "because the engine was disabled. The crank pin or strap connected with a rod had given out, and he did not know which." Talcott said there were a half-dozen passengers on the hurricane deck when Hurd made the statement. "There was considerable confusion among them," Talcott added. "The captain was frustrated as well as the rest."[22]

Sterns Hatch, a hotelkeeper from Des Moines who had been a deputy marshal at Rock Island at the time of the *Afton* collision, gave a deposition in which he testified that he had a conversation with Captain Hurd on the levee "some two or three hours after the occurrence." Hatch asked Hurd how far the *Afton* had gotten above the bridge pier "before she swung around," and Hurd had answered "the boat was thirty or forty feet above the pier." Hatch then asked Hurd what had caused the boat to swing around in the draw of the bridge. "I can hardly answer that question," Hurd answered, "but for some cause her machinery on that side did not work well, and the boat got on a shear and the pilot could not straighten her and she came round against the bridge."[23]

Robert Lowers was a resident of Davenport who saw the fire that engulfed the *Afton* from his home. Like many others on both sides of the river, he went down to the bank to see what had caused the conflagration. In the office of a firm called Lawler and Company he found a crowd gathered around a man who was addressed as the "captain" of the boat. "Someone asked the captain if the boat was insured," Lowers said. "The captain replied that she was insured against fire, but the bridge was the cause of the fire." Lowers said he was not certain that the man who said these words was in fact the captain of the *Afton*, but added, "My impression is that it is the same man as I have just been introduced to as Captain Hurd, but I cannot state positively."[24]

D. Clarence McNeil, a physician and surgeon from Camanche, Iowa, a small town about forty miles upriver from Rock Island, was a passenger on the steamboat *Vienna* when the *Effie Afton* collided with the bridge. While he was still on board the *Vienna* McNeil saw the *Afton* strike the bridge's right-hand pier and swing around under the span. As soon as the *Vienna* docked at Rock Island he made his way out to the bridge and onto the *Afton*. "The *Afton* had not swung clear round and under before I got to her," McNeil said. He helped passengers who were scrambling to get off the stricken boat, some onto the bridge and others onto the *J. B. Carson*, which had pulled up to the *Afton*. McNeil said he heard two men talking. "One of the men was tall," McNeill said. "Fresh complexion; sandy whiskers; his hair lighter than his whiskers, and a little appearance of baldness. The other was a man of dark hair and whiskers about the same length as the first one but heavier. The dark-haired man says, 'Well, she is insured.' The other says, 'No, she's lost.' The other said 'I thought she was insured,' and the reply was, 'She is, but only against fire.' By this time three or four persons had joined the group, and one of them said to the parties, 'It is a pity she don't burn. She is good for nothing,' and with an oath said, 'I would burn her and get the insurance.'" McNeill got the impression that the sandy-haired man was the captain because "he appeared to be giving orders." "After hearing this conversation," McNeill continued, "I started to go down on the pier, and heard the cry of fire. A man immediately run down to see, and came back and reported that a stove had been turned over, but the fire was put out." McNeill continued to help passengers get off, then went on shore and from there back to the *Vienna*, where he sat down to breakfast. After a while he again heard the cry of fire. He "got up from the table and looked out and saw the flames just bursting out." McNeil said that "it was at least an hour and a half from the time I first saw her swing around against the bridge until the fire broke out."[25]

Following McNeil's shocking testimony, the defense attorneys offered the depositions of some of the plaintiffs' witnesses and recalled some of their own live witnesses to exhibit inconsistencies or clarify points that had been insufficiently covered in the principal presentations. In all, the defense had presented, through depositions or live testimony, more than thirty witnesses. The *Chicago Tribune* told its readers that "the mass of testimony put in by the defence has been truly formidable."[26] Combined with the more than eighty witnesses presented by the plaintiffs, the jurors had a lot of evidence to help them make their decision.

Before he finally closed his case, however, Judd wanted to make one last point. It was a point that he thought important, and potentially powerful. While Benjamin Brayton was still on the stand, Judd offered a written statement certified by the superintendent of the Chicago and Rock Island Railroad showing the number of trains, train passengers, and freight tonnage that had passed over the bridge from September 8, 1856, through August 8, 1857—a key period in the life of the young span. If admitted into evidence, the statement had the potential of doing great damage to the plaintiffs' case, so their lawyers lost no time in objecting to it. T. D. Lincoln argued that the question to be decided in the trial was whether the Rock Island Bridge interfered "with the free and easy navigation of the river," and that could not be answered by showing how much traffic passed over the bridge. The bridge was "equally an obstruction no matter how much business was done upon it." To allow this evidence to come in "would lead to endless evidence upon the comparative commerce of rivers and railroads."[27]

Joseph Knox argued the point for the defense. He said that his clients viewed the river as a "free stream." But it was "a startling doctrine" to assert that "however great the public necessities of the Union," they could not be shown in a court of law, "for it amounted to saying that a bridge could not be built," a doctrine that "could not be tolerated in this country where the greatest good of the greatest number was sought." The "true doctrine was that these varying interests should be made to harmonize, each giving as much as it can." Knox referred to the Peoria Bridge case, in which John McLean was the judge, as a precedent for the proposition that the interests of bridges and river traffic should harmonize. "The Court there said that the right of free navigation of the Illinois River was not inconsistent with the right of the State to provide means of crossing by bridges or otherwise," Knox explained. "Such bridges do not essentially injure the navigation. The interests are coexistent and neither can impair or destroy the other."[28]

Abraham Lincoln's argument on this vital point followed Knox's.

He gave a history of the Peoria Bridge case—a history he was well acquainted with, having been one of the attorneys in the case. He said that the defense in the current litigation "expected to try this case with the admission that the bridge must not be a material obstruction." But he thought there was "a qualification to the obstruction in all cases—the materiality of it—and that was to be affected by the necessity of the bridge." The plaintiffs held that their vested interest in free navigation "could not be interfered with," but the courts were beginning to decide otherwise, "conforming, as they should do, to the nature and wants of our country."[29]

Answering Lincoln, Hezekiah Wead accused the defendants of arguing that, because the bridge was "an immense advantage," the boat owners were not entitled to recover for their loss. If this argument was accepted, Wead said, the Mississippi would no longer be a "free navigable stream." The question to be decided in the case was not how much traffic was passing over the bridge—or how much there might be in the future—but whether the bridge was an obstruction. If the extent of future traffic over the bridge could be considered, Wead asked, "where would it end? . . . Would the rule be varied with each successive year?"[30]

As Judge McLean considered the attorneys' arguments on this question, he reviewed the already famous Wheeling Bridge case, in which the Supreme Court had originally ruled that the suspension bridge over the Ohio River was a material obstruction to navigation, but then had been overruled by Congress, which declared the bridge a lawful span and required steamboats passing under it not to interfere with its elevation or structure. McLean had written the Supreme Court's original opinion in *Wheeling Bridge*[31] and vigorously dissented from his colleagues' subsequent decision to submit to the will of Congress.[32]

It seemed that McLean still harbored some bitterness about the result in *Wheeling Bridge*, for he observed that, because of it, "not a steamboat from Pittsburgh can pass without leveling its chimneys." McLean thought the evidence offered by the defendant had "little bearing" on the issues of the present case, but he ruled that it could be admitted for the limited purpose of showing "the necessity of a bridge." It could not be considered, however, for the purpose of taking away "the nature of the obstruction."[33]

With that, Norman Judd read from the bridge superintendent's statement. It showed that from September 8, 1856, to August 8, 1857, inclusive, 12,586 freight cars had passed over the Rock Island Bridge. Those same cars had been loaded with 125,860 tons of freight. In the same period, 74,179 passengers had crossed over the bridge.[34]

These numbers may, in Judge McLean's mind, have had "little bearing" on the case. But the numbers were large, and large numbers have a certain power. The jurors, not the judge, would decide the future of the Rock Island Bridge, and when they did so, it was by no means clear that they would disregard the very impressive volume of commerce that was already passing over it.

ELEVEN

A Virtual Triumph

≈

The last witnesses were heard on Saturday, September 19, the eleventh day of the trial. Closing arguments began on Monday, September 21. Henry Binmore had terminated his reports from Chicago when the witnesses' testimony ended, so there are no accounts in his newspaper of any of the attorneys' closing speeches. The *Chicago Tribune* ended its courtroom reports at the same time, telling its readers that "the case is now being argued" and "we have not room for a synopsis, even, of the very able arguments of Counsel."[1] But Robert Hitt continued to report from the courtroom. His accounts in the *Chicago Press* thus constitute the only printed reports of the attorneys' arguments. Although set forth at some length in the *Press*, Hitt's reports are actually abbreviated summaries of what he considered the most important remarks made by the lawyers.

As lead attorney for the steamboat owners, Hezekiah Wead had the right to speak first.[2] He began by emphasizing the significance of the case. Certainly no one in the courtroom that day had any doubt that the case was an important one, but Wead's remarks reinforced the point. He insisted that his clients had not brought their suit to prevent bridges from spanning the Mississippi, but solely to recover damages for the loss of the *Effie Afton*. He noted a certain arrogance in the claims of the bridge owners. They were "a grasping corporation," he said, and to any complaint about the bridge or its location, they turned and said, "In prohibiting us you are ruining the great commercial cities." But the question to be decided was simply whether the Rock Island Bridge was an obstruction. "The law is that the citizens of the United States have a right to the free navigation of the Mississippi River," Wead said. "It has been eloquently called the 'Father of Waters.' Care has always been taken to keep it free from all obstructions."

Wead dismissed testimony about the difficulties steamboats had in navigating the Rock Island Rapids. "We have shown that boats were detained by the bridge," he said, "and they bring us proof that boats were detained by the rapids." The issue was whether the bridge was an obstruction, not the rapids. He also minimized Seth Gurney's testimony that 958 boats had passed through the bridge after August 4, 1856, and only seven had been injured. "Suppose that be true," Wead said. "If out of a thousand boats seven must be injured, is not that an obstruction?" But how many boats the length of the *Effie Afton* had passed through? There had been only one, Wead said, and that showed that the bridge had "destroyed the navigation for such boats. Such boats have been shut out.... The old adage is, 'Figures cannot lie,' but I shall show you before I get through that this old man's figures do lie."

Wead spoke at some length about the difficulties that pilots encountered in attempting to pass through the draw of the bridge, and the collisions that followed, and he spoke at even greater length about the law that he thought was applicable to those collisions. He gave the official citations of published cases, some decided in the U.S. Circuit Courts, some in state supreme courts, and read from them. And he called on T. D. Lincoln to read some more. If the jurors were not already "nid, nod, and noddin'," this reading of dry, technical legal opinions was well calculated to help them do so.

Joseph Knox was the next attorney to address the jury.[3] Speaking in behalf of the bridge owners, he agreed with Wead about the great importance of the case, but he disagreed about almost everything else. He reviewed the involvement of the St. Louis Chamber of Commerce in the suit—an involvement that T. D. Lincoln of Cincinnati had objected to every time it came up in the testimony. Answering Wead's charge that the bridge builders claimed the right to build their bridge wherever they wanted, Knox asserted: "We contend not that we have a right to shut off navigation, but that we have a right to build a bridge, if not materially obstructing navigation. . . . We believe the bridge is placed in the very best manner. Is it reasonable that it should not have been so placed? Would sensible and skillful men, knowing the magnitude of the investment, having so much at stake, have knowingly placed an obstacle to navigation there, which the law would remove? Common sense will show us that men in such a case would place it in the best manner possible."

Knox reminded the jury that on the morning of the *Effie Afton*'s collision with the bridge, the pilot Nathaniel Parker had backed the boat out of its place at the Rock Island dock and promptly struck a ferry boat, breaking some of the *Afton*'s guard chains. Then, going up to the draw of the bridge, he "took a race with the *J. B. Carson*, passed her on the Iowa or Davenport side, just before she got to the draw." In passing the *Carson*, Knox said, the *Afton* "must have been driven over into the eddy." Yet Parker continued ahead, striking one of the piers of the bridge with full force. "Was that ordinary care and skill?" Knox asked. "Running a race with another boat, getting into the eddy at the foot of the pier, and then running against the stone pier with all her might?"

Knox chided the plaintiffs' attorneys for "various absurdities" in their evidence, and he defended Seth Gurney against Wead's accusation that the bridge caretaker was lying. "Humble as Gurney is," Knox said, "no man is wealthier in a character for unswerving integrity. Why not bring his neighbors here to testify as to his character, if they wished to attack him? . . . We have introduced here six engineers," Knox continued, "Jervis, Harris, Tracy, Gilbert, Brayton and Mason, and no other six engineers in this country stand higher. . . . These six men say that those piers are as well located and as well constructed in form as they can be."

The Rock Island Bridge was, Knox said, "a work of which the country ought to be proud." He referred to reports that a similar bridge was being planned across the Mississippi from the Illinois shore to St. Louis. It was odd, he thought, that the business leaders of the Missouri city were adamantly opposed to the bridge at Rock Island but willing to accommodate one on their home turf. He sneered, "A bridge must not be built unless it brings trade to the great metropolis of all Pikedom." ("Pikedom" was a contemptuous term, originally applied to Missourians from Pike County but later used to describe any region inhabited by rubes and ruffians.)

Knox's long argument—begun on Monday afternoon, the twelfth day of the trial, and concluded on Tuesday morning—ended with calm words. He was "trying to fairly and truly represent the case," he said, and he "was willing to leave it to a jury of just men." His speech was followed by the customary afternoon break, which gave the courtroom spectators a welcome moment of quiet before the beginning of Abraham Lincoln's argument.[4]

W̲e know a good deal from sources other than the newspapers how Lincoln must have appeared to the Chicago jurors when he rose to address them that September afternoon in 1857. He had over the years adopted familiar habits that inevitably followed him into the courtroom in the Saloon Building. Herndon said that when his part-ner addressed a jury he was "awkward, ungainly, odd. Sometimes his hands, for a short while, would hang by his side. . . . He used his head a great deal in speaking, throwing or jerking or moving it now here and now there, now in this position and now in that, in order to be more emphatic, to drive the idea home." He "never beat the air, never sawed space with his hands, never acted for stage effect; was cool, careful, earnest, sincere, truthful, fair, self-possessed, not insulting, not dictatorial; was pleasing, good-natured." Herndon reminded us that Lincoln's voice was "shrill, squeaking, piping," but as he con-tinued to speak it "became harmonious, melodious, musical, if you please, with face somewhat aglow; his form dilated, swelled out, and *he rose up a splendid form,* erect, straight, dignified."[5]

As detailed in Hitt's transcript, Lincoln began his speech in a characteristically Lincolnian way by telling the jury that "he did not purpose to assail anybody, that he expected to grow earnest as he proceeded but not ill-natured." He acknowledged that there was "some conflict of testimony in the case," but there had been many witnesses, and "one quarter of such a number of witnesses seldom agree and even if all were on one side, some discrepancy might be expected. We are to try and reconcile them, and to believe that they are not intentionally erroneous as long as we can."

It was a typically Lincolnian beginning for what was, in reality, to be a hard-hitting speech—Lincoln assuring the jurors that he did not intend to be disagreeable before he proceeded (in a subtly agreeable way) to be disagreeable. He wanted the jury to like him, and he knew that the first words he spoke to them would help to win them over. He was telling the jury that he was an agreeable sort of lawyer, that he had no accusations to make against his opponents in the case, that if the testimony offered by the witnesses on the two sides conflicted, it was no more than what "might be expected."

Lincoln continued by assuring the jury that "he had no prejudice against steam boats or steamboat men, nor any against St. Louis, for he supposed they went about this matter as other people do in their situation." St. Louis, he continued, "as a commercial place may desire that this bridge should not stand as it is adverse to her commerce, diverting a portion of it from the river; and it may be that she supposes that the additional cost of railroad transportation upon the productions of Iowa will force them to go to St. Louis if this bridge is removed. The meetings in St. Louis are connected with this case only as some witnesses are in it[,] and thus has some prejudice added color to their testimony."

With another piece of subtle rhetoric, Lincoln had reinforced one of the key arguments of the defendants in the case: that the St. Louis Chamber of Commerce had fomented this litigation, that the steamboat interests in the Missouri city were behind the lawsuit, and that in defending the Rock Island Bridge against the claims of the owners of the *Effie Afton* he and his colleagues were only standing up to a powerful interest opposed to any and all bridges over the Mississippi. And he had introduced this potentially explosive theme in a way that few would recognize as an attack on his opponents in the case. He was saying, in effect, that the purpose of this trial was not only to reach a fair and just result for the parties. It was to oppose the "prejudice" of a powerful interest in a powerful city where steamboats reigned supreme.

"The last thing that would be pleasing to me," Lincoln said, "would be to have one of the great channels extending almost from where it never freezes to where it never thaws blocked up, but there is a travel from east to west whose demands are not less important than that of those of the river. It is growing larger and larger, building up new countries with a rapidity never before seen in the history of the world." Lincoln alluded to "the astonishing growth of Illinois, having grown within his memory to a population of a million and a half; to Iowa and the other young rising communities of the northwest."

Lincoln told the jurors that the "current of travel" on the railroads, which he and his colleagues represented, had "its rights as well as that north and south. If the river had not the advantage in priority and legislation we could enter into free competition with it and we could surpass it. This particular railroad line has a great importance and the statement of its business during a little less than a year shows this importance. It is in evidence that from September 8th, 1856, to August 8th, 1857, 12,586 freight cars and 74,179 passengers passed over this bridge. Navigation was closed four days short of four months last year, and during this time while the river was of no use this road and bridge were valuable. There is too a considerable portion of time when floating or thin ice makes the river useless while the bridge is as useful as ever. This shows that the bridge must be treated with respect in this court and is not to be kicked about with contempt."

Lincoln was making good use of Seth Gurney's written record of steamboats that had passed through the Rock Island Bridge. He was also determined to remind the jury that, unlike steamboats, railroads and railroad bridges did not have to shut down when freezing weather descended on the Upper Mississippi. The river was completely closed by ice for a good part of every year, impassable to all river traffic, yet railroads, their freight, and their passengers continued to move.

"The other day," Lincoln observed, "Judge Wead alluded to strife of the contending interests and even a dissolution of the Union." This was certainly one of the most troubling undercurrents of the trial. In the great war between the North and the South that was quickly approaching (although nobody could appreciate just how quickly), Lincoln would be the most powerful defender of the Union, the champion of the nation created by the Founding Generation but menaced by the growth of quarreling regional interests. As president during the Civil War, he would address the national crisis with powerful words and eloquent phrases. Now, however, he responded to suggestions that the Union might be endangered by opposition to bridges over the Mississippi with a cliché: "The proper mode for all parties in this affair is to 'live and let live' and then we will find a cessation of this trouble about the bridge."[6] If Hitt's transcription of Lincoln's words was literally correct (newspaper accounts of extemporaneous speeches often departed in varying degrees from the actual words spoken), it was a disappointing, even banal response to a troubling threat, and plainly could not compare with the eloquence that Lincoln would summon a few years later when actually confronted with threats to the Union.

"What mood were the steamboat men in when this bridge was burned?" Lincoln asked. "Why there was a shouting and ringing of bells and whistling on all the boats as it fell. It was a jubilee, a greater celebration than follows an excited election." He referred to Seth Gurney's written record of the boats that had passed through the bridge. "From April 19th, 1856, to May 6th—seventeen days—there were twenty accidents and all the time since then there have been but twenty hits, including seven accidents so that the dangers of this place are tapering off and as the boatmen get cool the accidents get less. We may soon expect if this ratio is kept up that there will be no accidents at all."

Lincoln then addressed Wead's denigration of the floats that the bridge engineers had used to study the currents that passed through the bridge. Wead had argued that floats were not a reliable indication of the difficulties that boats encountered at the bridge, because "there was a difference between a float and a boat." But Lincoln did not remember that Wead "indulged us with an argument in support of this statement. Is it because there is a difference in size? Will not a small body and a large one float the same way under the same influence? True a flat boat will float faster than an eggshell and the eggshell might be blown away by the wind, but if under the *same influence* they would go the same way. Logs, floats, boards, various things the witnesses say all show the same current."

Lincoln next spoke of "the angular position of the piers." These words signaled that he was about to reveal his understanding of things mechanical and to call on the geometric insights he had acquired in his long study of Euclid.[7] He was also to demonstrate his remarkable ability to remember facts and figures. Unlike most other trial lawyers, Lincoln rarely took notes while listening to the testimony of witnesses. "Notes are a bother," he once told Hiram Beckwith, a fellow lawyer, "taking time to make, and more to hunt them up afterward. Lawyers who do so soon get the habit of referring to them so much that it confuses and tires the jury."[8] Henry Clay Whitney insisted that Lincoln "took *no* notes, but remembered everything quite as well as those who did so." Whitney told of one trial in which all the court lawyers except Lincoln insisted that a witness had sworn "so-and-so," but "it turned out that Lincoln was correct and that he recollected better than the united bench and bar."[9] The testimony that the jurors in Judge McLean's courtroom had listened to was long, voluminous, and technical, yet Lincoln was willing to show them how much of it he remembered—and how much of it he really understood.

"What is the amount of the angle?" he asked. "The course of this river is a curve and the pier is straight. If a line is produced from the upper end of the long pier straight with the pier to a distance of 350 feet and a line is drawn from a point in the channel opposite this point to the head of the pier, Colonel Mason says they will form an angle of twenty degrees. But the angle if measured at the pier is seven degrees, that is we would have to move the pier seven degrees to make it exactly straight with the current. Would that make the navigation better or worse? The witnesses of the plaintiff seem to think it was only necessary to say that the pier formed an angle with the current and that settled the matter. Our more careful and accurate witnesses say that though they had been accustomed to seeing the piers placed straight with the current, yet they could see that here the current had been made straight by us in having made this slight angle; that the water now runs just right, that it is straight and cannot be improved. They think that if the pier was changed the eddy would be divided and the navigation improved."

This was a technical argument, not one that was calculated to appeal to the jurors' emotions, but one that would impress them with Lincoln's command of the facts of the case. Admirers of the Rock Island Bridge believed that the structure was an engineering triumph of sorts, a technical victory over a formidable natural obstacle, and evidence of human progress in an age that longed for progress. Jurors might be persuaded to support the bridge in the current litigation if they believed that it furthered their economic interests, the swift and efficient transportation of freight and passengers through a rapidly expanding section of the country whose future was inevitably linked to progress. But they might also be won over to the bridge's side by the knowledge that the span was a mechanical success. It was erected to unite the eastern and western banks of the greatest river in North America with iron rails. Lincoln's task in the current trial was to convince the jurors that the bridge had accomplished its goal—and that it had done so well.

"I am not now going to discuss what is a material obstruction," Lincoln told the jurors. With these words he was skirting the key issue in the case, but doing so in a typically Lincolnian way. The root question that lay behind all the other questions in the trial was whether the Rock Island Bridge was a "material obstruction." On the answer to that question all the other questions in the trial largely depended. Yet the question was as much legal as it was factual. It was not Lincoln's style to try to explain the law to juries. He did not like to read from statute books or published cases and thus try to instruct jurors on the law correctly applicable to the cases he tried. He knew that such arguments would induce "nid, nod, and noddin'." "Rather," according to Hiram Beckwith, "he would turn to opposing counsel or to the bench and say to the jury, 'These gentlemen will allow, or the Judge, if need be, will tell you, that the law of the case is thus or so.'"[10] Now, following that practice, he was content to say: "We do not greatly differ about the law. The cases produced here are I suppose proper to be taken into consideration by the court in instructing a jury. Some of them I think are not exactly in point but I am still willing to trust his honor, Judge McLean, and take his instructions as law."

If Lincoln was not willing to discuss the law governing material obstructions, he was willing to discuss another important issue in the case. It was his contention, and that of his colleagues for the defense, that the *Effie Afton*'s tragic collision with the Rock Island Bridge was attributable not to the mere presence of the bridge in the river, not to the angling position of the piers in the river channel, but to want of skill and care in the operation of the steamboat. If the boat was not operated carefully—if its pilot was guilty of negligence in his handling of the boat on the morning of the fateful disaster—the owners of the *Afton* could not recover for their loss. It was, to state it simply, their own fault, for they put the *Afton* in the river, they employed the pilot and crew members who had charge of it on May 6, 1856, and they were ultimately responsible for what happened to it at Rock Island.

"What is reasonable skill and care?" Lincoln asked. "This is a thing of which the jury are to judge. I differ from the other side when it says that they are bound to exercise no more care than was taken before the building of the bridge. If we are allowed by the legislature to build the bridge, when a pilot comes along it is unreasonable for him to dash on heedless of this structure which has been *legally put there*. The *Afton* came there on the fifth and lay at Rock Island until next morning. When a boat lies up the pilot has a holiday, and would not any of [you] jurors have then gone around to the bridge and gotten acquainted with the place? Pilot Parker has shown here that he does not understand the draw. I heard him say that the fall from the head to the foot of the pier was four feet; he needs information. He could have gone there that day and seen there was no such fall. He should have discarded passion[,] and the chances are that he would have had no disaster at all. He was bound to make himself acquainted with the place."

Lincoln referred to the testimony of Joseph McCammant, the regular pilot of the *Afton*, who was aboard the boat when it collided with the bridge but not at the wheel. "McCammant says the current and the swell coming from the long pier drove her against the long pier. In other words drove her toward the very pier from which the current came! It is an absurdity, an impossibility." Lincoln had by this time given up his subtlety and indirection for clear, sharp words. Testimony offered by the other side was "absurd," "impossible"—strong words that carried strong impressions. "The only reconciliation I can find for this contradiction is in a current which White says strikes out from the long pier and then like a ram's horn turns back, and this might have acted somehow in this manner."

Lincoln was ready to impress the jury a second time, now with his understanding of how the river currents flowed under the Rock Island Bridge, his understanding of geometric shapes and angles, and his memory for details. "I shall try to prove," he said, "that the average velocity of the current through the draw with the boat in it should be five and a half miles an hour; that it is slowest at the head of the pier and swiftest at the foot of the pier. Their lowest estimate in evidence is six miles an hour, their highest twelve miles. This was the testimony of men who had made no experiment, only conjecture. We have adopted the most exact means. The water runs swiftest in high water and we have taken the point of nine feet above low water. The water when the *Afton* was lost was seven feet above low water or at least a foot lower than our time. Brayton and his assistants timed the instruments. The best instruments known in measuring currents. They timed them under various circumstances and they found the current five miles an hour and no more. They found that the water at the upper end ran slower than five miles; that below it was swifter than five miles, but that the average was five miles."

Lincoln now employed one of his most effective forensic techniques: asking questions that, by their very force, impelled the answer. Lincoln scholar Douglas L. Wilson has written of Lincoln's "remarkable gift for the interrogatory mode of exposition, exploring complex issues by asking pointed questions."[11] It was a gift he made frequent use of when he was president, asking questions about government policy that could only be answered as he intended them to be answered. ("Are all the laws, *but one* to go unexecuted, and the government itself go to pieces, lest that one be violated?" he asked at the time that he first suspended the writ of habeas corpus.)[12] It was equally effective when he was addressing a jury: "Shall men who have taken no care, who conjecture, some of whom speak of twenty miles an hour, be believed against those who have had such a favorable and well improved opportunity? They should not even *qualify* the result. Several men have given their opinion as to the distance of the steamboat *Carson* and I suppose if *one* should go and *measure* that distance you would believe him in preference to all of them."

Lincoln now spoke about the depth of the river channel under the bridge, the width of the draw, the total area that was covered by water, and the speed of the current at different water depths. It was a heady, almost numbing, dose of figures, speeds, distances, and directions. Could the jurors follow all that Lincoln was telling them? Probably not—but they could still be impressed by the seemingly effortless way in which he conveyed this very complicated information to them. His voice, no doubt, carried a tone of assurance. He was dealing with facts, and when he spoke of facts he did so with confidence. And, as always, he spoke honestly. Lawyers who observed Lincoln in hundreds, even thousands, of trials, were unanimous in their estimate of Lincoln's basic integrity, in the courtroom as well as in his political life. "He seemed entirely ignorant of the art of deception or of dissimulation," said Henry Clay Whitney.[13]

Lincoln continued to speak about the cross-currents that the plaintiffs and the plaintiffs' witnesses claimed impeded the progress of boats through the draw. "But can these men's testimony be compared with the nice, exact, thorough experiments of our witnesses?" he asked. He reviewed the extensive tests that the defense witnesses had made with floats and their conclusion that the floats showed no cross-currents. "Can you believe that these floats go across the currents?" he asked. "It is inconceivable that they could not have discovered every possible current. How do boats find currents that floats cannot discover?"

The court day had come to an end. The jurors, no doubt, were tired. The septuagenarian judge who presided over the crowded courtroom may have been fatigued. And Lincoln himself may have been weary. A lawyer who addresses a jury for hours on end may be physically exhausted by the effort, but he is rarely mentally

exhausted. If, like Lincoln, the lawyer believes in the case he is arguing, he wants to continue his argument. He wants to persuade the
jury that his clients are in the right and to do all he can to assure
that they will prevail over their opponents.

L incoln had been spending his evenings in Chicago in the Tremont
House. At least one of his evenings, however, was spent with Norman Judd and his wife in their house on the shore of Lake Michigan.
It may have been after he made his closing argument in the *Afton*
case—at least that case was on the minds of the Judds and the visiting
lawyer as they enjoyed their tea and sat outside the house enjoying
the view of the Chicago harbor. Lincoln was in a talkative mood,
eager to converse about subjects other than steamboats and bridges
on the Mississippi. As night fell, he spoke about the stars in the sky
above them and about biblical passages he had studied (Lincoln was
not a regular churchgoer, though he was a keen and lifelong student
of the Bible). He told the Judds about the lecture he had prepared
(or was then preparing) on discoveries and inventions. In its completed form, he was to deliver this lecture six times between 1858
and 1860, although not to enthusiastic audiences (the subject was not
well suited to his speaking talents, or at least not of sufficient interest
to his lecture audiences to hold their attention).[14] When the night
air grew chilly, the Judds and their guest went inside, where Lincoln
stretched his long limbs over the sofa and continued his musings.
After Lincoln left, Norman Judd remarked that he was "constantly
more and more surprised at Mr. Lincoln's attainments and the varied knowledge he has acquired during years of constant labor at
the Bar, in every department of science and learning. A professor at
Yale could not have been more interesting or more enthusiastic."[15]

Joseph Knox also spent at least one evening with the Judds during
the *Afton* trial. Mrs. Judd recalled that it was after Lincoln had delivered the first part of his closing argument and that Knox was not
pleased with how Lincoln had performed. "He sat down at the dinner table in great excitement," Mrs. Judd remembered, saying, "Lincoln has lost the case for us. The admissions he made in regard to the

currents in the Mississippi at Rock Island and Moline will convince the court that a bridge at that point will always be a serious and constant detriment to navigation on the river." Mrs. Judd recalled, however, that her husband did not agree. He said that Lincoln's admission in regard to the currents were facts that could not be denied, but that they only proved that the bridge should have been built at a different angle to the stream, and that a bridge so built could not injure the river as a navigable stream."[16]

Lincoln resumed his argument on Wednesday, September 23. Aware, no doubt, that the jurors were growing weary of all they had heard thus far, Lincoln assured them that he would "conclude as soon as possible," but he had some more points that he wanted to make. He said that the colored map that the plaintiffs had at one point brought into the court showed that the alleged cross-currents "did not exist." He had a model of the boat, which he used to explain that "the boat struck on the lower shoulder of the short pier as she swung around in the splash door, then as she went on around she struck the point or end of the pier where she rested. Her engineers," Lincoln said, "say the starboard must have struck the upper point of the pier so far back as not to disturb the wheel."

Lincoln addressed the suggestions made by various plaintiffs' witnesses that the bridge at Rock Island should have been a suspension bridge, or that it should not have been a bridge at all but a tunnel dug under the river. He said there was no practicability in the project of building a tunnel under the river, for there "is not a tunnel that is a successful project in this world." (Lincoln was apparently unaware that tunnels had been successfully dug under the Thames River in London.) The suspension bridge was similarly impracticable. "A suspension bridge cannot be built so high," Lincoln said, "but that the chimneys of the boats will grow up till they cannot pass. The steamboat men will take pains to make them grow. The cars of a railroad cannot without immense expense rise high enough to get even with a suspension bridge or go low enough to get through a tunnel; such expense is unreasonable."

According to Hitt's newspaper report, Lincoln concluded with the observation that he had "much more to say, many things he could suggest to the jury, but he wished to close to save time." Precisely how long Lincoln spoke was not reported, though it is clear that his closing remarks extended over parts of two days.[17] It was also evident that T. D. Lincoln had not yet had his chance to argue the case, and his closing speech was a long one, for Hitt reported that it took seven hours to deliver.[18] What T. D. Lincoln's remarks were was left to conjecture, however, for they were not printed in the newspapers. Then followed Judge John McLean's charge to the jury, also a long—even droningly long—recapitulation of the evidence and the legal issues presented in the trial. Abraham Lincoln had expressed his opinion that McLean had "considerable vigor of mind," and his jury charge proved Lincoln right. It included detailed and precise summaries of the testimonies of dozens of witnesses that demonstrated, if nothing else, that the seventy-two-year-old judge was paying attention to what all of the witnesses had said during the trial.[19]

McLean's charge included some general observations about the river, the bridge, and the case the jurors were now called on to decide. "To any one who will take a general view this is high evidence of a rising and prosperous country," the judge said. "Bountiful as Providence has been in supplying our country with great lakes and mighty rivers, they are found inadequate to the wants of society. They are the great arteries of commerce, but like the human system, the body cannot be preserved in its healthful vigor unless the veins shall connect with the arteries and impart health and action to every part." The Mississippi and other navigable rivers were "within the commercial power of Congress," McLean said, and "subject to its regulation," but "to specify what shall be a legal structure of a bridge, over any of our rivers, would be attended with great difficulty. The same river would require different regulations to meet its various localities. Upon the whole, perhaps no better rule can be suggested than that which the courts have adopted. It is a safe rule and it is adapted to all rivers and all localities. The bridge must be so constructed as not materially to obstruct navigation."

But what, in legal contemplation, constituted an "obstruction"? McLean asked. And when was an "obstruction" a "material obstruction"? To try to arrive at any answer to this question, McLean thought it was necessary to resort to the dictionary. "To obstruct is to hinder, not to prevent," he said. "It is used in the sense, that some inconvenience, expense or delay may be imposed, but these shall be so limited as not to be serious, such as are not material in the prosecution of commerce."

And if the bridge was a drawbridge, what requirements did the law impose on it? "A draw in a bridge must be convenient and safe," McLean explained. "Not, that such an accommodation must be adapted to the use of ignorant pilots or boatmen. All commercial arrangements or accommodations, are made with reference to the presumption of law, that any one who assumes the responsibility of navigating a steamboat or other vessel, is qualified to discharge so responsible a duty, and if he fail in such duty for want of capacity, care or knowledge, his employer must suffer.... Gentlemen of the Jury," McLean said, "you can apply the above rule to the case in hand. Was the *Effie Afton*, in attempting to pass the draw, conducted with care and competent skill?" McLean now concluded:

> Upon the whole, gentlemen, I feel bound to say, if you believe from the evidence, the plaintiffs' witnesses were not mistaken in regard to the cross-currents and eddies in the draw, which endangered the passage by steamboats, and that there was no want of due care and skill in the management of the *Effie Afton* in attempting to pass through the draw which resulted in her total loss, you will find for the plaintiffs the value of the boat including the insurance money, which, by agreement of counsel, may be considered as a part of the damages to be recovered. But if you shall believe from the evidence, that there are no currents or eddies in the draw, which form a material obstruction to the passage of it, by boats which ply upon the river, and that the *Effie Afton*, in attempting to pass the draw, was not managed with that degree of care and skill which prudent and competent officers would be expected to exercise, in such a case, you will find for the defendant.

The case was now in the hands of the jury. It was about four o'clock in the afternoon of Thursday, September 24, the fifteenth day of the trial.[20] The jurors had listened to more than one hundred witnesses, some engineers with lofty reputations as experts, some steamboat pilots with years of experience on the western rivers, some mere bystanders who had observed the events at Rock Island on May 6, 1856. They had heard long hours of argument from skillful attorneys who had studied the facts of the case from almost every possible angle and yet could not agree on precisely what had happened on the tragic day, or who was legally responsible for the losses suffered. Perhaps Henry Binmore had been right when, at the beginning of the trial, he had drolly told his readers in St. Louis that experts would "of course differ" on the issues in the case, and that "the men who should know all about it, disagreeing, a jury of twelve men who *know nothing* about it will be called on to decide the scientific question."[21]

The deliberations continued until well after dark. The jurors returned to the courtroom once or twice with questions for the judge. What, they asked, was the precise meaning of the legal term "expert"? McLean supplied them with additional instructions that may or may not have helped them. It was past nine o'clock when the jurors returned a final time to inform the waiting judge and attorneys of the outcome of their deliberations.[22]

The law required that if a verdict was rendered, it be unanimous.[23] But the jurors were not unanimous. They had voted in favor of the bridge by a vote of nine to three.[24] The owners of the *Effie Afton* had failed in their attempt to assess damages against the span. All of the efforts they had brought against it had failed. The jury was hung.

The day after the trial ended, the *Chicago Press* said that the divided jury vote was "practically a verdict for the defendants. The bridge—that great link between the East and the West—will stand unmarred. The damages claimed by the owners of the *Effie Afton*, though not wholly lost, they have failed to recover."[25] The *Chicago Daily Democrat* editorialized that the hung verdict was "virtually a triumph for the bridge."[26]

The fact that the jury was hung meant the case was not yet entirely over, however, and that the legal future of the Rock Island Bridge had yet to be finally decided.

TWELVE

The Bridge Stands

≈

T he failure of the jurors to reach a unanimous verdict required
Judge McLean to dismiss them and return the case to the court's
calendar for future trial. Whether a new jury would actually be
summoned to the Saloon Building courtroom was largely in the
hands of Jacob Hurd, Alexander Kidwell, and Joseph Smith. They
could insist on a new trial or not—the choice was theirs. Lincoln
and his fellow defense attorneys had beaten back the boat owners'
first attempt to bring down the Rock Island Bridge with a judgment
for damages. The bridge still spanned the river. Trains still crossed
it daily carrying passengers and freight from Illinois into Iowa and
back again. If the plaintiffs wanted a new trial, they needed some
assurance that the new trial would produce tangible results. The
result that they most favored, of course, was the demolition of the
bridge, but a hefty judgment for damages could do a lot to help bring
about that result.

Only three weeks after the Chicago trial ended Hezekiah Wead
wrote Hurd, who had returned to his home in Ohio, urging him not
to be discouraged. Wead was sure that if competent engineers could
be brought from St. Louis to Rock Island to "actually find out how
the current affects boats in the draw," they would prevail in a new
trial.[1] Wead wrote Hurd again in November advising him that he had
written Congressman Cadwallader Washburn of Wisconsin asking
him to introduce a bill in Congress allowing a change of venue in the
case (the law did not then authorize such a change). Wead and Hurd
clearly believed that their failure to win a verdict in Chicago was due

to the pro-bridge, anti-steamboat bias of the jurors there and that if they could try the case before jurors elsewhere they would win it.

On November 30, Josiah W. Bissell, the St. Louis–based engineer who had designed a suspension bridge over the Mississippi at St. Louis that was never built, and who later prepared a map of the Rock Island Bridge designed to warn steamboat operators that it was a hazard to navigation, wrote Hurd from Cincinnati, where he was making arrangements with T. D. Lincoln to go on with what he called "the Chamber of Commerce suit" against the bridge. Bissell said the St. Louis Chamber had left the matter "entirely in my hands," and he intended "to do it up thoroughly." He had given T. D. Lincoln some new information about the "river pirates" they were fighting, and he was going to Davenport to gather more. Bissell noted that the St. Louis Chamber had already spent $1,200 on the litigation and was willing to advance another $600, although it expected Hurd to sign a note for repayment of the money.[2]

Wead had apparently broached the idea to Hurd of approaching Senator Stephen A. Douglas with the suggestion that he join the plaintiffs' team in a retrial, although Wead was not certain whether Douglas had already received a retainer from the railroad. On December 28, Hurd wrote Douglas, who was then in Washington embroiled in a bitter debate about the admission of Kansas to the Union. A pro-southern convention in Kansas had submitted a pro-slavery state constitution to President Buchanan, but Douglas had condemned the process by which the constitution was adopted as "a mockery and insult."[3] In the letter, marked "confidential," Hurd asked the Illinois senator to advise him by mail if he was "retained by the R.R. Bridge Co. in the case of J.S. Hurd (myself) et. al., vs. said Co. The case to which I refer is for the recovery of damages for the loss of the steamer *Effie Afton* May 6, '56, at the Rock Island Bridge." If Douglas had not been retained by the Bridge Company, Hurd wanted to procure his services, and he hinted that he would pay him well. "I shall certainly *beat* the Co.," Hurd said, "& desire your cooperation, also that you may share in the result." Hurd then revealed his sympathy with popular sovereignty, the controversial political doctrine that Douglas had advanced in his Kansas-Nebraska bill of

1854 and that had enhanced his reputation as one of the Democratic Party's national leaders. Hurd continued:

> Politically I have the people in this portion of my state (southern Ohio) and the adjoining portion of Kentucky all right on the Popular Sovereignty question. Permit me to refer you to Judge H. W. Wead of Peoria, Ill, (one of my attys in the case referred to) who will vouch for my loyalty. It is needless for me to say to you the attention of (not only) the American People—but the civilized world is upon yourself as the champion and standard bearer of a cherished doctrine.[4]

Douglas was, of course, a lawyer as well as a powerful politician. He had been an associate justice of the Illinois Supreme Court from 1841 to 1843, although his service there was not particularly impressive (according to one of his biographers, "he made up in energy and quickness for what he lacked in depth and understanding").[5] Hurd's appeal to Douglas seems to have been based as much in political sympathy for the senator as in admiration for his legal ability. He enclosed a steamboat ticket with the letter, inviting Douglas to travel on the river free of charge.[6] Hurd apparently did not know that Douglas was as much a champion of railroads as Lincoln—Douglas once said that "no man can keep up with the spirit of the age who travels on anything slower than the locomotive."[7]

There is no evidence that Douglas ever answered Hurd's invitation. As far as the surviving record shows, the man who was within half a year to become the opponent of Abraham Lincoln in a series of bitterly argued political debates that catapulted Lincoln into national prominence never joined Hurd's legal team in the *Effie Afton* case.

Wead was also making efforts to enlist the U.S. Army Corps of Engineers in the fight against the bridge. Not long after the end of the Chicago trial, he contacted Congressman Washburn who, on January 4, 1858, introduced a resolution in the House of Representatives instructing the House Committee on Commerce "to inquire if the railroad bridge across the Mississippi river, at Rock Island, Illinois, is a serious obstruction to the navigation of said river; and if so, to report to this House what action, if any, is necessary on the part of the Government to cause such obstruction to be removed."[8] Washburn was a Republican and a political supporter of Abraham Lincoln, as was his brother, Illinois congressman Elihu B. Washburne (Elihu added an *e* to the family name to recall its English roots), but both represented districts with close ties to river traffic. Cadwallader Washburn's district in southwest Wisconsin was a rich source of the timber that was floated down the Mississippi in rafts, and Elihu B. Washburne represented the lead- and silver-rich district around Galena, Illinois, so it was not surprising that they sympathized with the steamboats. Elihu B. Washburne was the congressman who rendered the report to the House of Representatives in April, a report that described the Rock Island Bridge as "a material and dangerous obstruction to the navigation of the Mississippi river" but declined to recommend any federal action against it because the courts had "full and ample power to remedy any evil that may exist."[9]

Not satisfied with this report, the St. Louis Chamber of Commerce urged some senators and representatives to undertake yet another study of the Rock Island Bridge, this one to be conducted by a specially appointed board of military engineers. The result was a report that was submitted to Secretary of War John B. Floyd—a former governor of Virginia who was soon to become a general in the Confederate army—in March 1859. Noting that it had been facilitated by Josiah Bissell, the new report concluded that the bridge had been poorly designed and located and that it was "not only an obstruction to the navigation of the river, but one greater than there was any occasion for." But like the earlier Washburne report it made no recommendation for any action.[10]

For all the available record reveals, Lincoln's involvement in the *Effie Afton* case ended when he received the fee for his participation in the Chicago trial. He had been retained for his courtroom skills and had little or nothing to do with the legal proceedings that preceded the courtroom battle, so there was no reason for him to continue to represent the Bridge Company after the trial. He was busy with many other cases in the last days of 1857 and the first half of 1858, some in the courts of Illinois's Eighth Judicial Circuit, even more in the Illinois Supreme Court and the U.S. courts in Springfield and Chicago. His fee for his *Effie Afton* work was apparently $400, for he deposited that amount in his Springfield bank account on September 26, 1857.[11] Norman Judd, however, was of counsel to both the Bridge Company and its affiliated railroads, so he continued to work on the litigation in its later stages—which were quite extensive.

On May 7, 1858, a man named James Ward filed suit in the U.S. District Court for the District of Iowa asking for a court order declaring the Rock Island Bridge a "common and public nuisance."[12] Ward was a resident of St. Louis and a part owner of three steamboats that regularly plied the Mississippi between St. Louis and St. Paul.[13] The defendant named in his suit was the Iowa-based Mississippi and Missouri Railroad Company. Unlike Hurd's suit in Chicago, which sought to recover damages for the loss of the *Effie Afton*, Ward's Iowa suit did not seek damages—although he did complain that his boats had been injured by the bridge. Instead he alleged that the bridge was erected in violation of treaties, acts of Congress, and his own rights of navigation of the river. And he asked that it "be abated and removed."[14]

Since Ward was a citizen of Missouri, and the Mississippi and Missouri Railroad Company was an Iowa corporation, the district court in Iowa had jurisdiction over the parties under the Diversity of Citizenship Clause of the U.S. Constitution.[15] Whether the court had jurisdiction over the subject matter of the suit (the Rock Island Bridge) was another and, as it eventually turned out, critical issue. In any case, Ward's suit did not entitle him to a jury trial, for actions asking for equitable remedies (such as abatement of a nuisance) are not covered by the constitutional guarantee of trial by jury.[16]

What Ward's suit did entitle him to was a hearing before Iowa's U.S. District Judge James M. Love. Love was a Virginia-born appointee of President Franklin Pierce and, as it happened, a friend of Samuel Miller, one of Ward's attorneys in the suit. Miller was one of Iowa's most interesting lawyers, for he had been a physician in his native Kentucky before gaining admission to the bar and moving across the Mississippi to Iowa in 1850. His move was inspired in part by his opposition to slavery and in part by his conviction that Keokuk's location on the Mississippi about 150 miles below Rock Island destined it to become a great commercial center.[17] River traffic and a thriving steamboat presence would, in Miller's view, contribute to Keokuk's future, while the bridge at Rock Island would seriously threaten it by diverting transportation to the railroad. Love, who was a former partner of Miller's own legal partner in Keokuk, apparently shared that opinion, although he did not share Miller's politics, for Miller was a Republican and Love a Democrat.[18]

Acting through the St. Louis Chamber of Commerce and the St. Louis City Council, steamboat interests in the Missouri city contributed large sums to finance Ward's lawsuit.[19] Extensive depositions were taken, some as far away as Detroit, Cincinnati, and even New York City, before Judge Love issued his decree in April 1860, agreeing with Ward that the bridge was a nuisance and ordering that it be torn down.[20] Since the jurisdiction of the federal court for Iowa extended only to the middle of the Mississippi, however, Love could not order the total demolition of the Rock Island Bridge, only the portion of it on the Iowa side of the state line—a line that ran down the middle of the river. So he ordered the demolition of the piers and superstructure that were in Iowa, but not those that were in Illinois.[21]

The case was appealed to the United States Supreme Court, where it was argued on December 18, 1862. The nation was then in the midst of the war that pitted armies commanded by Confederate president Jefferson Davis, an old foe of the Rock Island Bridge, against forces commanded by United States president Abraham Lincoln, the bridge's onetime defender. Strangely, Samuel Miller had by that time become a member of the Supreme Court, thanks to an appointment by Lincoln in July 1862.[22] (Lincoln apparently knew nothing of Miller before he appointed him except that he was reputed to be a skillful lawyer and that his appointment was warmly recommended by prominent politicians in Iowa.)

As the former attorney for James Ward, Miller of course recused himself from the Supreme Court appeal. On January 20, 1863, a decision was announced by Associate Justice John Catron of Tennessee, a southern Democrat who, despite his state's secession from the Union, remained loyal to the federal government. Concluding that if there was in fact any obstruction to navigation at Rock Island, it was on the Illinois side of the bridge, Catron announced that the Iowa court had no authority over it, for the Iowa court's jurisdiction extended only up to the state line. Ordering the removal of the Iowa portion of the bridge would not solve any problems, since the facts did not show any obstruction on the Iowa side of the river. When T. D. Lincoln of Cincinnati, who was James Ward's attorney in the Supreme Court, argued that the public was entitled to the free navigation of the whole river from bank to bank, Catron scoffed. "According to this assumption," the Tennessean wrote, "no lawful bridge could be built across the Mississippi anywhere; nor could the great facilities to commerce accomplished by the invention of railroads, be made available where great rivers had to be crossed." Judge Love's order was reversed.[23]

Three more efforts were made to bring down the Rock Island Bridge, two that were legal and another that, judging from newspaper reports, was bizarrely illegal.

Dissatisfied with the Supreme Court's ruling that the U.S. District Court in Iowa had no jurisdiction over the Illinois portion of the Rock Island Bridge, steamboat owners began a new effort against the bridge, this time in the U.S. District Court for the Northern District of Illinois. This court, of which Thomas Drummond was the presiding judge, was located in Chicago, where the original lawsuit against the bridge had come to grief with a hung jury. The new action aimed to overcome the problem of dealing with Chicago jurors by invoking the district court's admiralty jurisdiction.

Admiralty law concerns itself with maritime matters, including the rights and duties of ship owners and operators, both on the high seas and in inland navigable waters. The U.S. Constitution assigns jurisdiction in admiralty cases to the U.S. District Courts but, following the English practice, exempts them from trial by jury.[24]

The new action was begun with the filing of a libel—the initial pleading in admiralty cases—against the bridge by the Galena,

Dubuque, Dunleith, and Minnesota Packet Company. This company, often called the Minnesota Packet Company for short, had lost a large steamboat named the *Grey Eagle* when it collided with the Rock Island Bridge on May 9, 1861, and sank. Like the *Effie Afton*, the *Grey Eagle* had been built at Cincinnati at considerable expense, with some reports saying that it cost more than $60,000. Unlike the earlier boat's, however, the *Grey Eagle*'s collision resulted not just in the loss of the boat but also in seven deaths.[25] The libel asked the district court to impose a lien for $70,000 against the Illinois portion of the bridge. The Mississippi and Missouri Railroad Company and others intervened as claimants, filing formal objections to the court's admiralty jurisdiction. Their objections were quickly sustained by the district court and, on appeal, by the circuit court, and the libel was dismissed without trial.

A second appeal was then taken to the United States Supreme Court, where a decision was announced on December 30, 1867. Sustaining the lowers courts' dismissal, Associate Justice Stephen J. Field of California—like Samuel Miller, a Lincoln appointee to the High Court—wrote the opinion for a unanimous Court. "A maritime lien can only exist upon moving things engaged in navigation," Field wrote, "or upon things which are the subjects of commerce on the high seas or navigable waters. It may arise with reference to vessels, steamers and rafts, and upon goods and merchandise carried by them. But it cannot arise upon anything which is fixed and immovable, like a wharf, a bridge, or real estate of any kind. Though bridges and wharves may aid commerce by facilitating intercourse on land or the discharge of cargoes, they are not in any sense the subject of maritime lien."[26]

In August 1860, residents of both Chicago and St. Louis were shocked by news that Josiah Bissell and a young attorney from Rock Island named Walter F. Chadwick had been arrested in Chicago for conspiracy to set fire to the Rock Island Bridge.[27] News of the arrests quickly spread to the East Coast, where the *New York Times* reported that "evidence of the plan formed to burn the bridge is said to be conclusive."[28] The *Chicago Press and Tribune* told its readers that, about a year earlier, a large quantity of combustible material had been discovered on the span by the bridge watchman, who successfully removed it before it could be ignited. The authorities suspected an attempted arson and, from that time forward, kept "vigilant eyes" on the bridge.[29] According to the *Press and Tribune*, Bissell had come to Chicago the following April and offered to give a private detective who had previously done some work for him $5,000 to "cause the bridge to be burned." He told the detective that lawsuits would never be effective to remove the span, "but let it once be burned and we'll get out an injunction against rebuilding it. Do you see?"[30]

Alerted to the plot by the detective, the authorities prepared a trap. When a suspicious package came from St. Louis addressed to the detective, it was taken to a room where the grand jury was meeting and found to contain fifty champagne bottles "filled with a highly combustible, treacle-like fluid known as 'Greek Fire.'" One of the bottles was opened and a portion of its contents was poured into a saucer and lit, unleashing a fire which "well-nigh burned up the jury room."[31] Bissell and Chadwick, who was alleged to have acted as Bissell's accomplice, were quickly arrested and indicted. The *Davenport Gazette* reflected much of the outrage felt by pro-railroad interests when it wrote that Bissell "has for years been smelling around this bridge and doing dirty work among steamboat men to collect evidence of its being an obstruction to navigation. In a thousand ways he has proved himself an unscrupulous, unprincipled knave, utterly unworthy of the confidence of any honest man, much less of such a body as the St. Louis Chamber of Commerce. His arrest on this charge has not surprised us, for we have long believed, and even intimated in these columns, that he was none too good to burn the bridge if he could get the chance."[32]

Freed on bail advanced by business interests in St. Louis, Bissell went to trial a few months later. His lawyer argued that the charges against him had been manufactured to prevent him from continuing to act as the St. Louis Chamber of Commerce's agent in attempts to bring down the bridge, and that the bridge owners wanted to "destroy him and remove him out of the way."[33] Chamber of Commerce officials from the Missouri city admitted that Bissell was acting in their behalf but denied that he had been authorized to do anything illegal. However strong the evidence against Bissell and Chadwick had seemed at first, and however sure the river men in St. Louis were that Chicago jurors favored railroad interests over those of steamboats, convictions could not be obtained. The jury returned a verdict of not guilty, apparently on the curious ground that the indictment did not properly state that the Illinois end of the bridge touched the city of Rock Island and that the Illinois court thus lacked jurisdiction of the case.[34]

Still convinced that he could not obtain a fair jury trial in Chicago, Jacob Hurd filed a second, and separate, suit for damages sustained in his loss of the *Effie Afton*, this time in an Illinois state court, where the jury pool would be uncontaminated by Chicagoans. Hurd's initial filing was in February 1859, in the circuit court for Rock Island County, but before it could be brought to trial, opposition from the railroads and its attorneys forced several changes of venue. The suit finally wound up in the circuit court for McDonough County, Illinois, where, in 1875, the judge dismissed it.[35]

It had been nearly twenty years since the *Effie Afton* struck the bridge and burned, and in all of that time every effort that creative lawyers in Illinois and deep-pocketed steamboat owners in St. Louis could conceive had failed to bring down the bridge. By 1875, even Jacob Hurd had left the scene, for he had been killed in 1866 by a boiler explosion on the steamboat *W. R. Carter* near Vicksburg. His body was never recovered.[36]

THIRTEEN

The Great and Durable Question

≈

More people had probably seen Lincoln in action in the *Effie Afton* trial than in any of his previous courtroom battles, for the crowded city of Chicago was fast becoming the legal as well as the commercial and transportation center of the Middle West, and the bridge controversy had excited greater attention than any other struggle of Lincoln's legal career. The spectators who filled Judge McLean's courtroom day after day had been impressed by the lanky Springfielder's ability to handle himself "on his feet," as courtroom lawyers routinely must. But a new opportunity to display Lincoln's talents to the general public was revealing itself in the form of a series of debates with Stephen A. Douglas, who was seeking reelection to the Senate.

Lincoln was eager to become Douglas's Republican opponent in 1858, in part to redeem himself from his disappointing failure to win election to the Senate in 1855, in part because he had fundamental disagreements with Douglas about slavery in the United States. His growing reputation as a skillful lawyer was not the only dividend he won in the *Effie Afton* trial, for that hectic two weeks in the courtroom of Judge McLean had brought him and Norman Judd closer together. As Judd watched Lincoln's courtroom performance, his respect for Lincoln's legal abilities had grown along with his sense that Lincoln had a real political future.

After his role in foiling Lincoln's senatorial ambitions in 1855, Judd had abandoned his Democratic affiliation, joined Lincoln in the new Republican Party, and won election to the influential post of Republican state chairman. Once merely courtroom colleagues, Judd and Lincoln were now political allies. When the Republican state convention convened in Springfield in June 1858, Judd called the delegates to order, certified their credentials, and led an enthusiastic delegation from Cook County that paraded through the hall with a banner proclaiming "Cook County for Abraham Lincoln." Lincoln scholar Allen C. Guelzo has called the convention "an unsullied triumph for Norman Judd's organizing skills."[1] It was only the second time in American history that a candidate for election to the U.S. Senate had been nominated by a major party, and though the act was not formally binding—the senator would not be elected by popular vote but by the state legislators chosen in the upcoming fall election—it was an important boost for Lincoln's chances.[2] Accepting the nomination, Lincoln gave his famous "House Divided Speech," setting out his views on the future of slavery in the United States in prose that reverberated through Illinois and beyond.

Repeating a biblical phrase, as he often did, Lincoln told the delegates who nominated him that "'A house divided against itself cannot stand.' I believe this government cannot endure, permanently half *slave* and half *free*." He continued: "I do not expect the Union to be *dissolved*—I do not expect the house to *fall*—but I *do* expect it will cease to be divided. It will become *all* one thing, or *all* the other. Either the *opponents* of slavery, will arrest the further spread of it, and place it where the public mind shall rest in the belief that it is in course of ultimate extinction; or its *advocates* will push it forward, till it shall become alike lawful in *all* the States, *old* as well as *new*— *North* as well as *South*."[3] Lincoln made a powerful argument against the spread of slavery into the western territories, condemning Senator Douglas's doctrine of popular sovereignty as "a mere deceitful pretense for the benefit of slavery,"[4] for it permitted a simple majority of the voters in a territory—all white men, of course—to decide whether slavery would or would not be permitted in the territory.

Douglas did not care whether slavery was "voted *down* or voted *up*," but Lincoln did. He charged that Douglas had been part of a conspiracy among President James Buchanan, former President Franklin Pierce, and Chief Justice Roger B. Taney of the U.S. Supreme Court to nationalize slavery. The supposed conspiracy centered around Taney's controversial decision in *Dred Scott v. Sandford,* announced in Washington on March 6, 1857, only a few months before Lincoln joined Judd in the defense of the *Effie Afton* trial. It was not Lincoln's first reference to *Dred Scott*; he had roundly criticized the decision in a speech in Springfield in June, 1857.[5] It was one of his most forceful, however, and it would set the tone for much of his debate with Douglas in the upcoming election.

On July 24, in part at the urging of Judd, Lincoln wrote Douglas, asking him to meet him in a series of debates in different parts of Illinois.[6] Judd personally tracked Douglas down and delivered the letter to him in Chicago, reacting with restraint when the senator berated him for having abandoned the Democratic Party.[7] Douglas was much more famous than Lincoln and did not want to share his celebrity with his lesser-known opponent, but he knew that a refusal to debate Lincoln would seem cowardly. So he set dates on which he would meet Lincoln in seven of Illinois's congressional districts.

The *Dred Scott* decision was one of the principal subjects in the debates, as was Douglas's Kansas-Nebraska Act and his doctrine of popular sovereignty, and both men's views on slavery. Douglas revealed himself on the debate platforms as an unabashed white supremacist. "I say to you, in all frankness, gentlemen, that in my opinion a negro is not a citizen, cannot be, and ought not to be under the constitution of the United States," he declared in the debate at Charleston, Illinois, on September 18. "I say that this government was created on the white basis. It was made by white men, for the benefit of white men and their posterity forever, and never should be administered by any except white men."[8] Douglas reaffirmed his belief in popular sovereignty, saying that if a state chose to "keep slavery forever, it is not my business, but its own; if it chooses to abolish slavery, it is its own business—not mine. I care more for the great principle of self-government, the right of the people to rule, than I do for all the negroes in Christendom."[9]

Prodded by Douglas's persistent race-baiting and the knowledge that racial prejudice was pervasive in Illinois, as it also was in other northern states, Lincoln made some very racist statements of his own—statements that in later years would haunt (and, in the views of many, stain) his memory. In the debate at Charleston, Illinois, on September 18, he said: "I am not, nor ever have been in favor of bringing about in any way the social and political equality of the white and black races[.] . . . I am not nor ever have been in favor of making voters or jurors of negroes, nor of qualifying them to hold office, nor to intermarry with white people; and I will say in addition to this that there is a physical difference between the white and black races which I believe will for ever forbid the two races living together on terms of social and political equality."[10] But even as he was making these statements, he made it very clear that, in contrast to Douglas, he believed that slavery was wrong, that its spread into the western territories should be stopped, and that it should be placed "in the course of ultimate extinction."[11] At Galesburg, Illinois, on October 7, he said that he regarded slavery "as a moral, social and political evil."[12] At Quincy, Illinois, on October 13, he affirmed his belief that blacks were "entitled to all the rights enumerated in the Declaration of Independence—the right of life, liberty and the pursuit of happiness," and that they were "as much entitled to these as the white man." If the black man "is not my equal in many respects," Lincoln said, "in the right to eat the bread without leave of anybody else which his own hand earns, he is my equal and the equal of Judge Douglas, and the equal of every other man."[13] (Lincoln consistently called Douglas by his early judicial title.) Lincoln acknowledged that there was a great difference of opinion in the country about slavery, but he thought that "the difference of opinion, reduced to its lowest terms, is no other than the difference between the men who think slavery is wrong and those who do not think it wrong."[14]

Douglas proclaimed his support for the *Dred Scott* decision because it was "delivered by the highest judicial tribunal on earth, a tribunal established by the Constitution of the United States for that purpose, and hence that decision becomes the law of the land, binding on you, on me, and on every other good citizen, whether we like it or not."[15] Lincoln argued that the *Dred Scott* decision was based on false premises and that those false premises gave rise to its false conclusions.[16] He pointed out that controversial court decisions had in the past been reversed or disregarded by other branches of the government. He pointed in particular to President Andrew Jackson's rejection of the Supreme Court decision in *McCulloch v. Maryland*,[17] upholding the constitutionality of the second Bank of the United States.[18] Jackson was the hero of Douglas's Democratic Party, but he persisted in his belief that the bank was unconstitutional despite the Supreme Court's contrary pronouncement, and he vetoed its recharter. Lincoln argued that Supreme Court decisions could, and should, be overruled when it was determined that they were wrong. He did not propose to resist the *Dred Scott* decision. He did not "propose that when Dred Scott has been decided to be a slave by the court, we, as a mob, will decide him to be free." But he did oppose the Supreme Court's decision "as a political rule which shall be binding on the voter," and he declared that he and the Republican Party proposed "so resisting it as to have it reversed if we can, and a new judicial rule established upon this subject."[19]

The legal issues in the *Effie Afton* and *Dred Scott* cases were starkly different, but their political consequences were mutually reinforcing. Without *Effie Afton*, Lincoln might not have won the enthusiastic political support of Norman Judd in 1858 and beyond (or if he had won it, it might not have been as strong). Without Judd's participation in the Republican state convention in Springfield in 1858, Lincoln might not have won the party's senatorial nomination (or if he had won it, it might not have been as enthusiastic). Without the nomination and Judd's support during the ensuing campaign, Lincoln's profile might not have risen as high as it did. And without Lincoln's vigorous and eloquent disagreement with the *Dred Scott* decision, voiced in his debates with Douglas, he might never have won the Republican presidential nomination in 1860 and gone on to win that year's election.

There is no question that Lincoln's debates with Douglas in 1858 were a springboard to his election as president of the United States. Shorthand reports of the debates were, ironically, taken down by the same two reporters who had covered the *Effie Afton* trial: Henry Binmore and Robert R. Hitt. Binmore had left the St. Louis *Missouri Republican* and was now working for the pro-Douglas *Chicago Times*, while Hitt was engaged by the pro-Lincoln *Chicago Press and Tribune.*[20] First printed in Chicago, then copied in newspapers all over Illinois and beyond, reports of the debates helped to acquaint voters with the positions of Douglas and Lincoln on the great issues they debated and to increase popular interest in the election.

When the voters went to the polls in November, the statewide candidates of the Republican Party received more votes than their Democratic opponents, but the malapportionment of legislative districts resulted in a Democratic majority in the legislature, and Douglas won another term as senator.[21] Lincoln was initially depressed by his defeat and wrote one of his old friends, "I now sink out of view, and shall be forgotten." In the same letter, however, he said, "I am glad I made the late race. It gave me a hearing on the great and durable question of the age, which I could have had in no other way," adding, "I believe I have made some marks which will tell for the cause of civil liberty long after I am gone."[22] And he prepared a compilation of his debates with Douglas for publication in book form (using Binmore's reports of Lincoln's words and Hitt's reports of Douglas's), confident that it would find a receptive audience. He was right, for when *The Political Debates between Hon. Abraham Lincoln and Hon. Stephen A. Douglas* was issued in 1860, it became a runaway best-seller.[23]

In August 1859, Lincoln made a trip into Iowa with Ozias M. Hatch, the Illinois secretary of state. He traveled from Springfield to St. Joseph by train, then boarded a steamboat for the trip up the Missouri River to Council Bluffs, where Norman Judd owned land. Judd's note to Lincoln was coming due, and Judd had proposed to give him a new note secured by some of his land in the Iowa town.[24] Lincoln inspected the property, met some of the leading citizens in the town, and on August 13 gave a speech in the Council Bluffs Concert Hall on the subject of slavery and its expansion into the western territories. Iowans were for the most part supportive of Lincoln's strong opposition to the Kansas-Nebraska Act and Stephen Douglas's doctrine of popular sovereignty, and his speech went well.[25]

While he was in Council Bluffs, Lincoln met Grenville M. Dodge, a young railroad surveyor who was employed by the Mississippi and Missouri Railroad, then building its lines from Iowa City west to the Missouri River. Lincoln and Dodge conversed for a couple of hours, in the course of which Dodge pressed on him the idea that the best route for the projected railroad to the Pacific lay through Council Bluffs and Omaha and then followed the bed of the Platte River Valley toward the Rocky Mountains.[26]

Years later, Dodge—who served as a major general in the Union Army and afterward became the chief engineer of the Union Pacific Railroad—remembered Lincoln's enthusiasm about the projected line. "He stated that there was nothing more important before the nation at that time than the building of the railroad to the Pacific Coast," Dodge recalled. "He ingeniously extracted a great deal of information from me."[27] Lincoln decided to accept Judd's property as collateral, which Judd deeded to him on November 11, 1859. On their way home, Lincoln and Hatch traveled aboard a steamboat that ran aground in the Missouri River and delayed their arrival back in Springfield.[28]

In October 1859, Lincoln received an invitation to make a much longer trip, this time to New York to address a group of eastern Republicans at Henry Ward Beecher's Plymouth Church in Brooklyn.[29] When he arrived in New York in February 1860, he found that the venue for the speech had been changed to Manhattan's Cooper Union. He had carefully prepared for the speech he delivered at the Cooper Union on February 27, spending long hours in the Illinois State Library researching the history of slavery in the early days of the United States. His speech—ninety minutes long—reiterated the themes he had expressed in his debates with Stephen Douglas, including his views on the *Dred Scott* case, which he had continued to refine since his debate with Douglas in 1858. The speech demonstrated to Easterners the passion and eloquence that Illinoisans had seen and heard in 1858.[30] In a letter to his wife, Lincoln said that the Cooper Union speech "went off passably well and gave me no trouble whatever."[31] In New York, however, it created a deep impression, inspiring Horace Greeley of the *New York Tribune* to comment: "No man ever before made such an impression on his first appeal to a New York audience."[32] The *Tribune* printed the speech in pamphlet form, and in Illinois it was republished by Springfield's *Illinois State Journal.*[33]

Despite his political activity, Lincoln continued to apply himself to his legal practice in early 1860. It was, after all, the means by which he supported himself and his family, and if he did not take on clients and appear in court he would soon find himself in financial distress. The attorney for William Jones, a wealthy Chicago banker who owned some land along the city's lakeshore, had for more than a year been asking Lincoln to join him in the trial of an important real estate case that was scheduled for the U.S. Circuit Court in the spring of 1860. Lincoln's trial calendar was already congested, and his supporters in the Illinois Republican Party were making plans to put his name before the upcoming Republican National Convention as a candidate for the party's presidential nomination. But he found room for the trial on his calendar, and went up to Chicago in late March to prepare for it.

Formally titled *Johnston v. Jones and Marsh* but informally called the Sand Bar case, the trial tested the ownership of a parcel of real estate formed by accretions of sand and gravel after the U.S. Army Corps of Engineers straightened the Chicago River and built two piers into Lake Michigan in the 1830s. It was recognized throughout Illinois as one of the most bitterly contested cases in Chicago's history, for the disputed land (part of a larger tract formed by the accretions) was deemed to be worth hundreds of thousands—perhaps even as much as a million—dollars. Litigation in the case had begun in 1849 and already spanned three jury trials and one appeal to the United States Supreme Court, none of which had effectively settled the rights of the parties.[34] The upcoming trial would be the fourth, and if sustained by the Supreme Court, it would finally end the legal wrangling.

Lincoln was one of four lawyers for William Jones who opposed three lawyers for William S. Johnston when the case went before the jury on March 23. He took an active part in the questioning of witnesses and the presentation of final arguments, all of which ended on April 4 with a verdict in favor of Lincoln's client. Lincoln was pleased when, on the day the jury rendered its verdict, he received a fee of $350 for his work in the trial.[35] Predictably, the case was again appealed to the United States Supreme Court, which heard it in late 1861. Associate Justice Noah Swayne of Ohio, whom Lincoln had appointed to the Supreme Court following the April 1861 death of John McLean, announced the opinion affirming the decision of the jury in Chicago.[36]

The extent to which Lincoln's legal career had helped his political ambitions was vividly demonstrated when the Republican Party met in Chicago on May 16, 1860, just six weeks after the conclusion of the Sand Bar trial. Lincoln's managers there were Leonard Swett, Stephen T. Logan, Jesse W. Fell, Ward Hill Lamon, Norman Judd, and David Davis. All of these men were Illinois lawyers (although Davis had been elevated to the judgeship of the Eighth Judicial Circuit) who had known and worked with Lincoln for many years and become enthusiastic supporters of his candidacy for the party's presidential nomination. Judd, who had been Lincoln's co-counsel in the *Effie Afton* trial and played a major role in his 1858 campaign for election to the Senate, gave the nominating speech for Lincoln, and David Davis acted as his manager during the balloting.

Against the opposition of New York's William H. Seward, Pennsylvania's Simon Cameron, Ohio's Salmon P. Chase, and Missouri's Edward Bates, all better-known politicians with greater national reputations than the Illinoisan now nicknamed "the Rail-Splitter," Lincoln seemed at the outset to have little chance of capturing the presidential nod; but with the help of his lawyer friends, and the growing realization that all of the other candidates had weaknesses, he succeeded on the third ballot and, on May 18, won the nomination.[37] In the presidential election that was held on November 6, Lincoln won more popular votes than any of his three opponents (Stephen Douglas, John C. Breckinridge, and John Bell), and on March 4, 1861, he was inaugurated in Washington, D.C., as the nation's sixteenth president.

FOURTEEN

History's Verdict

≈

The day before Lincoln received the Republican convention's presidential nomination, the party adopted its platform for the coming campaign. The document began by restating positions the Republican Party had already made well known: opposition to the spread of slavery into the western territories, condemnation of the reopening of the African slave trade (which it condemned as "a crime against humanity and a burning shame to our country and age"), an "abhorrence" for "all schemes for disunion, come from whatever source they may," and support for the admission of Kansas into the Union as a free state. It added a strong position favoring protection for the rights of recent immigrants to the United States (thus opposing the nativist, or anti-Catholic policies of the Know-Nothing Party), favoring the adoption of a homestead act, which would give western settlers access to lands beyond the Mississippi, supporting a tariff that would "encourage the development of the industrial interests of the whole country," and advocating federal aid for the construction of the long-sought-after railroad to the Pacific. In emphatic language, the platform declared that "a railroad to the Pacific Ocean is imperatively demanded by the interests of the whole country" and "the federal government ought to render immediate and efficient aid in its construction."[1]

In his formal acceptance of the nomination, Lincoln made it clear that the platform met his "approval" and that it would be his "care not to violate, or disregard it, in any part."[2] After his inauguration he made serious—and mostly successful—efforts to carry out this promise, despite the overwhelming distractions that the secession of the southern states presented to him: the massive defiance of federal law that secession represented; the military attacks on Fort Sumter, South Carolina, and other federal properties; the threat of a military invasion of the national capital; the need to assemble an army sufficient to beat back the southern threats and raise revenues adequate to fund the war effort; the conviction that slavery was at the heart of the crisis, and the growing conviction that it was his duty as president to meet it with emancipation; and his overarching passion to preserve the Union, a "nation, conceived in liberty, and dedicated to the proposition that 'all men are created equal,'" whose preservation he regarded as "the last best hope of earth."[3]

On May 20, 1862, President Abraham Lincoln signed the promised Homestead Act, giving 160 acres of public land to each settler who would occupy and improve it for five years.[4] Then, on July 1, 1862, he signed the Pacific Railway Act, pledging federal aid for the construction of the railroad to the Pacific Ocean. Among other things, the Railway Act promised generous subsidies in the form of land grants and credits for the construction of the railroad; it also authorized the president to fix the width (gauge) of all of the rail lines built west and to establish the geographical point at which the rails should begin their westward course.[5] Only one day later, he signed the so-called Morrill Act, which made generous grants of federal land to the states and territories for the creation of agricultural colleges.[6] Nine days later, on July 11, 1862, he signed an act creating a federal arsenal at Rock Island, a move deemed necessary for the support of Union forces after the Confederate capture and destruction of the U.S. Arsenal at Harpers Ferry, Virginia.[7] On January 21, 1863, acting pursuant to the authority granted him in the Pacific Railway Act, he issued an order setting the gauge of the railroad from the Missouri River to the Pacific Ocean at five feet.[8] (Congress, however, countermanded his order on March 3, setting the gauge at four feet eight and a half inches—a width used in the eastern states and popularly called the "standard gauge.")[9] On November 17, 1863, two days before he delivered his immortal address on the battlefield at Gettysburg,

Pennsylvania, he fixed the point at which the Pacific railroad would begin as "so much of the Western boundary of the State of Iowa as lies between the North and South boundaries of the United States Township, within which the City of Omaha is situated" (that is, a point directly opposite Council Bluffs, Iowa).[10] On June 9, 1864, he delivered a message acknowledging his nomination for a second term as president in which he stated (among many other things) that he and his party were "in favor of the speedy construction of the Railroad to the Pacific coast."[11] On July 2, 1864, he signed an act amending the Pacific Railway Act of 1862, increasing the federal aid for the construction of the railroad by doubling the land grants and guaranteeing the payment of interest on bonds sold to raise cash for construction.[12]

The Pacific railroad was actually two railroads, one that built eastward from California under the direction of the California-incorporated Central Pacific Railroad Company, and a second that moved westward from Council Bluffs and Omaha under the direction of the federally incorporated Union Pacific. Construction was delayed, in part by the demands of the incorporators—many of whom had greater appetites for personal profit than for the actual laying of rails—and in part by the deserts and canyons, rivers and soaring mountain ranges that lay between the Missouri River and the Pacific Ocean.

The failure of the plaintiffs in the *Effie Afton* case to bring down the Rock Island Bridge enabled the span to remain open to rail traffic through the end of the 1850s and into the 1860s. New settlers passed over the span into Iowa and the surrounding territories, bringing with them predominantly anti-slavery and pro-Union sentiments. If Jefferson Davis had been successful in locating the first railroad bridge over the Mississippi in the South, much the same might have been true in that region: slaveholders and their supporters could have crossed the river from east to west in great numbers, increasing their force in Missouri, Arkansas, Louisiana, and Texas.

The success of Lincoln and his colleagues in defending the Rock Island Bridge also made the bridge and the railroads that crossed it important players in moving troops and freight during the Civil War. Fighting along the river brought normal steamboat traffic to a virtual halt while railroad traffic over the Rock Island Bridge continued, even accelerated. Throughout the conflict, trains crossed over the Mississippi at Rock Island, moving passengers and freight. When President Lincoln first called for a volunteer regiment from Iowa, ten times the required number of Iowans responded. Every call for volunteers from Iowa was met with enthusiasm, so by the end of the fighting Iowa could boast that more than seventy-six thousand of its men, including forty-six Iowa regiments, four batteries of light artillery, nine regiments of cavalry, and thousands of replacement units, had served in the Union Army.[13]

The railroads of the North greatly exceeded those of the South in the mileage covered, permitting Union forces to move over long distances and providing efficient transportation routes for the massive amounts of provisions, supplies, equipment, and armaments they needed to sustain their efforts.[14] By itself, the Rock Island Bridge was not essential to Union victory, but as part of a massive—and ever expanding—network of rails extending from the Atlantic seaboard across the Mississippi and beyond, it contributed significantly to the Union Army's military successes. The Civil War was, in fact, the "first true railroad war" in history, with iron rails carrying fighting men and all that it takes to sustain them on a scale never before seen in history.[15]

The fighting between the North and South drew to a close as Union General Ulysses S. Grant accepted the surrender of Confederate General Robert E. Lee at Appomattox Court House, Virginia, on April 9, 1865. Lincoln's life was ended by an assassin's bullet in Ford's Theatre in Washington on April 14, 1865, and the institution of slavery was brought to a final end in the United States with the ratification of the Thirteenth Amendment to the Constitution on December 6, 1865. All of this happened before the golden spike was driven into the last tie uniting the eastern and western halves of the Pacific Railway at Promontory Summit, Utah, on May 10, 1869. But the golden spike symbolized the triumph of an idea and the force behind it.

* * *

The Rock Island Bridge proved to be a durable survivor, even after it was partially destroyed by the *Effie Afton*. As locomotives and cars increased in weight and speed, and as the volume of the traffic that crossed the bridge grew, the span was strengthened, first by the addition of suspension cables that enhanced the load-bearing capacities of the timber trusses, then by the replacement of the original, flat-topped trusses with higher and heavier trusses that formed arches at the top of each of the spans. All of this work was done on the original piers and with only minimal interruptions to the flow of train traffic across the river.[16]

Then, in March 1868, the bridge was struck by two natural disasters. The first was a massive ice floe brought down the river by the severe cold of the winter and then exacerbated by heavy rains and an early thaw that cracked the ice, formed it into what the *Davenport Gazette* described as "icebergs," and created a kind of a gorge between the two banks of the river. The ice crashed into the bridge, damaging the piers and the spans above them so badly that trains could not pass over.[17] Engineers and a crew of workers were promptly summoned from Chicago to lay rails down to the river from the depots in Rock Island and Davenport so freight could be carried across the river by ferries while repairs were begun.[18] Then, just six days later, the bridge was hit by a wind so fierce that the *Gazette* called it a tornado.[19] Six men were on the span when the wind struck; three were injured, and one was sent to his death in the icy water below.[20] Nature in the form of ice and wind had spoken louder than any of the steamboat men or lawyers ever could. Defiant of the twin disasters, railroad officials and engineering crews worked furiously to rebuild the bridge, and just over six weeks later they were able to reopen it to rail traffic.[21] The *Gazette* called the rebuilding effort "a speedy and thorough operation" that evidenced "great skill" on the part of the bridge managers and engineers.[22]

Even before this work was completed, however, plans were afoot to replace the entire bridge with a new structure. These plans arose in part from the government's wish to expand the arsenal it had established on Rock Island during the war and make more of the island available for buildings and roadways, in part from an awareness by both government officials and railroad engineers that the bridge needed to be more stable and better positioned. As early as June 27, 1866, Congress authorized the construction of a new bridge, to be located at the western end of the island, about 1,500 feet downriver from the original site.[23] The government and the Rock Island Railroad—officially known as the Chicago, Rock Island and Pacific Railroad Company after August 1866—formally agreed that the new span would be owned by the government but financed and maintained by both the government and the railroad, which was granted a right-of-way across the new structure and free use of it for its trains.[24]

In 1867, Congress appropriated $200,000 for the erection of the bridge, on the express condition that the railroad first secure its required payment of half of the cost of construction and maintenance.[25] In 1868, the federal lawmakers authorized the secretary of war to begin the construction of the new bridge on the understanding that after it was ready for use, the railroad company would remove the old bridge and the old railroad track leading up to it. At the same time Congress specified that its total expenditure on the project should not exceed $1 million.[26] Welcoming the government as partners in the new span, the railroad promptly complied with its obligations, providing half of the cost of construction and maintenance and removing the old bridge from the island and the river channel.

Built of iron and now called the Government Bridge, the new structure had two decks. The lower was designed to accommodate wagons and horses, while the upper supported a single railroad track. Two walkways, each five feet wide, extended beyond the trusses on either side of the lower deck to accommodate foot traffic.[27] Extending from Rock Island to Davenport, the bridge was a little more than 1,600 feet long.[28] It rested on six piers that rose from the riverbed. Like its predecessor, the new bridge permitted steamboats and other river traffic to pass through a draw span, 366 feet long and operated by two hydraulic jacks. Unlike the earlier structure, however, the draw span was located next to the island shoreline rather than over the main river channel.[29] Completed in 1872, the Government

Bridge was formally transferred to the Rock Island Arsenal in February 1873.[30]

The new bridge stood for more than twenty years, at which time it was apparent that a stronger and heavier span was needed to support the larger locomotives and rail cars of the era. In 1895, construction was begun on a new bridge designed by a young Polish-born engineer named Ralph Modjeski who, from his base in Chicago, would later design iconic bridges over the Hudson River in New York, the Delaware River in Philadelphia, the Detroit River between Michigan and Ontario, Canada, and San Francisco Bay in California.[31] Resting on the existing piers, the new bridge consisted of all-steel trusses and an all-steel swing span. Like its predecessor, it had two decks, an upper level with tracks that would accommodate two-way train traffic and a lower level for road traffic. Completed in 1896, the new bridge was still owned by the federal government, still called the Government Bridge, and still open to the use of the Chicago, Rock Island and Pacific Railroad.[32]

For a while, the bridge accommodated street trolleys as well as trains. The Rock Island Railroad continued to use the span as its locomotives raced from Chicago across the Mississippi and on to distant destinations in Colorado, Texas, New Mexico, and even—by a joint agreement with the Southern Pacific Railroad—California. Although the Rock Island ceased its operations in 1980, other railroads continued to use the bridge well into the twenty-first century.

Congress's willingness to assist railroad corporations to build lines across rivers like the Mississippi, and even across the Great Plains and the Rocky Mountains to the Pacific Coast, did not arise out of hostility to the steamboats, or evidence unwillingness to help them navigate the great rivers. Adopting the argument Lincoln made to the jury in the *Effie Afton* trial, Congress agreed that there was room for both steamboats on and railroads crossing over the Mississippi. Steamboats could continue to navigate the great river, and railroads could cross it with their spans.

Beginning after the Civil War, Congress authorized extensive river improvement projects designed to deepen the steamboat channels. They straightened the river in places, built levees to prevent flooding in times of high water, erected wing dams to help raise the water level in dry seasons, blasted rock from the river bottom to remove rocks and deepen the channels, and excavated canals to ease the passage of boats over and around rapids, sand bars, and other natural obstructions to navigation. In the 1880s, the Army Corps of Engineers began a program of constant river improvements that continued well into the twenty-first century.[33] As a result, the appearance of the river changed mightily. The Mississippi that Mark Twain knew and loved in the middle of the nineteenth century became a nostalgic memory. Steamboat safety was improved, and the river became more hospitable to barges and rafts that moved sand and gravel and coal and oil from one river town to another, but commerce on the river was not appreciably enhanced.

Congress also facilitated the construction of more bridges over the great river. Shortly after it authorized the construction of the first Government Bridge at Rock Island, it laid down rules for future bridges that would be built across the Mississippi. Set forth in an act of Congress approved by President Andrew Johnson in 1866, the rules were initially designed to meet a proposal for the construction of a railroad bridge across the river at Quincy, Illinois. They were quickly expanded to apply to railroad bridges at Burlington, Iowa; Hannibal, Missouri; Prairie du Chien, Wisconsin; Keokuk, Iowa; Winona, Minnesota; Dubuque, Iowa; St. Louis, Missouri; and even Kansas City, Missouri.[34] The rules stated that it would be "lawful" to build either a continuous span bridge or a drawbridge at any of those locations, but only if the bridge complied with specific requirements.[35]

The 1866 act was evidence, if any was needed, that bridges were now being built at key locations up and down the Mississippi, and that many more were planned. The Rock Island had been the first railroad bridge to span the mighty river; despite its legal difficulties, it had proven that such a crossing could effect a marvelous revolution in transportation. Between 1869, the year the Pacific Railway was completed, and 1872, the Rock Island Bridge served as the most direct link across the Mississippi River, connecting the East Coast by way of Chicago with the West Coast via the transcontinental rail-road.[36] By 1879, more than 85 percent of the farm products shipped from states along the Mississippi went east by rail and only 15 percent by way of the river.[37]

The 1857 trial that Abraham Lincoln took part in in Chicago, fol-lowed by a host of successful legal battles in other courts, had proven not only that such a bridge was legal and could be defended in court against its enemies. It had also helped to prove that the bridge made economic sense, for all the litigation was expensive, but the bridge and the railroad that spanned it continued to make money. By 1880, thirteen railroad bridges had crossed the Mississippi between St. Louis and St. Paul;[38] by 1886, the number had grown to fifteen, and by 1888, sixteen.[39]

St. Louis, once the economic powerhouse of the Mississippi Val-ley, was left behind, a laggard in the race to acquire railroad con-nections. There were, of course, powerful men in the Missouri city who, from the first, understood that railroads would one day be an important part of the transportation network that was rapidly spreading across the upper Midwest. They strove valiantly to bring down the Rock Island Bridge, but they were not averse to building such a bridge to connect their own city with the east bank of the river. The suspension bridge that Josiah Bissell designed before 1857 proved that there was interest in railroads in St. Louis. But the money men of the river city fought among themselves for the glory (and the profit) of building the first railroad bridge, and Bissell's plan, as well as many others, fell by the wayside.

Competing bridge projects were announced in the early 1860s, but the funds necessary to make them a reality were not forthcom-ing.[40] It was not until 1867 that work was actually begun on a railroad bridge at St. Louis. It was designed by James Eads, a successful busi-nessman who had spent many years on the Mississippi as a salvager, diving to the bottom of the river to rescue wrecked steamboats and other craft that had come to grief in the river and sunk in murky waters.[41] Eads had never designed a bridge, but he knew the river bottom, and he knew it well. The bridge that he planned for St. Louis was much different from the Rock Island Bridge, or any other

Mississippi River span built up to that time. It had massive stone piers sunk deep in the river channel and soaring spans of steel that arched high above the surface of the water. Opened in 1874, the Eads Bridge was the first permanent crossing of the Mississippi River below its confluence with the Missouri River.[42] It was immediately acclaimed as an engineering wonder, but the railroads that crossed it into Illinois did not make as much money as Eads or his backers expected, and within a year the bridge fell into receivership.[43] Trains still used it—in greater and greater numbers as the years passed by—while steamboat traffic declined. By 1890, the total rail business out of St. Louis was twelve times the river traffic; by 1900, it was thirty-two times; by 1906, it was one hundred times.[44]

Bridges came more slowly to the Lower Mississippi. The first bridge to cross the river south of the mouth of the Ohio was opened at Memphis in 1892. A bridge was opened at Vicksburg in 1930 and at New Orleans in 1935. By the end of the twentieth century, more than two hundred bridges spanned the Mississippi from its headwaters in Minnesota to its mouth below New Orleans.[45]

From the time the railroads first crossed the Mississippi, farm produce and passenger transport, at one time the mainstays of steamboat business on the river, declined rapidly. Trains were so much faster, so much more dependable, and at the same time so much more economical, that river traffic found it harder and harder to compete. The endless destinations that could be reached by railroads and the fact that trains could run almost all year round, while steamboats could not proceed through ice or over shallow riverbeds when the water level was low, added to the steamboats' woes. A new America was being forged. It was one in which the railroads played a key role. Powerful locomotives on iron rails were racing forward, while ponderous steamboats on winding rivers were steadily losing ground.

One kind of business that favored the river traffic continued even after the others had nearly disappeared, however. Lumber from the forests of Minnesota and Wisconsin, essential to build new homes for the growing population of the Mississippi Valley and beyond, was ideally suited to river transportation, for logs are wood and wood floats on water. Great quantities of northern lumber were floated down the Mississippi on rafts and barges from 1870 to 1915. But the timber harvesting practices of the period were savage and unforgiving, with clear-cutting prevailing almost everywhere. When the forests at last disappeared, so did the logs, and so did lumber rafting on the Mississippi.[46] By 1915, river transportation had ceased to be a competitive—or even very important—part of inland transportation in the United States.[47]

It had been a long and bitter struggle between the railroads and the steamboats, but the railroads in the end prevailed. The jurors that heard Lincoln's *Effie Afton* argument in Chicago in 1857 had been unable to reach a legally binding verdict: they clearly favored the bridge over the steamboat, but not unanimously. They were hung. Only a few decades later, however, the sequence of events compelled a decision the jurors could not make. The railroads, and the bridge that first carried them across the great river, had won. History had rendered its verdict.

While history was rendering its verdict on the railroads and the bridges, it was also rendering a verdict on the Springfield attorney who helped to defend the first railroad bridge built over the river. By the early twentieth century, Abraham Lincoln had become a towering figure in an almost mythical American past, a martyred president remembered as the Savior of the Union and the Great Emancipator. Other parts of the Lincoln story were also being recognized, however: his work to make the nation economically strong and healthy; his championing of roads and schools and railroads; and his work as a courtroom advocate.

The story of the *Effie Afton* case adds a measure of real history to the heroic Lincoln mythology. It reminds us that before he went to Washington, Lincoln was also a resourceful lawyer who, in a crowded Chicago courtroom in 1857, helped to bind the nation together with iron rails, to bridge the mightiest river on the continent, and to turn the nation toward an economic future of strength and vitality. In these ways, too, he contributed mightily to the making of America.

ACKNOWLEDGMENTS

Writing this book has been a labor of both effort and joy. Research for the story took me to many archives and libraries, and to the geographic location where much of the extraordinary story of the *Effie Afton* case was played out: the grand intersection of water and land that lies between Rock Island, Illinois, and Davenport, Iowa, in the region now known as the Quad Cities. The Legal Papers of Abraham Lincoln were an indispensable source of much of the historical data on which the story rests, but previous works of scholarship relating to the Mississippi River, the development of steamboats in the nineteenth century, and the advance and eventual domination of the river by the railroads and the bridges that carried them across the river were also invaluable.

My familiarity with the legal history of the period, and my own experiences as a courtroom lawyer, helped me understand the grand drama that Abraham Lincoln took part in in the U.S. Circuit Court in Chicago in 1857. And my travels brought me in contact with people who acquainted me with bits of the story along the way. I cannot remember them all, but I can thank them all, and must content myself with naming just a few of those who deserve special appreciation: Daniel W. Stowell, director and editor of the Papers of Abraham Lincoln in Springfield, Illinois; James M. Cornelius, curator of the Lincoln Collection at the Abraham Lincoln Presidential Library and Museum in Springfield; Jan Perone, newspaper librarian at the Lincoln Presidential Library and Museum, and Jennifer Erickson, in the Audio-Visual collection of the same great institution; Diane Mallstrom of the Genealogy and Local History Department at the Public Library of Cincinnati and Hamilton County in Cincinnati; Debbie Bainter of the circuit clerk's office in the McDonough County Courthouse, Macomb, Illinois; Orin R. Rockhold, Bobbi Jackson, and Kathleen Seusy of the Rock Island County Historical Society in Moline, Illinois; Jodie Creen Wesemann, museum specialist–registrar at the Rock Island Arsenal Museum in Rock Island, Illinois; Bryon Andreasen, former editor of the *Journal of the Abraham Lincoln Association*; Jason Emerson, historian, Lincoln scholar, and author of (among other books) *Lincoln the Inventor* and *Giant in the Shadows: The Life of Robert T. Lincoln*; James F. Shearouse, reference librarian at the Rock Island Public Library; Robert L. Romic of the Technical Library of the U.S. Army Corps of Engineers in Rock Island; Lori B. Bessler, reference librarian at the Wisconsin Historical Society in Madison; Eunice Schlichting, Christina Kastell, and Christine Chandler of the Putnam Museum of Science and Natural History in Davenport; Jennifer Stibitz of the University of Wisconsin Library in Madison; Peter A. Hansen, editor of the Railway and Locomotive Historical Society's *Railroad History*; Cara Randall, librarian at the California State Railroad Museum Library in Sacramento; Rodney A. Ross of the Center for Legislative Archives at the National Archives in Washington, D.C.; Lori Cox-Paul, director of archival operations, and Jake Ersland, archivist, at the National Archives in Kansas City; Mike Widener, rare book librarian at the Lillian Goldman Law Library at Yale Law School; Barbara DeWolfe and Janet Bloom of the William L. Clements Library at the University of Michigan in Ann Arbor; Patti Hinson of the Mariners' Museum Library in Newport News, Virginia; Lauren Leeman, reference specialist at the State Historical Society of Missouri in Columbia; Joleene Fluegel, historical consultant at the Geneseo Public Library in Geneseo, Illinois; and William Riebe of Davenport, Iowa, retired land surveyor for the U.S Army Corps of Engineers at Rock Island and indefatigable railroad buff, whose studies of the structure of the bridges at Rock Island were based on original plans and drawings derived from the archives of the Rock Island Arsenal.

I have benefited greatly from the insights and suggestions of Matthew Carnicelli, my agent; Bob Weil, the publishing director of Liveright; and Phil Marino, whose fine editing has done much to make this a good book.

Thanks to them all.

TIMELINE

1809   FEBRUARY 12. Lincoln is born near Hodgenville, Kentucky.

1811–12 Steamboat *New Orleans* becomes the first steamboat west of the Appalachians, traveling all the way from Pittsburgh to New Orleans.

1814–15 Steamboat *Enterprise* becomes the first steamboat to engage in regular commerce on the Ohio and Mississippi Rivers.

1816   MAY. U.S. Army begins construction of Fort Armstrong on Rock Island in the Mississippi River. Construction is completed the following year.

DECEMBER. Traveling by flatboat, the Lincoln family moves from Kentucky to southern Indiana.

1816–17 Steamboat *Washington* becomes the first steamboat to make a round trip from Louisville to New Orleans and back.

1818   Six steamboats are built at Cincinnati, which is emerging as the chief boat-building port on the western rivers.

1826   Construction begins on the Louisville and Portland Canal, designed to bypass the Falls of the Ohio and allow cargo and passengers to travel all the way from Pittsburgh to New Orleans without changing boats or waiting for high water. Construction is completed in 1830.

1828   SPRING. Lincoln travels by flatboat from Rockport, Indiana, to New Orleans. He and his traveling mate sell the flatboat and its cargo in New Orleans and return to Indiana by steamboat.

1830   MARCH. Lincoln moves from Indiana to Illinois, traveling with his father and family.

1831   MARCH. At the age of twenty-one, Lincoln leaves his family and travels down the Sangamon River to New Salem, Illinois.

    APRIL–JULY. With two other men, Lincoln makes a second flatboat trip to New Orleans and back.

1832   EARLY. Lincoln works with a crew of laborers clearing the way for the first steamboat passage on the Sangamon River.

    APRIL–JULY. Lincoln is mustered into military service at Fort Armstrong on Rock Island. He has joined other volunteers to serve in a conflict with the Sauk and Fox Indians that becomes known as the Black Hawk War. At Fort Armstrong, he is elected captain of his company.

    AUGUST 6. Lincoln is defeated in his first bid for election to the Illinois state legislature.

1833   DECEMBER 31. The slave later known as Dred Scott arrives at Fort Armstrong with his owner, a U.S. Army surgeon.

1834   AUGUST 4. Lincoln wins his second bid for election to the Illinois state legislature, where he is active in support of transportation projects.

1836   MAY. Fort Armstrong is decommissioned. Dred Scott's owner takes him to Fort Snelling, Wisconsin Territory (later Minnesota).

    JUNE. Construction begins on the Illinois and Michigan Canal, a water link between the Illinois and Chicago Rivers that will accommodate boat traffic from the Mississippi to Chicago.

    SEPTEMBER 9. The Illinois Supreme Court admits Lincoln to the practice of law.

1837 MARCH 1. Lincoln's name is entered on the roll of attorneys by the Illinois Supreme Court clerk. He moves to Springfield and forms a partnership with John Todd Stuart, a prominent lawyer he met at Fort Armstrong.

1838 Lincoln handles most of the law partnership's business while Stuart campaigns for Congress against Lincoln's future political nemesis, Stephen A. Douglas.

 AUGUST 6. Stuart is elected to Congress, and Lincoln is reelected to the Illinois state legislature.

1841 APRIL. Lincoln becomes the junior partner of Stephen T. Logan, another prominent Springfield lawyer.

1842 MAY 13. The Northern Cross is the first railroad to reach Springfield, Illinois. Poorly built and equipped, it is soon abandoned. In 1853, it is reborn as the Great Western Railroad.

 NOVEMBER 4. Lincoln marries Mary Todd of Kentucky.

1844 DECEMBER. Upon the amicable dissolution of his partnership with Logan, Lincoln accepts William (Billy) Herndon as his junior partner.

1846 AUGUST 3. Lincoln is elected to Congress, to take office in December 1847.

1847 JULY. Lincoln makes his first visit to Chicago as a delegate to the River and Harbor Convention, where he meets Norman Judd and other prominent lawyers and politicians.

 OCTOBER 25. Lincoln and his family leave Springfield on a nearly six-week-long journey to Washington, D.C., where he is to serve in Congress. They travel by stagecoach to Alton, Illinois, cross the Mississippi to St. Louis, then take a riverboat down the Mississippi to the Ohio and up that river to its junction with the Kentucky River, which in turn brings them to Frankfort, Kentucky. They take the Lexington and

Ohio Railroad for a short trip to Lexington, where they visit Mrs. Lincoln's family. Their journey east from Lexington may include travel by steamboat as well as in stagecoaches and trains.

DECEMBER 2. Lincoln and his family arrive in Washington.

DECEMBER 6. Lincoln takes his seat in Congress.

1848   FEBRUARY 27. The Illinois legislature charters the Rock Island and La Salle Railroad Company and authorizes it to construct a railroad from Rock Island to the Illinois River terminus of the Illinois and Michigan Canal.

LATE SEPTEMBER–EARLY OCTOBER. Lincoln and his family travel by steamboat through the Great Lakes from Buffalo to Chicago. Seeing another steamboat that has run aground in the Detroit River, Lincoln develops an idea for "an Improved Method of Lifting Vessels over Shoals."

DECEMBER 7. Lincoln returns to Washington for the second session of his congressional term.

1849   MARCH 7. While attending Congress, Lincoln argues the case of *Lewis v. Lewis* before Chief Justice Roger Taney and the associate justices of the U.S. Supreme Court.

MARCH 10. Still in Washington, Lincoln applies for a patent for his invention of "an Improved Method of Lifting Vessels over Shoals."

MAY 22. Lincoln's patent application is approved as Patent No. 6,469.

1851   FEBRUARY 7. The Chicago and Rock Island Railroad is incorporated in Illinois by an amendment to the charter of the Rock Island and La Salle Railroad Company.

FEBRUARY 10. The Illinois legislature incorporates the Illinois Central Railroad Company.

DECEMBER. Lincoln represents an insurance company in the trial of *Columbia Insurance Co. v. Peoria Bridge Company*, seeking damages sustained when a canal boat and its cargo were lost by crashing into a bridge over the Illinois River. When the jury fails to agree on a verdict, the parties reach an out-of-court settlement.

1852 FEBRUARY. In the landmark case of *Pennsylvania v. Wheeling and Belmont Bridge Co.*, the U.S. Supreme Court decides that the suspension bridge over the Ohio River at Wheeling, Virginia (later West Virginia), interferes with steamboat navigation and must be raised to a greater height or torn down. Justice John McLean of Ohio, who will preside over the *Effie Afton* trial in 1857, writes the opinion.

AUGUST 31. Congress overrules the Supreme Court, declaring the Wheeling Bridge a lawful structure and requiring captains and crews of steamboats on the Ohio River to regulate their vessels so as not to interfere with its elevation or construction.

1853 JANUARY 17. The Illinois legislature charters the Railroad Bridge Company to build a railroad bridge over the Mississippi from Rock Island, Illinois, to Davenport, Iowa, "in such a manner as shall not materially obstruct or interfere with the free navigation of said river."

FEBRUARY 5. The Iowa legislature charters the Mississippi and Missouri Rail Road Company to build a railroad spanning the state from Davenport on the Mississippi to Council Bluffs on the Missouri River.

JULY. Construction starts on an approach to the Rock Island Bridge.

SEPTEMBER. Secretary of War Jefferson Davis refuses requests for a right-of-way across land formerly held by the military at Rock Island.

1854   FEBRUARY 22. On George Washington's birthday, the first trains of the Chicago and Rock Island Railroad arrive in Rock Island City.

FEBRUARY 28. Lincoln argues the important tax case of *Illinois Central v. County of McLean* in the Illinois Supreme Court. Unable to reach a decision, the court orders a rehearing.

MAY 30. President Franklin Pierce signs the Kansas-Nebraska Act, opening western territories to slavery under the doctrine of "popular sovereignty" and arousing political opposition from Lincoln and others.

JUNE 5. As the work of locating the piers and constructing the bridge begins, dignitaries gather at Rock Island and six steamboats take twelve hundred distinguished citizens and celebrants up the Mississippi from Rock Island to St. Paul, Minnesota, and back. John A. Dix, president of the Chicago and Rock Island Railroad, tells the crowd "we are on the way to the Pacific; and we intend to go there."

JULY. The U.S. marshal and two high army officers arrive at Rock Island with orders to stop the laying of track.

AUGUST. An Iowa congressman charges that Jefferson Davis is opposed to bridging the Mississippi at Rock Island because he favors a southern over a northern railroad route to the Pacific.

DECEMBER. At the behest of Secretary of War Jefferson Davis and the U.S. attorney general, the U.S. attorney files suit to stop the construction of the Rock Island Bridge. The case is referred to Supreme Court Justice John McLean for trial in Washington, D.C.

1855   FEBRUARY. Lincoln is nearly elected to the United States Senate by the Illinois legislature. He ascribes his loss in large part to the opposition of Democratic state senator Norman Judd.

JULY. In *United States v. Railroad Bridge Company*, Justice McLean refuses to issue an injunction to stop the construction of the Rock Island Bridge, saying that a lawsuit for damages may be filed if a boat is injured by the span. Work on the bridge accelerates.

SEPTEMBER. Lincoln goes to Cincinnati to take part in the important patent trial of *McCormick v. Manny*, but he is rebuffed by lead attorney Edwin Stanton, his future secretary of war.

NOVEMBER. Construction of the 430-ton steamboat *Effie Afton* is completed in Cincinnati.

WINTER. Scaffolds are erected on solid ice that extends across the Mississippi as the superstructure of the Rock Island Bridge is put in place.

1856 JANUARY. Lincoln reargues the tax case of *Illinois Central v. County of McLean* in the Illinois Supreme Court. He will eventually receive a fee of $5,000 for his work in this case in behalf of the Illinois Central Railroad.

APRIL 21–22. The first locomotives pass over the Rock Island Bridge.

MAY 5. The *Effie Afton* arrives at Rock Island from St. Louis, intending to proceed through the bridge and on to St. Paul. High winds persuade its captain and crew to pause until the following morning.

MAY 6. The *Effie Afton* approaches the bridge at a high rate of speed, crashes into it, erupts in flames, and sinks. When a section of the bridge catches fire and falls into the river, steamboats nearby blow whistles and ring bells in celebration.

JUNE 19. The newly organized Republican Party opens its first national convention in Philadelphia. John C. Frémont is nominated for president. Lincoln receives 110 votes for the vice presidential nomination but loses to William L. Dayton of New Jersey.

SEPTEMBER 8. Damage to the Rock Island Bridge has been repaired, and trains again cross the span.

SEPTEMBER 27. Construction of the Illinois Central Railroad is completed.

OCTOBER. Jacob Hurd, principal owner of the *Effie Afton*, files a suit for damages against the Rock Island Bridge in the U.S. Circuit Court in Springfield. Formally titled *Hurd et al v. The Railroad Bridge Company*, the suit is popularly called the *Effie Afton* case.

NOVEMBER 19–29. Lincoln successfully represents the defendants in a sensational murder trial in Springfield.

DECEMBER 16. Steamboat owners and businessmen meet in the Merchants' Exchange in St. Louis and appoint a committee "to take measures to remove the railroad bridge from the Mississippi river" at Rock Island.

1857 SPRING. The *Effie Afton* case is moved from Springfield to Chicago, as attorneys gather more than a thousand pages of depositions from important witnesses in Illinois, Missouri, and other states.

MARCH 6. In Washington, Chief Justice Roger Taney announces the U.S. Supreme Court's decision in *Dred Scott v. Sandford*, summarily denying Dred Scott's claim to be a free man. The decision outrages Lincoln and gives rise to one of his most powerful political arguments.

JULY 7. Lincoln is in Chicago, where he agrees to join Norman Judd and two other attorneys in the defense of the *Effie Afton* trial.

JULY 9. Lincoln appears in the U.S. Circuit Court and successfully argues for a new date for the *Effie Afton* trial.

FIRST WEEK OF SEPTEMBER. Lincoln arrives in Chicago. With a party of lawyers and engineers he travels to Rock Island on a special railroad car from Chicago to study the bridge in preparation for the upcoming trial.

SEPTEMBER 8. The *Effie Afton* trial opens in Chicago before Justice John McLean and a jury of twelve men.

SEPTEMBER 9–19. Witnesses testify and depositions are read.

SEPTEMBER 22–23. Lincoln delivers a long closing argument.

SEPTEMBER 25. The jury announces that it is unable to reach a verdict. Three jurors favor the plaintiffs' claim for damages, while nine believe that the bridge is not a "material obstruction" to steamboat traffic. Justice McLean provides the opportunity of a new trial.

DECEMBER 28. Jacob Hurd writes Senator Stephen Douglas, asking him to become his attorney in a new trial, but Douglas is occupied by government business in Washington.

1858   JANUARY 4. The Committee of Commerce of the House of Representatives is instructed to begin an investigation into the Rock Island Bridge to determine if it is a serious obstruction to the navigation of the Mississippi and, if so, what action the government should take "to cause such obstruction to be removed."

APRIL 15. The Commerce Committee report says that the bridge is a "material and dangerous obstruction," but the committee is "disinclined to recommend any action by Congress" because the courts have "full and ample power to remedy any evil that may exist."

MAY 7. James Ward, a prominent St. Louis steamboat owner, files suit in the U.S. District Court for Iowa asking that the bridge be declared a nuisance and that the court order its removal.

JUNE 16. Meeting in the State Capitol in Springfield, the Republican state convention endorses Lincoln for election to the United States Senate. Accepting the nomination, Lincoln gives his famous "House Divided Speech."

JULY 24. Norman Judd, who has joined Lincoln in the Republican Party, personally delivers a letter from Lincoln to Senator Douglas proposing a series of debates for the senatorial campaign. Douglas agrees.

AUGUST 21. Lincoln and Douglas meet in Ottawa, Illinois, for their first debate.

OCTOBER 15. Lincoln and Douglas meet for the last of their seven debates in Alton, Illinois.

1859   FEBRUARY 14. Jacob Hurd begins a new suit for damages against the Chicago and Rock Island Railroad. Begun in Rock Island but ultimately moved to McDonough County, Illinois, the suit is never brought to trial and is finally dismissed in 1875.

JUNE. Some malicious persons attempt to set fire to the Rock Island Bridge.

AUGUST. Lincoln travels to Council Bluffs, Iowa, where he addresses a large audience on the principles of the Republican Party and surveys the site for the beginning of a railroad to the Pacific.

1860   FEBRUARY 27. Lincoln speaks at Cooper Union in New York.

APRIL 3. In the suit filed by James Ward in Iowa, U.S. District Judge John M. Love declares the Rock Island Bridge a public nuisance and orders that the three piers and superstructure on the Iowa side of the river be torn down. His order is appealed to the U.S. Supreme Court, which will issue its decision in 1863.

MAY 18. Lincoln is nominated for president by the Republican National Convention in Chicago.

AUGUST 7–9. Josiah W. Bissell and Walter F. Chadwick are arrested and indicted in Chicago for conspiracy to burn the Rock Island Bridge.

NOVEMBER 6. Lincoln prevails in the popular election for president.

DECEMBER 20. South Carolina is the first of eleven states to adopt ordinances of secession from the Union.

1861   FEBRUARY 11–23. Lincoln travels to Washington by train.

MARCH 4. Lincoln is inaugurated as president.

1862   MAY 20. Lincoln signs the Homestead Act, giving a plot of 160 acres of land to each settler who will occupy and improve it for five years.

JULY 1. Lincoln signs a federal income tax law and an "act to aid in the Construction of a Railroad and Telegraph Line from the Missouri River to the Pacific Ocean."

JULY 2. Lincoln signs the Morrill Act, authorizing land grants to agricultural and mechanical colleges in every state.

JULY 11. Lincoln signs an act establishing a federal arsenal at Rock Island.

1863   JANUARY 20. The U.S. Supreme Court reverses the Iowa district court decision in *Mississippi and Missouri Railroad Company v. Ward*, stating that because the jurisdiction of the Iowa court extends only to the middle of the river, removing the bridge on the Iowa side would solve nothing in the matter of obstruction, and if Love's decision were upheld, "no lawful bridge could be built across the Mississippi anywhere."

JANUARY 21. Lincoln issues an order setting the uniform width (gauge) of the proposed Pacific railroad from the Missouri River to the Pacific Ocean at five feet.

MARCH 3. Counteracting Lincoln, Congress sets the width of the proposed Pacific railroad track at four feet eight and a half inches ("standard gauge").

NOVEMBER 17. Lincoln establishes the starting point for the Pacific railroad in Omaha, Nebraska.

1864   JUNE 9. In a message acknowledging his nomination for a second term as president, Lincoln states that he and his party "are in favor of the speedy construction of the Railroad to the Pacific coast."

NOVEMBER 4. Lincoln is reelected.

1865   MARCH 4. Lincoln is inaugurated for his second presidential term.

APRIL 14. Lincoln is assassinated.

1866   FEBRUARY 2. Jacob Hurd dies in a steamboat explosion on the *W. R. Carter* near Vicksburg.

JUNE 27. Congress authorizes the construction of a new bridge across the Mississippi at Rock Island. It is built on the same piers as the first.

JULY 9. The Mississippi and Missouri Railroad Company is acquired by the Chicago and Rock Island Railroad to form the Chicago, Rock Island and Pacific Railroad Company.

1867–72 The U.S. Army Corps of Engineers opens a channel in the Rock Island Rapids two hundred feet wide and four and a half feet deep.

DECEMBER 30. The U.S. Supreme Court decides the case of *Galena, Dubuque, Dunleith, and Minnesota Packet Co. v. Rock Island Bridge,* upholding a decision of the U.S. District Court for the Northern District of Illinois dismissing an admiralty suit brought against the Rock Island Bridge. Justice Stephen J. Field writes the majority opinion, holding that "though bridges and wharves may aid commerce by facilitating intercourse on land, or the discharge of cargoes, they are not in any sense the subjects of maritime lien." This decision marks the effective end of the Rock Island Bridge litigation.

1868   MARCH 10. A massive ice floe crashes into the Rock Island Bridge, damaging the piers and span so badly that trains cannot pass over it.

MARCH 16. The bridge is seriously damaged by a wind so fierce that the local newspaper calls it a tornado. Three men on the bridge are injured, and a fourth is killed.

APRIL 23. Reconstruction of the bridge is completed, and trains again pass over it.

JULY 20. Congress authorizes the construction of a new bridge a short distance downriver from the existing span. The government will build the bridge, but the railroad will pay half of the construction cost. The new span will be called the Government Bridge.

1869   MAY 10. Leland Stanford drives a golden spike into the railroad at Promontory Summit, Utah, marking the connection of the Central Pacific and the Union Pacific Railroads and the completion of the long-sought railroad across the continent to the Pacific.

MAY 11. The Chicago, Rock Island and Pacific Railroad finishes its rail connection to Council Bluffs, thus linking it with the railroad across the continent to the Pacific. However, the official connection is reserved for the Cedar Rapids and Missouri River Railroad.

JULY. Construction of the Government Bridge at Rock Island begins.

1872 NOVEMBER. The Government Bridge opens for traffic.

1874 JULY 4. The Eads Bridge at St. Louis is opened to rail traffic. It is the first bridge over the Mississippi at St. Louis.

1875 SEPTEMBER 28. The Circuit Court of McDonough County, Illinois, dismisses Jacob Hurd's last suit against the Rock Island Bridge.

1879 More than 85 percent of the surplus produce of the trans-Mississippi states now goes east by rail and only 15 percent by water.

1880 Thirteen railroad bridges now cross the Mississippi between St. Louis and St. Paul.

1895 Congress authorizes construction of a new Government Bridge, to be built of steel on the piers of the existing bridge.

1896 The new Government Bridge opens to rail traffic.

1907 Congress decides that the channel in the Rock Island Rapids must be deepened to six feet.

1980 Nearly 130 years after its founding, the Rock Island Railroad is liquidated in bankruptcy. The Government Bridge at Rock Island continues to be used by automobiles, trucks, busses, and other railroads. Although the original bridge is long gone, modest monuments on both sides of the river mark its former location.

NOTES

ABBREVIATIONS USED IN NOTES

CP	*Chicago Press*
CT	*Chicago Tribune*
CWL	*Collected Works of Abraham Lincoln*, ed. Roy P. Basler. 9 vols. New Brunswick, NJ: Rutgers University Press, 1953–55.
DG	*Davenport Gazette*
HI	*Herndon's Informants: Letters, Interviews, and Statements about Abraham Lincoln*, ed. Douglas L. Wilson and Rodney O. Davis with the assistance of Terry Wilson. Urbana and Chicago: University of Illinois Press, 1998.
HL	*Herndon's Lincoln by William H. Herndon and Jesse W. Weik*, ed. Douglas L. Wilson and Rodney O. Davis. Urbana and Chicago: Knox College Lincoln Studies Center and University of Illinois Press, 2006.
PAL:LDC	*Papers of Abraham Lincoln: Legal Documents and Cases*, ed. Daniel W. Stowell and others. 4 vols. Charlottesville: University of Virginia Press, 2008.
PJD	*Papers of Jefferson Davis*, ed. Lynda Laswell Crist and Mary Seaton Dix. Vol. 5, 1853–55. Baton Rouge: Louisiana State University Press, 1985.
RIA	*Rock Island Argus*
RHP	Robert R. Hitt Papers, Library of Congress
SLMR	St. Louis *Missouri Republican*
Stat	United States Statutes at Large
Ward	*James Ward v. The Mississippi and Missouri Railroad Company*, District Court of the United States for the District of Iowa, Middle Division, RG 21, National Archives and Records Administration, Central Plains Region, Kansas City, MO.

INTRODUCTION

1 As chartered by the Illinois legislature on January 17, 1853, the bridge company was named the "Railroad Bridge Company." *Private Laws of the State of Illinois, Passed by the Eighteenth General Assembly, Convened January 3, 1853* (Springfield, IL: Lanphier and Walker, 1853), 329–30. See discussion in chapter 4.

2 Guelzo, *Abraham Lincoln, Redeemer President,* 171.

3 Burlingame, *Abraham Lincoln: A Life* 1:337.

4 Neely, *Lincoln and the Triumph of the Nation,* 36.

5 Thomas, *Abraham Lincoln: A Biography,* 157.

6 At the time of this writing, the only book about the case is Larry A. Riney, *Hell Gate of the Mississippi: The Effie Afton Trial and Abraham Lincoln's Role in It* (Geneseo, IL: Talesman Press, 2006).

7 PAL:LDC 2:324, 2:331, 2:338–39. Lincoln's most famous murder trial was that of William "Duff" Armstrong, also known as the Almanac trial (1858). PAL:LDC 4:1–48. This was the subject of the 1939 motion picture starring Henry Fonda titled *Young Mr. Lincoln.* See Steiner, *An Honest Calling,* 6, 180n3.

8 PAL:LDC 2:11, 2:43; see Steiner, *An Honest Calling,* 103–36.

9 A wire suspension bridge for pedestrians, horses, mules, carriages, and swine was opened in January 1855 at the site later occupied by the Hennepin Avenue Bridge in Minneapolis. Torn apart by a high wind in March 1855, it was repaired and stood until 1875. Costello, *Climbing the Mississippi River Bridge by Bridge* 2:94.

10 U.S. Const., Art. I, sec. 8, cl. 3 (giving Congress the power to regulate "commerce with foreign nations, and among the several states"). See Ely, "Lincoln and the Rock Island Bridge Case."

11 See U.S. Const., Art. VI, cl. 2: "The Constitution, and the laws of the United States which shall be made in pursuance thereof, . . . shall be the supreme law of the land; and the judges in every state shall be bound thereby, anything in the Constitution or laws of any State to the contrary notwithstanding."

12 "An Ordinance for the Government of the Territory of the United States Northwest of the River Ohio, Adopted by the Congress under the Articles of Confederation," July 13, 1787, sec. 4.

13 See *Pennsylvania v. Wheeling and Belmont Bridge Company,* 54 U.S. [13 Howard] 518 (1852); 59 U.S. [18 Howard] 421 (1855). See also discussion in chapter 4.

14 Martin, *Railroads Triumphant,* 278; see discussion in Ely, "Lincoln and the Rock Island Bridge Case."

15 *Dred Scott v. Sandford,* 60 U.S. [19 Howard] 393, 407, 446, 450. See discussion in chapter 4.

16 CWL 2:495.

17 See discussion in chapter 13.

18 Stampp, *America in 1857,* vii.

19 McPherson, *Battle Cry of Freedom*, 188–92. The Panic began on August 24 and expanded dramatically during September, while Lincoln was in Chicago engaged in the *Effie Afton* trial, forcing the closure of banks across the country and plunging many individuals and businesses into financial insolvency.

20 Stampp, *America in 1857*, viii.

21 See, e.g., Guy C. Fraker, *Lincoln's Ladder to the Presidency: The Eighth Judicial Circuit* (Carbondale and Edwardsville: Southern Illinois University Press, 2012); Roger Billings and Frank J. Williams, eds., *Abraham Lincoln, Esq.: The Legal Career of America's Greatest President* (Lexington: University Press of Kentucky, 2010); Brian Dirck, *Lincoln the Lawyer* (Urbana and Chicago: University of Illinois Press, 2007); Mark E. Steiner, *An Honest Calling: The Law Practice of Abraham Lincoln* (DeKalb: Northern Illinois University Press, 2006); Allen D. Spiegel, *A. Lincoln, Esquire: A Shrewd, Sophisticated Lawyer in His Time* (Macon, GA: Mercer University Press, 2002); John P. Frank, *Lincoln as a Lawyer* (Urbana: University of Illinois Press, 1961); John J. Duff, *A. Lincoln: Prairie Lawyer* (New York: Bramhall House, 1960); Albert A. Woldman, *Lawyer Lincoln* (Boston: Little, Brown, 1937).

22 Paludan, *The Presidency of Abraham Lincoln*, 303.

23 Paludan, "'Dictator Lincoln': Surveying Lincoln and the Constitution," 8, 10.

24 Neely, *Lincoln and the Triumph of the Nation*, 110–11.

25 Ibid., 209.

26 Ibid., 111.

27 Dirck, "A. Lincoln, Respectable 'Prairie Lawyer,'" 73.

28 Dirck, *Lincoln the Lawyer*, 142.

29 Holzer, "Reassessing Lincoln's Legal Career," 8, 10, 15.

30 Williams, "Lincoln's Lessons for Lawyers," 19–36.

31 Ibid., 36.

32 Typed transcript in RHP, as printed in PAL:LDC 3:360.

33 Daniel W. Stowell, editor of the Papers of Abraham Lincoln, to author, March 7, 2013.

34 The Papers of Abraham Lincoln is a long-term project to identify, image, and publish all documents written by or to Lincoln during his lifetime. See Papaioannou and Stowell, "Dr. Charles A. Leale's Report on the Assassination of Abraham Lincoln," 40n1.

1. A GREAT HIGHWAY OF NATURE

1 Rivers vary in length and width as they meander or straighten and as soil is added to or eroded from their banks or deltas. The figures given here are from National Park Service, Mississippi River Facts, http://www.nps.gov/miss/riverfacts.htm, accessed November 23, 2012.

2 Monette, "The Progress of Navigation and Commerce," 480.

3 Twain, *Life on the Mississippi*, 1.

4 Ibid., 2.

5 Anfinson, *The River We Have Wrought*, 15; Tweet, *History of Transportation on the Upper Mississippi and Illinois Rivers*, 9.

6 Anfinson, *The River We Have Wrought*, 16.

7 SLMR, September 20, 1857, 1.

8 Petersen, "The 'Virginia,' the 'Clermont' of the Upper Mississippi," 351–53.

9 Anfinson, *The River We Have Wrought*, 16; Fremling, *Immortal River*, 184; Beltrami, *Pilgrimage in America*, 159–60.

10 Hunter, *Steamboats on the Western Rivers*, 43–45; Tweet, *History of Transportation on the Upper Mississippi and Illinois Rivers*, 19.

11 Tweet, *History of Transportation on the Upper Mississippi and Illinois Rivers*, 19.

12 Ibid., 44.

13 Primm, *Lion of the Valley*, 149 (by 1837, Duncan's Island was a two-hundred-acre island covered with cottonwood trees; there was a mere trickle of water between it and the shore).

14 Tweet, *History of Transportation on the Upper Mississippi and Illinois Rivers*, 44–45; Thomas, *Robert E. Lee: A Biography*, 90–91, 94–96; Primm, *Lion of the Valley*, 151 (by 1855 Duncan's Island "was a memory").

15 Hunter, *Steamboats on the Western Rivers*, 61–120 (structural evolution of the western steamboat).

16 Page, "The *Effie Afton* Case," 3.

17 Latrobe, *The First Steamboat Voyage on the Western Waters*, 6–32; Kane, *The Western River Steam-Boat*, 45.

18 Dorsey, *Master of the Mississippi*, 89–90; *American Telegraph* [Brownsville, Pa.], December 14, 1814.

19 *Lloyd's Steamboat Directory*, 44–45; Tweet, *History of Transportation on the Upper Mississippi and Illinois Rivers*, 13.

20 Tweet, *History of Transportation on the Upper Mississippi and Illinois Rivers*, 13–14; Primm, *Lion of the Valley*, 108.

21 *Cincinnati: A Guide to the Queen City and Its Neighbors*, 57.

22 Trescott, "The Louisville and Portland Canal Company, 1825–1874," 686–708.

23 *Cincinnati: A Guide to the Queen City and Its Neighbors*, 58.

24 Fowle, "A Famous Interference Case: Lincoln and the Bridge," 614–15.

25 Campanella, *Lincoln in New Orleans*, 10–13.

26 Burlingame, *Abraham Lincoln: A Life* 1:42.

27 Campanella, *Lincoln in New Orleans*, 27–29.

28 Rice, *Reminiscences of Abraham Lincoln*, 270–80.

29 Campanella, *Lincoln in New Orleans*, 31.

30 PAL:LDC 3:322n41; Campanella, *Lincoln in New Orleans*, 35–141.

31 Campanella, *Lincoln in New Orleans*, 128–33.

32 CWL 4:63.

33 CWL 1:320, 4:63.

34 HI, 17, 34, 44; Campanella, *Lincoln in New Orleans*, 148–49.

35 Donald, *Lincoln*, 43–44; HI, 34, 442, 639.

36 CWL 3:29. Holzer, *The Lincoln-Douglas Debates*, 36–37, points out that the phrase "beau ideal of a statesman" has been quoted so many times "it has entered the historical language," but he cautions that it may not be precisely what Lincoln said in this debate, for the *Chicago Times*'s published version of this quote was that Lincoln called Clay "my beau ideal of a *great man* [emphasis added]," not "statesman."

37 Holt, *Rise and Fall of the American Whig Party*, 2; see Speech of Henry Clay on American Industry, in the House of Representatives, March 30 and 31, 1824, in F. W. Taussig, *State Papers and Speeches on the Tariff* (Cambridge, MA: Harvard University, 1893), 252–316.

38 Meyers, *The Jacksonian Persuasion*, 10–14; Magliocca, *Andrew Jackson and the Constitution*, 48–60.

39 Magliocca, *Andrew Jackson and the Constitution*, 29–33; Holt, *Rise and Fall of the American Whig Party*, 66.

40 Heidler and Heidler, *Henry Clay*, 229.

41 CWL 2:221.

42 Zobrist, "Steamboat Men versus Railroad Men," 160.

43 *Laws of the State of Illinois, Tenth General Assembly, at their Session Commencing December 5, 1836, and ending March 6, 1837* (Vandalia: William Walters, Public Printer, 1837), 121–51.

44 HL, 128.

45 Burlingame, *Abraham Lincoln: A Life* 1:114–22, 144. Boritt, *Lincoln and the Economics of the American Dream*, 9, says that Lincoln was not the leader, but he was one of the important champions, of the 1837 improvement system.

46 Angle, *"Here I Have Lived,"* 83–90.

47 James K. Polk, Veto Message, August 3, 1846, in Messages and Papers of the Presidents, http://www.presidency.ucsb.edu/ws/index.php?pid=67936. Presidential vetoes of internal improvement plans were based on constitutional objections. Boritt, *Lincoln and the Economics of the American Dream*, 4.

48 "Speech of Mr. Lincoln of Illinois," SLMR, July 12, 1847, 2.

49 CWL 1:480–90.

50 There were at least forty-nine such cases. PAL:LDC 3:321.

51 Ibid.

52 S. F. Dixon, *Substituted Liabilities: A Treatise on the Law of Subrogation* (Philadelphia: George W. Childs, 1862), 151.

53 *Columbus Insurance Company v. Peoria Bridge Company*, 6 McLean 70–76 (7th Cir. 1853); an earlier opinion was rendered in the same case sustaining a demurrer to the defendants' claim that, because the bridge was authorized by an act of the Illinois legislature, the bridge company could not be liable. See *Columbus Insurance Co. v. Curtenius*, 6 McLean 209-221 (7th Cir. 1853). The act of the legislature was dated January 26, 1847.

54 PAL:LDC 3:205–24.

55 Emerson, *Lincoln the Inventor,* 4; Temple, *Lincoln's Connections with the Illinois and Michigan Canal, His Return from Congress in '48, and His Invention,* 35.

56 HL, 188–89; Emerson, *Lincoln the Inventor,* 6, 83n18.

57 The attorney was Zenas C. Robbins. Emerson, *Lincoln the Inventor,* 15–17.

58 CWL 2:33.

59 Neely, *Abraham Lincoln Encyclopedia,* 162; Emerson, *Lincoln the Inventor,* 27, 33.

2. NO OTHER IMPROVEMENT

1 Boorstin, *The Americans,* 18.

2 Frey, *Encyclopedia of American Business History and Biography: Railroads in the Nineteenth Century,* 20–21; Stover, *Routledge Historical Atlas of the American Railroads,* 13.

3 Frey, *Encyclopedia of American Business History and Biography: Railroads in the Nineteenth Century,* 1988.

4 McPherson, *Battle Cry of Freedom,* 12.

5 CWL 1:5–6.

6 *Laws of the State of Illinois, Tenth General Assembly, at their Session Commencing December 5, 1836, and ending March 6, 1837* (Vandalia: William Walters, Public Printer, 1837), 121–51.

7 Starr, *Lincoln and the Railroads,* 25–31.

8 Ibid., 31.

9 Ibid., 34; Angle, *"Here I Have Lived,"* 144.

10 Starr, *Lincoln and the Railroads,* 33.

11 Angle, *"Here I Have Lived,"* 152–53; see *Laws of the State of Illinois, Passed by the Fifteenth General Assembly, at Their Session, Begun and Held in the City of Springfield, December 7, 1846* (Springfield: Charles H. Lanphier, Public Printer, 1847), 109–11.

12 Starr, *Lincoln and the Railroads,* 38.

13 Burlingame, *Abraham Lincoln: A Life* 1:253–57; Starr, *Lincoln and the Railroads,* 47.

14 Although he offers no particular evidence, Starr, *Lincoln and the Railroads,* 48, says that the Lincolns traveled by stage from Lexington to Covington, Virginia, and then on to Winchester, Virginia, where the Winchester and Potomac Railroad took them north to Harpers Ferry and a connection with the Baltimore and Ohio Railroad. DeRose, *Congressman Abraham Lincoln,* 75, says that the Lincolns traveled by stage to Winchester, Virginia, and thence by train to Washington. Temple, "Mary Todd Lincoln's Travels," 181, states that the Lincolns left Lexington for Maysville, Kentucky (on the Ohio River), whence they went up the river to Wheeling, and then took the National Road (a stagecoach road) to its connection with the Baltimore and Ohio. Riddle, *Congressman Abraham Lincoln,* 12, states that it is probable that the Lincolns took the river route.

15 Stover, *Routledge Historical Atlas of the American Railroads,* 18.

16 Holzer, *Lincoln President-Elect,* 305–96.

17 Angle, *"Here I Have Lived,"* 152.

18 Ibid., 162–63.

19 *Laws of the State of Illinois, Passed by the Ninth General Assembly, at their Second Session, Commencing December 7, 1835, and ending January 18, 1836* (Vandalia: J. Y. Sawyer, Public Printer, 1836), 129–38.

20 PAL:LDC 4:358; Starr, *Lincoln and the Railroads*, 40–41; Stover, *Routledge Historical Atlas of the American Railroads*, 32.

21 9 Stat. 466–67.

22 PAL:LDC 2:373; 4:358.

23 *Private Laws of the State of Illinois Passed at the First Session of the Seventeenth General Assembly, Begun and Held at the City of Springfield, January 6, 1851* (Springfield: Lanphier and Walker, 1851), 61–74.

24 Frey, *Encyclopedia of American Business History and Biography: Railroads in the Nineteenth Century*, 193; PAL:LDC 2:374.

25 Stover, *Routledge Historical Atlas of the American Railroads*, 23.

26 Steiner, *An Honest Calling*, 63–64.

27 PAL:LDC 2:307n10.

28 PAL:LDC 2:209.

29 PAL:LDC 2:448.

30 Illinois Const., Art. 9, sec. 5 (1848).

31 *Private Laws of the State of Illinois Passed at the First Session of the Seventeenth General Assembly Begun and Held at the City of Springfield, January 6, 1851* (Springfield: Lanphier and Walker, 1851), 71–72.

32 *Illinois Central Rail Road v. County of McLean*, 17 Ill. 291 (1856).

33 HL, 218. According to Herndon, the official who declined to pay the bill was "supposed to have been the superintendent George B. McClellan who afterwards became the eminent general." However, McClellan did not begin his employment at the Illinois Central until January 1857. His initial post was chief engineer; he was promoted to vice president in 1858. The railroad's refusal to pay the bill was before January 1857, when Lincoln filed his suit against it. HL, 281n20, says: "McClellan could not have been the official involved."

34 PAL:LDC 2:406–11.

35 Ibid.

36 Ibid.

37 Dooley, "Lincoln and His Namesake Town," 136.

38 See Emerson, *Giant in the Shadows*, 29.

39 Frey, *Encyclopedia of American Business History and Biography: Railroads in the Nineteenth Century*, 111, 118.

40 *Private Laws of the State of Illinois, Passed at the First Session of the Seventeenth General Assembly, Begun and Held at the City of Springfield, January 6, 1851* (Springfield: Lanphier and Walker, 1851), 47–50.

41 Petersen, "The Rock Island Comes," 293; Larkin, *John B. Jervis*, 8–14, 60, 89–91, 169n12, 170n27.

42 Hayes, *Iron Road to Empire*, 12–30; Petersen, "The Rock Island Comes," 287–300; Frey, *Encyclopedia of American Business History and Biography: Railroads in the Nineteenth Century*, 119.

43 *The Rail-Roads, History and Commerce of Chicago,* 10.

44 Hayes, *Iron Road to Empire,* 29–30.

45 Peterson, "The Grand Excursion of 1854," 313.

46 Sedgwick, "The Great Excursion to the Falls of St. Anthony," 321.

47 Hayes, *Iron Road to Empire,* 31–32.

48 *Private Laws of the State of Illinois, Passed by the Eighteenth General Assembly, Convened January 3, 1853* (Springfield: Lanphier and Walker, 1853), 329–30.

49 Rock Island's Family Tree, http://home.covad.net/~scicoatnsew/rihist1 .htm#2_5_1853.

50 Frey, *Encyclopedia of American Business History and Biography: Railroads in the Nineteenth Century,* 436–37.

51 Cooper, *Jefferson Davis, American,* 257–58.

52 Ibid., 257.

53 See letter from Jefferson Davis to William R. Cannon, December 7, 1853, in PJD 5:142. See also discussion in chapter 4.

54 10 Stat. 1031–37.

55 Faulk, *Too Far North, Too Far South,* 131–39.

3. HIS PECULIAR AMBITION

1 See Pratt, "The Genesis of Lincoln the Lawyer," 3–10, tracing Lincoln's interest in the law from his early days in Indiana to his residence in New Salem, Illinois, and stating: "For years he had been attracted to the law."

2 Borrett, *Out West: Letters from Canada and the United States,* 253.

3 Burlingame, *Abraham Lincoln: A Life* 1:7.

4 HI, 115; HL , 50.

5 CWL 1:8.

6 CWL 4:65.

7 Madison "never joined the bar; he never had a client or a case." Sarah Mary Bilder, "James Madison, Law Student and Demi-Lawyer" (2010), *Boston College Law School Faculty Papers,* paper 363, http://lawdigitalcommons.bc.edu/ lsfp/363.

8 He was admitted to the bar of the Illinois Supreme Court in September 1836 but not officially enrolled until March 1, 1837. Steiner, *An Honest Calling,* 37; HL, 121; PAL:LDC 1:xxix–xxx.

9 Rice, *Reminiscences of Abraham Lincoln,* 240.

10 Steiner, "Abraham Lincoln and the Rule of Law Books," 1298–99.

11 HI, 534; HL, 121; CWL 4:65.

12 HI, 14.

13 HI, 450; HL, 78–79.

14 CWL 2:82.

15 HL, 122. In the final tabulation, Stuart won his election over Douglas by only 36 votes out of a total vote of 36,405. Johannsen, *Stephen A. Douglas,* 68.

16 Thomas, "Lincoln and the Courts," 163.

17 PAL:LDC 4:356.
18 Daniel W. Stowell, editor of the Papers of Abraham Lincoln, to author, March 7, 2012; PAL:LDC 1:xii.
19 Burlingame, *Abraham Lincoln: A Life* 1:36–37, 64–65.
20 Robert T. Lincoln to John F. Dillon, January 5, 1901, as quoted in Emerson, *Giant in the Shadows: The Life of Robert T. Lincoln*, 33.
21 HL, 194; Whitney, *Life on the Circuit with Lincoln*, 69.
22 CT, December 29, 1895.
23 PAL:LDC 1:xxxvi.
24 Steiner, "Does Lawyer Lincoln Matter?" 49.
25 Thomas, "Lincoln and the Courts," 177.
26 *Lewis v. Lewis*, 48 U.S. [7 Howard] 776 (1849); PAL:LDC 1:xxxix; Lupton, "Basement Barrister: Abraham Lincoln's Practice before the United States Supreme Court," 47–58; McGinty, *Lincoln and the Court*, 18.
27 PAL:LDC 1:22.
28 HI, 635–36.
29 Whitney, *Life on the Circuit with Lincoln*, 233.
30 Ibid., 233–34.
31 PAL:LDC 4:291–95.
32 Whitney, *Life on the Circuit with Lincoln*, 63.
33 Ibid.
34 PAL:LDC 4:224–26.
35 HL, 194.
36 For a comprehensive survey of Lincoln's life on the Eighth Judicial Circuit and a compelling argument that the circuit and the lawyers Lincoln worked with there propelled him to the presidency, see Fraker, *Lincoln's Ladder to the Presidency*.
37 Dirck, *Lincoln the Lawyer*, 154.
38 Whitney, *Life on the Circuit with Lincoln*, 62–63.
39 HI, 349.
40 Rice, *Reminiscences of Abraham Lincoln*, 333–34.
41 Burlingame, *Abraham Lincoln: A Life* 1:60.
42 Donald, *Lincoln*, 537.
43 Whitney, *Life on the Circuit with Lincoln*, 236.
44 Ibid., 233.
45 Ibid.
46 Ibid., 236.
47 Arnold, *Life of Abraham Lincoln*, 84.
48 HL, 208–9.
49 HI, 529.
50 HL, 209.
51 HL, 210.
52 HL, 210–11. Before 1853, arguments in the Illinois Supreme Court were limited to two hours (three by special permission). In 1858, the time limit was set at one hour without special permission. Thomas, "Lincoln and the Courts," 171.

53 PAL:LDC 1:16.
54 PAL:LDC 1:17.
55 CWL 2:81.
56 HL, 293–94.

4. THE FIRST BRIDGE OVER THE FIRST RIVER

1 Adams, *History of Braintree, Massachusetts*, 76.
2 Wood, "New England Toll Bridges," 164.
3 Rock Island's modern name is Arsenal Island. This was derived from the U.S. Army Arsenal built there during the Civil War and was thought to avoid confusion with the nearby city of Rock Island. The historic name is used in this book.
4 Merrick, *Old Times on the Upper Mississippi*, 296.
5 Fowle, "The Original Rock Island Bridge across the Mississippi River," 58.
6 Nothstein, "The First Railroad Bridge to Cross the Mississippi," 1–2.
7 *The Autobiography of Ma-Ka-Tai-Me-She-Kia-Kiak, or Black Hawk*, 57.
8 Slattery, *Illustrated History of the Rock Island Arsenal and Arsenal Island* 1:36.
9 William C. Davis, *Jefferson Davis: The Man and His Hour*, 49–51; Slattery, *Illustrated History of the Rock Island Arsenal and Arsenal Island* 1:39.
10 Burlingame, *Abraham Lincoln: A Life* 1:67.
11 CWL 3:512.
12 HI, 362.
13 Donald, *Lincoln*, 45.
14 CWL 1:510.
15 Burlingame, *Abraham Lincoln: A Life* 1:71.
16 See discussion in chapter 2.
17 VanderVelde, *Mrs. Dred Scott*, 74–75. Fehrenbacher, *The Dred Scott Case*, 244, says that the slave built a cabin for Dr. Emerson on the opposite side of the river (now Iowa). VanderVelde, 75, 345n50, says it is more likely that the cabin was built by a hired man who was also a friend of Dr. Emerson and who stayed there after Emerson left.
18 "An Ordinance for the Government of the Territory of the United States Northwest of the River Ohio, adopted by the Congress under the Articles of Confederation, July 13, 1787, sec. 4, provided: "There shall be neither slavery nor involuntary servitude in the said territory, otherwise than in punishment of crimes whereof the party shall have been duly convicted." The legal principle that a slave became free when taken by his or her owner to a jurisdiction where slavery was not authorized by law derived from the English case of *Somerset v. Stewart*, in which Lord Chief Justice Mansfield said that the status of a slave was "so odious, that nothing can be suffered to support it, but positive law." *Somerset v. Stewart*, Lofft 1, 19, (K.B. 1772). If the law of the place did not sanction slavery, it was deemed illegal. See Fehrenbacher, *The Dred Scott Case*, 53–56. For the long history and complex permutations of Mansfield's decision in England and the United States, see Wiecek, "*Somerset*: Lord Mansfield and the Legitimacy of

Slavery in the Anglo-American World," 86–147. For Dred Scott's origins and travels with his master, see Fehrenbacher, *The Dred Scott Case*, 239–49.

19 3 Stat. 545–48, sec. 8, providing: "That in all that territory ceded by France to the United States, under the name of Louisiana, which lies north of thirty-six degrees and thirty minutes north latitude, not included within the limits of the state, contemplated by this act [Missouri], slavery and involuntary servitude, otherwise than in punishment of crimes, whereof the parties shall have been duly convicted, shall be, and is hereby forever prohibited."

20 *Dred Scott v. Sandford*, 60 U.S. [19 Howard.] 393, 407 (1857).

21 See discussion in chapter 13. For a more extensive review of the *Dred Scott* case and Lincoln's criticism of it, see McGinty, *Lincoln and the Court*, 38–64.

22 House Executive Document No. 51, 35th Congress, 2nd Session, 1859, 3, as quoted in Agnew, "Jefferson Davis and the Rock Island Bridge," 4–5.

23 10 Stat. 28–29.

24 *Private Laws of the State of Illinois, Passed by the Eighteenth General Assembly, Convened January 3, 1853* (Springfield: Lanphier and Walker, 1853), 329–30. The charter was reprinted in RIA, April 17, 1857, 2.

25 *Private Laws of the State of Illinois, Passed by the Eighteenth General Assembly, Convened January 3, 1853* (Springfield: Lanphier and Walker, 1853), 329–30.

26 *McCulloch v. Maryland*, 17 U.S. [4 Wheaton] 316, 405 (1819).

27 Ibid., 421.

28 Ibid.

29 *Pennsylvania v. Wheeling and Belmont Bridge Company*, 54 U.S. [13 Howard.] 518, 558 (1852).

30 Monroe, *The Wheeling Bridge Case*, 3.

31 *Pennsylvania v. Wheeling and Belmont Bridge Company*, 54 U.S. [13 Howard] 518, 568 (1852).

32 Ibid., 578.

33 Ibid., 591.

34 Ibid., 603.

35 10 Stat. 110–12.

36 Monroe, *The Wheeling Bridge Case*, 150.

37 *Pennsylvania v. Wheeling and Belmont Bridge Company*, 59 U.S. [18 Howard] 421, 430–31 (1855).

38 Act of March 19, 1847, as quoted in *Pennsylvania v. Wheeling and Belmont Bridge Co.*, 54 U.S. [13 Howard] 518, 565 (1852).

39 PJD 5:249.

40 Ibid.

41 Ibid.

42 Agnew, "Jefferson Davis and the Rock Island Bridge," 7.

43 Ibid., 9.

44 DG, August 21, 1854.

45 Ibid.

46 PJD 5:142.

47 *New York Herald*, November 29, 1854, quoted in PJD 5:23n1.

48 PJD 5:250; *Opinions of the Attorneys General* 6:670–79.

49 Nothstein, "The First Railroad Bridge to Cross the Mississippi," 7.

50 "Rock Island Bridge," *American Railroad Journal*, September 30, 1854, 615, reporting from *St. Louis Intelligencer.*

51 "Rock Island Bridge," *American Railroad Journal*, September 9, 1854, 573.

52 PJD 5:89–90.

53 Bill of complaint, quoted in Zobrist, "Steamboat Men versus Railroad Men," 164.

54 Agnew, "Jefferson Davis and the Rock Island Bridge," 9–10; PAL:LDC 3:310.

55 *United States v. The Railroad Bridge Company*, 6 McLean 517, 525 (7th Cir. 1855).

56 Ibid., 536.

57 Ibid., 539.

58 Ibid., 538.

5. A COLLISION OF INTERESTS

1 SLMR, September 20, 1857.

2 Petersen, "The Rock Island Comes," 293.

3 PAL:LDC 3:326n50.

4 Brayton, "The Crossing of the River," 49; Riebe, "The Government Bridge," 70; Hayes, *Iron Road to Empire*, 45.

5 PAL:LDC 3:341n83.

6 Fowle, "The Original Rock Island Bridge across the Mississippi River," 59; *The Rail-Roads, History and Commerce of Chicago*, 55.

7 Starr, *Lincoln and the Railroads*, 92.

8 *The Rail-Roads, History and Commerce of Chicago*, 11.

9 The bridge measurements varied slightly, depending on who gave them. These were taken from the careful study done by William Riebe. See Riebe, "The Government Bridge," 70. When Benjamin B. Brayton testified in open court, he stated that the width of the draw on the Illinois side was 116 feet and that on the Iowa side was 111 feet. See discussion in chapter 10.

10 *The Rail-Roads, History and Commerce of Chicago*, 11.

11 Brayton, "The Crossing of the River," 49.

12 Ibid.

13 Hayes, *Iron Road to Empire*, 44–45.

14 Downer, *History of Davenport and Scott County* 1:334.

15 Hayes, *Iron Road to Empire*, 45.

16 Nothstein, "The First Railroad Bridge to Cross the Mississippi," 9.

17 RIA, April 23, 1856.

18 Agnew, "Jefferson Davis and the Rock Island Bridge," 13.

19 Tweet, *History of Transportation on the Upper Mississippi and Illinois Rivers*, 21.

20 Primm, *Lion of the Valley*, 164.

21 Ibid., 192.

22 Zobrist, "Steamboat Men versus Railroad Men," 161.

23 See discussion in chapter 2.

24 Page, "The *Effie Afton* Case," 3.

25 PAL:LDC 3:310n8.

26 SLMR, September 13, 1857; Page, "The *Effie Afton* Case," 3.

27 Page, "The *Effie Afton* Case," 3–4; PAL:LDC 3:310–11.

28 SLMR, September 14, 1857.

29 The author acknowledged the naming of the boat in a letter to the *Cincinnati Commercial* in December 1855. See Elwin L. Page, "Who Was 'Effie Afton'?" 2.

30 Ibid., 1.

31 For a good summary of the life and career of Sarah Elizabeth Harper Monmouth and her connection to the *Effie Afton*, see Elwin L. Page, "Who Was 'Effie Afton'?"

32 SLMR, September 12, 1857.

33 Page, "The *Effie Afton* Case," 3.

34 Ibid., 3–4.

35 Ibid., 4.

36 Ibid.

37 "My first acquaintance with the navigation of the Upper Mississippi river was in May 1856." Deposition of Jacob S. Hurd, October 5–8, 1858, in *James Ward v. The Mississippi and Missouri Railroad Company*, United States District Court, Southern District of Iowa, RG 21, National Archives, Central Plains Region, Kansas City, MO, hereafter cited as *Ward*.

38 Page, "The *Effie Afton* Case," 4.

39 Testimony of Ozias Blinn, SLMR, September 11, 1857.

40 Deposition of Jacob S. Hurd, October 5–8, 1858, in *Ward*; SLMR, September 14, 1857.

41 SLMR, September 14, 1857; *Daily Illinois State Register*, May 12, 1857; Deposition of Jacob S. Hurd, October 5–8, 1858, in *Ward*.

42 Deposition of Jacob S. Hurd, October 5–8, 1858, in *Ward*.

43 SLMR, September 11, 1857.

44 Ibid.

45 The *Afton* overtook and passed the *Carson* in such a way "as to draw attention to her." RIA, September 12, 1857.

46 Ibid.

47 RIA, May 7, 1856.

48 RIA, May 8, 1856.

49 *St. Louis Intelligencer*, May 12, 1856, reprinted in RIA, May 17, 1856, 2, and RIA (weekly edition), May 21, 1856.

50 RIA (weekly edition), May 21, 1856.

6. THE SUIT IS FILED

1 CWL 4:67.

2 10 Stat. 277.

3 CWL 4:67.

4 CWL 7:281.

5 Burlingame, *Abraham Lincoln: A Life* 1:377.

6 CWL 2:255.

7 Donald, *Lincoln*, 183–84.

8 Ibid., 184.

9 Washburne, "Abraham Lincoln in Illinois," 316.

10 CWL 2:307.

11 Whitney, *Life on the Circuit with Lincoln*, 150.

12 HI, 510.

13 Burlingame, *Abraham Lincoln: A Life* 1:339.

14 Parkinson, "The Patent Case That Lifted Lincoln into a Presidential Candidate," 107–8.

15 Dickson, "Abraham Lincoln at Cincinnati," 62.

16 Parkinson, "The Patent Case That Lifted Lincoln into a Presidential Candidate," 122.

17 Burlingame, *Abraham Lincoln: A Life* 1:340; see also Parkinson, "The Patent Case That Lifted Lincoln into a Presidential Candidate," 118.

18 *McCormick v. Talcott*, 61 U.S. [20 Howard] 402 (1857).

19 Burlingame, *Abraham Lincoln: A Life* 1:341.

20 CWL 2:342.

21 See Finkelman, "John McLean: Moderate Abolitionist and Supreme Court Politician," 539–63.

22 Burlingame, *Abraham Lincoln: A Life* 1:421.

23 Finkelman, "John McLean: Moderate Abolitionist and Supreme Court Politician," 532.

24 Donald, *Lincoln*, 193.

25 Ibid., 193–94.

26 CWL 2:323.

27 CWL 2:385.

28 1 Stat. 73–93 (Judiciary Act of 1789).

29 Palmer, *Bench and Bar of Illinois*, 1:315–20.

30 "In Memoriam: Corydon Beckwith," 133 *Illinois Reports*, 9–19.

31 Greve, *Centennial History of Cincinnati and Representative Citizens*, 2:619–22.

32 "A. Lincoln v. Timothy D. Lincoln," 4.

33 SLMR, July 14, 1857 (Wead says that "this suit was commenced in October last"). The newspaper account is the best source for the commencement of the suit and the contents of the court pleadings, since the original documents were lost in the Chicago fire of 1871.

34 RIA, July 17, 1857, reprinting article from SLMR.

35 RIA (weekly edition), December 25, 1856.

36 Zobrist, "Steamboat Men versus Railroad Men," 167.

37 Ibid.

38 Rock Island's Family Tree, http://home.covad.net/~scicoatnsew/rihist1.htm#2_5_1853.

39 Jackson, *Rails across the Mississippi*, 3, 5.

40 RIA, February 23, 1857, quoting from CT, February 12, 1857.

41 Ibid.

42 Jackson, *Rails across the Mississippi*, 3.

43 RIA, February 25, 1857, quoting from SLMR.

44 See, e.g., RIA, April 11, 1857; May 23, 1857.

45 RIA, April 15, 1857, quoting from *Galena Courier*.

46 RIA, April 21, 1857, quoting from *St. Louis Democrat*, April 17, 1857.

47 RIA, June 17, 1857.

7. PREPARING THE GROUND

1 *United States v. Railroad Bridge Company*, 6 McLean 517–39 (7th Cir. 1855); see discussion in chapter 4.

2 PAL:LDC 4:361.

3 See, e.g., Miers, *Lincoln Day by Day* 1:132, 241.

4 PAL:LDC 3:314n22, 4:344.

5 SLMR, July 13, 1857.

6 Ibid.

7 Nevins, "Seventy Years of Service: From Grant to Gorman," 17; Starr, *Lincoln and the Railroads*, 94–95; Duff, *A. Lincoln: Prairie Lawyer*, 129; see Burlingame, *Abraham Lincoln: A Life* 1:337 (quoting part of this conversation).

8 Nevins, "Seventy Years of Service: From Grant to Gorman," 17.

9 RIA, September 1, 1857.

10 Lincoln deposited the $4,800 in the Springfield Marine and Fire Insurance Co. in Springfield on August 12, 1857. Pratt, *Personal Finances of Abraham Lincoln*, 54.

11 Ibid., 54, 77–79, 137.

12 Andreas, *History of Chicago*, 1:180.

13 Hurlbut, *Chicago Antiquities*, 542.

14 Andreas, *History of Chicago*, 1:180.

15 Saltonstall, "A Recollection of Lincoln in Court," 636.

16 Andreas, *History of Chicago*, 1:180.

17 A deposition is a written record of out-of-court oral testimony. *Black's Law Dictionary*, 8th ed., ed. Bryan A. Garner (St. Paul, MN: Thomson West, 1999), 472.

18 SLMR, July 13, 1857; RIA, July 18, 1857.

19 SLMR, July 13, 1857; RIA, July 20, 1857.

20 5 Stat. 176–78.

21 SLMR, July 14, 1857; RIA, July 20, 1857.

22 5 Stat. 176–78.

23 *Pennsylvania v. Wheeling and Belmont Bridge Company*, 54 U.S. [13 Howard] 518, 579 (1852).

24 *United States v. Railroad Bridge Company*, 6 McLean 517, 539 (7th Cir. 1855). See discussion in chapter 4.

25 CWL 2:342.

26 CWL 4:36, 40, 46.
27 See McGinty, *Lincoln and the Court*, 23.
28 Swisher, *Taney Period*, 48.
29 *Dred Scott v. Sandford*, 60 U.S. [19 Howard] 393, 529–64 (1857).
30 CWL 2:400.
31 HI, 644–45; HL, 220.
32 Cahan, *A Court That Shaped America*, 40.
33 PAL:LDC 4:345; McGinty, *Lincoln and the Court*, 105, 110, 112, 114.
34 PAL:LDC 4:345.
35 SLMR, July 14, 1857; RIA, July 20, 1857.
36 Ibid.
37 Holzer, *Lincoln-Douglas Debates*, 11.
38 Burlingame, *Abraham Lincoln: A Life* 1:497–98.
39 Ibid. 1:497. Founded in 1847, the *Chicago Tribune* merged with the *Chicago Press* (sometimes called the *Chicago Democratic Press*) in 1858 and became known as the *Chicago Press and Tribune*. After November 1860, it resumed its name as the *Chicago Tribune*. For the reporting of Henry Binmore and Robert Hitt of the Lincoln-Douglas debates of 1858, see chapter 8.
40 PAL:LDC 3:316n26.
41 Ibid. The other two cases were *People v. Peachy Quinn Harrison*, a murder trial that Lincoln tried in the Sangamon County Circuit Court in 1859 (see PAL:LDC 4:137–92) and *Johnston v. Jones and Marsh*, an important real estate ejectment case (popularly called the Sand Bar case) that he tried in the U.S. Circuit Court in Chicago in 1860 (see PAL:LDC 3:384–453 and discussion in chapter 13).
42 SLMR, July 14, 1857; RIA, July 20, 1857.
43 SLMR, September 8, 1857.
44 CWL 2:413.
45 See, e.g., Burlingame, *Abraham Lincoln: A Life* 1:337; Duff, *A. Lincoln: Prairie Lawyer*, 337.
46 See Russell, *A-Rafting on the Mississip'*, 70–71; PAL:LDC 3:326. Fraker, *Lincoln's Ladder to the Presidency*, 104, says that Lincoln went to the bridge, hired a boat to pass under it, and floated debris past it as he studied the currents.
47 In a letter to Frank F. Fowle dated February 28, 1928, Joseph Benjamin Oakleaf (1858–1930), a prominent collector of Lincolniana, expressed the categorical opinion that Lincoln did not visit the bridge. See Fowle, Correspondence relative to "A Famous Interference Case," Abraham Lincoln Presidential Library, Springfield, Illinois. In *Hell Gate of the Mississippi*, 193–204, Larry Riney argues that Lincoln probably did not visit the bridge at all, at least not before the trial.
48 RIA, September 1, 1857.
49 "Lincoln's Visit to the Rock Island Bridge."
50 A printed copy of the letter is in PAL:LDC 3:327.
51 The text of the letter is set forth in PAL:LDC 3:327. CWL 2:414n2 says the letter is of "questionable authenticity." Riney, *Hell Gate of the Mississippi*, 195–202, calls

it "questionable." But Judd may not have known that Lincoln was already in Chicago when he wrote the letter, and he may have used a secretary to draft it.

52 PAL:LDC 3:326. On September 20, 1857, Mrs. Lincoln wrote: "Mr. L. is not at home, this makes the fourth week, he has been in Chicago." Miers, *Lincoln Day by Day*, 2:200. This indicates that he was in Chicago the first week in September.

53 Brayton, "The Crossing of the River," 49; Benjamin B. Brayton Jr. to Hilon A. Parker, Davenport, Iowa, February 10, 1903, Parker Papers, Clements Library, University of Michigan, Ann Arbor. Brayton misremembered the year in which the visit took place as 1858 (it was 1857). But his recollections were recorded nearly fifty years after the event and, in such circumstances, misremembering the year is understandable. Young Brayton's recollections were garbled and embroidered in later retellings of the events and eventually acquired the status of folklore. See, e.g., Nevins, "Seventy Years of Service: From Grant to Gorman," 18; Botkin and Harlow, *A Treasury of Railroad Folklore*, 114. But many of the events of Lincoln's life received similar treatment.

8. A VERY SERIOUS OBSTRUCTION

1 Binmore was identified only by the initial "B," while Hitt was identified as R. R. Hitt.

2 Palmer, *Bench and Bar of Illinois*, 1:513–14, 2:648–49.

3 SLMR, September 10, 1857; CT, September 9, 1857.

4 1 Stat. 73–92, sec. 29; see McDermott, *The Jury in Lincoln's America*, 33–35 (bystanders commonly called on to serve as jurors in Illinois and neighboring states); Bryan A. Garner, ed., *Black's Law Dictionary*, 8th ed. (St. Paul, MN: Thomson West, 2004) (talesman as person selected from among bystanders in court to serve as juror when original jury panel has become deficient in number).

5 CT, September 9, 1857; SLMR, September 10, 1857.

6 SLMR, September 10, 1857; CT, September 9, 1857.

7 See McDermott, *The Jury in Lincoln's America*, 11, 14, 26, 30, 49–50, 58–59.

8 CT, September 9, 1857.

9 CP, September 9, 1857.

10 Ibid.; September 24, 1857.

11 Palmer, *Bench and Bar of Illinois* 1:320.

12 SLMR, September 11, 1857.

13 Ibid.

14 Precise measurements of the draw openings, like other components of the bridge, varied, depending on who was giving them.

15 SLMR, September 11, 1857; a summation of "the points" of Wead's statement is in CT, September 9, 1857.

16 SLMR, September 11, 1857.

17 Ibid.; CT, September 9, 1857.

18 SLMR, September 12, 1857.

19 Ibid.; CP, September 10, 1857.

20 SLMR, September 12, 1857.

21 Ibid.; CT, September 10, 1857; CP, September 10, 1857.

22 Ibid.

23 SLMR, September 12, 1857; CT September 10, 1857.

24 Twain, *Autobiography of Mark Twain* 1:274–78.

25 High-pressure boilers forty-two inches in diameter were generally limited to a maximum pressure of 110 pounds per square inch; in boilers of greater or lesser diameter the pressure was adjusted upward or downward by reference to this standard. See 10 Stat. 61–75, sec. 9, *Third*.

26 SLMR, September 12, 1857.

27 Ibid.; CT, September 10, 1857.

28 SLMR, September 12, 1857.

29 Ibid.; CT, September 10, 1857.

30 SLMR, September 12, 1857.

31 SLMR, September 13, 1857.

32 Ibid.

33 Ibid.

34 Ibid.

35 Ibid.

36 Ibid.

37 Ibid.

38 Ibid.

39 In a reflective essay published in the *Missouri Republican* on September 16, Binmore said that he tried to "abstract" the testimony "so as to present depositions which are much alike on all the points of interest," though he claimed (not entirely accurately): "The oral testimony you have in full."

40 Saltonstall, "A Recollection of Lincoln in Court," 636–37. This article was published under the name of F. G. Saltonstall. Saltonstall was incorrectly identified in Wilson, *Intimate Memories of Lincoln*, 67, as "an able lawyer and shrewd judge of men." He was in fact a stock and bond broker (and sometime commission merchant) identified as such in various sources, including the U.S. Census for Chicago in 1880 and Chicago city directories for 1855–56, 1861, 1862, and 1864.

41 Saltonstall, "A Recollection of Lincoln in Court," 636.

42 Ibid., 637.

43 For references to Lincoln's whittling, see Donald, *Lincoln*, 170; Rice, *Reminiscences of Abraham Lincoln*, 294; Burlingame, *Abraham Lincoln: A Life* 2:293; Emerson, *Lincoln the Inventor*, 7. Lincoln's whittling was graphically portrayed in Steven Spielberg's 2012 motion picture, *Lincoln*.

9. A CHORUS OF PROTESTS

1 SLMR, September 14, 1857.

2 SLMR, September 13, 1857.

3 Ibid.

4 SLMR, September 16, 17, 1857.

5 SLMR, September 13, 1857.

6 Ibid.

7 Ibid.

8 SLMR, September 14, 1857.

9 SLMR, September 13, 1857.

10 SLMR, September 14, 1857.

11 SLMR, September 15, 1857.

12 CP, September 12, 1857.

13 SLMR, September 13, 1857.

14 SLMR, September 12, 1857.

15 SLMR, September 16, 1857.

16 Ibid.

17 Ibid.

18 Ibid.

19 Ibid.

20 SLMR, September 14, 1857.

21 SLMR, September 16, 1857.

22 SLMR, September 13, 1857.

23 SLMR, September 16, 1857.

24 Ibid.

25 SLMR, September 17, 1857.

26 Greenleaf, *A Treatise on the Law of Evidence*, 5th ed., 430 (emphasis in original); see Smith, *A Selection of Leading Cases on Various Branches of the Law*, 6th American ed., 2:106 ("testimony of a witness cannot be received for the purpose of supporting an issue, to which he is a party of record.").

27 *Bridges v. Armour*, 46 U.S. [5 Howard] 91, 94.

28 This rule was abandoned, in some cases by statutory enactments and in others by judicial decisions, barely half a century after the *Effie Afton* case was tried. See Wigmore, *Select Cases on the Law of Evidence*, 2nd ed., 150, explaining that the rule "gradually became incongruous." Even witnesses who are directly interested in a suit may have valuable information to impart; in fact, they often have information that cannot be supplied by any other witnesses.

29 SLMR, September 16, 1857.

30 DG, September 12, 1857.

31 SLMR, September 16, 1857.

32 *Illinois Daily Journal*, September 12, 1857.

10. THE BRIDGE ITSELF ON THE STAND

1 SLMR, September 17, 1857; CT, September 16, 1857.

2 Ibid.

3 See Doc. No. 203, affidavit of Seth Gurney dated November 12, 1856, in *Documents of the Assembly of the State of New York, Eightieth Session—1857*, vol. 3 (Albany: C. Van Benthuysen, 1857).

4 SLMR, September 18, 1857; CT, September 16, 1857.

5 Ibid.

6 "The common law rejects the testimony of parties, of persons deficient in understanding, of persons insensible to the obligation of an oath, *and of persons whose pecuniary interest is directly involved with the matter in issue*." *Halsted's Digest of the Law of Evidence* (New York: Jacob R. Halsted, 1856), 1 (emphasis added).

7 In his instructions to the jury, Judge McLean described the type of float used here as "the instrument of a staff with cross boards, graduated to float from two feet below the surface to twelve." SLMR, September 26, 1857.

8 SLMR, September 20, 1857; CT, September 17, 1857.

9 Larkin, *John B. Jervis*, xi, xii, xiv, xix, 6–15, 16–32, 36, 39, 48, 49, 51, 52, 56, 60, 61–80, 95, 110, 124–26.

10 Ibid., 126.

11 SLMR, September 20, 1857; CT, September 17, 18, 1857.

12 SLMR, September 20, 1857; CT, September 18, 1857.

13 Ibid.

14 Ibid.

15 Wood, *History of the Republican Party and Biographies of Its Supporters, Illinois Volume*, 250–53.

16 SLMR, September 21, 1857; CT, September 21, 1857.

17 SLMR, September 21, 1857; CT, September 18, 1857.

18 Magee, *The John Deere Way*, 4–5.

19 SLMR, September 21, 1857; CT, September 18, 1857.

20 SLMR, September 21, 1857; CT, September 21, 1857.

21 Ibid.

22 SLMR, September 20, 1857; CT, September 18, 1857.

23 Ibid.

24 SLMR, September 21, 1857.

25 Ibid.

26 CT, September 21, 1857.

27 Ibid.

28 Ibid.

29 Ibid.

30 Ibid.

31 *Pennsylvania v. Wheeling and Belmont Bridge Company*, 54 U.S. [13 Howard] 518 (1852). For discussion of the *Wheeling Bridge* case, see chapter 5.

32 *Pennsylvania v. Wheeling and Belmont Bridge Company*, 59 U.S. [18 Howard] 421,

437–49 (1856) (McLean, J., dissenting on ground that act of Congress was unconstitutional and void).
33 SLMR, September 22, 1857; CT, September 21, 1857.
34 Ibid.

11. A VIRTUAL TRIUMPH

1 CT, September 22, 1857.
2 Wead's closing argument as given here is taken from Hitt's summary in CP, September 22, 1857. See PAL:LDC 3:344–52 for a printed summary.
3 Knox's closing argument as given here is all taken from Hitt's summary in CP, September 23, 1857. See PAL:LDC 3:352–59 for a printed summary.
4 What we know of Lincoln's speech is derived from Robert Hitt's report in the *Chicago Press* and from a typed transcription of his notes preserved in the Library of Congress. Both of these sources identify Lincoln as the "Hon. Abram Lincoln." Both are somewhat shortened summaries, not full transcripts, of what Lincoln said; see CP, September 24, 1857; Robert R. Hitt Papers, Manuscript Division, Library of Congress, Washington, DC.
5 Burlingame, *Abraham Lincoln: A Life* 1:320.
6 RHP, as quoted in PAL:LDC 3:360.
7 See discussion in chapter 3.
8 CT, December 29, 1895.
9 Whitney, *Life on the Circuit with Lincoln*, 231 (emphasis added).
10 CT, December 29, 1895.
11 Wilson, *Lincoln's Sword*, 78.
12 McGinty, *The Body of John Merryman*, 102.
13 Whitney, *Life on the Circuit with Lincoln*, 232.
14 Emerson, *Lincoln the Inventor*, 35–53.
15 Judd, "An Evening with Mr. Lincoln," 520–23.
16 Ibid., 523–24.
17 CP, September 24, 1857.
18 RHP, as quoted in PAL:LDC 3:365.
19 The excerpts from McLean's charge given here are taken from CP, September 25, 1857. A printed account of the charge is in PAL:LDC 3:366–81.
20 CT, September 25, 1857.
21 SLMR, September 8, 1857.
22 CT, September 25, 1857.
23 In the nineteenth century, it was generally assumed that the Seventh Amendment to the U.S. Constitution required that juries in federal courts consist of twelve members and that their verdicts be unanimous. See *Springville City v. Thomas*, 166 U.S. 707 (1897) (unanimous verdict as essential feature of trial by jury in common-law cases); *American Publishing Co. v. Fisher*, 166 U.S. 464 (1897) (Utah statute authorizing jury verdict by vote of nine jurors unconstitutional). In the second half of the twentieth century, however, the United States Supreme

Court held that juries with fewer than twelve members will satisfy the amendment. See *Colgrove v. Battin*, 413 U.S. 149, 160 (1973) (jury of six members satisfies Seventh Amendment). The Seventh Amendment provides: "In suits at common law, where the value in controversy shall exceed twenty dollars, the right of trial by jury shall be preserved, and no fact tried by a jury, shall be otherwise re-examined in any Court of the United States, than according to the rules of the common law." The Seventh Amendment applies only to suits in federal court, not to those in state courts. It applies only to civil suits seeking monetary relief, not to those seeking equitable relief (injunctions, specific performance, or other nonmonetary remedies traditionally available only in the English courts of chancery). Further, the amendment does not apply to issues of maritime or admiralty rights.

24 CP, September 26, 1857; *Illinois Daily Journal*, September 28, 1857; *Chicago Daily Democrat*, September 26, 1857.

25 CP, September 25, 1857.

26 *Chicago Daily Democrat*, September 26, 1857.

12. THE BRIDGE STANDS

1 Wead to Hurd, October 15, 1857, Jacob S. Hurd Papers, Public Library of Cincinnati and Hamilton County, Cincinnati.

2 Bissell to Hurd, November 30, 1857, Jacob S. Hurd Papers, Public Library of Cincinnati and Hamilton County, Cincinnati.

3 Johannsen, *Stephen A. Douglas*, 591.

4 J. S. Hurd to Hon. S. A. Douglas, December 28, 1857, Stephen A. Douglas Papers, University of Chicago.

5 Johannsen, *Stephen A. Douglas*, 110.

6 Online catalog of Stephen A. Douglas Papers, University of Chicago.

7 Johannsen, *Stephen A. Douglas*, viii.

8 *Cong. Globe*, 35th Congress, 1st Session, January 4, 1858, 184.

9 "Railroad Bridge across the Mississippi River at Rock Island," April 15, 1858, 35th Congress, 1st Session, House Report No. 250, 5; SLMR, May 5, 1858.

10 Warren, *Report on Bridging the Mississippi River between Saint Paul, Minn., and St. Louis, Mo.*, 143–45.

11 PAL:LDC 3:381; Pratt, *Personal Finances of Abraham Lincoln*, 56, 162, 166.

12 The suit began with the filing of a bill in chancery. *Ward*; PAL:LDC 3:381.

13 *Ward*; SLMR, August 24, 1858.

14 SLMR, August 24, 1858.

15 U.S. Const., Art. III, sec. 2 (the judicial power extends to controversies "between citizens of different states").

16 The Seventh Amendment to the U.S. Constitution guarantees the right of trial by jury "in suits at common law, where the value in controversy shall exceed twenty dollars." A suit for abatement of a nuisance is an action in equity (often, particularly in the nineteenth century, called "chancery") and not a "suit at

common law," so there is no constitutional right to a jury trial in such a suit. See *Parsons v. Bedford*, 28 U.S. [3 Peters] 443, 446 ("courts of equity use the trial by jury only in extraordinary cases").

17 Ross, *Justice of Shattered Dreams*, 8, 10–11, 15, 16, 17, 19–25, 38–39; McGinty, *Lincoln and the Court*, 108–10.

18 Ross, *Justice of Shattered Dreams*, 39, 75.

19 *Chicago Press and Tribune*, November 20, 1858; June 18, 1859.

20 *Ward*; *Chicago Press and Tribune*, April 5, 1860.

21 Decree in *Ward*.

22 McGinty, *Lincoln and the Court*, 110.

23 *Mississippi and Missouri Railroad Company v. Ward*, 67 U.S. [2 Black] 485 (1863).

24 U.S. Const., Art. III, sec. 2 (the judicial power of the United States extends "to all cases of admiralty and maritime jurisdiction"). The Seventh Amendment guarantees trial by jury "in suits at common law, where the value in controversy shall exceed twenty dollars." The phrase "suits at common law" does not include suits in equity or of admiralty and maritime jurisdiction. *Parsons v. Bedford*, 28 U.S. [3 Peters] 433, 446. See 1 Stat. 77. sec. 9 (district courts have "exclusive original cognizance of all civil causes of admiralty and maritime jurisdiction," and "the trial of issues of fact, in the district courts, in all causes except civil causes of admiralty and maritime jurisdiction, shall be by jury"). In admiralty courts, causes are usually determined by the court without the aid of a jury. Benedict, *The American Admiralty, Its Jurisdiction and Practice*, 106. Under the Admiralty Rules adopted by the U.S. Supreme Court in 1842, an admiralty case is tried before the judge; there are no juries in admiralty proceedings proper. Hughes, *Handbook of Admiralty Law*, 2nd ed., 410.

25 Merrick, *Old Times on the Upper Mississippi*, 144, 189, 272.

26 *The Rock Island Bridge*, 73 U.S. 213, 216 (1867).

27 *Chicago Press and Tribune*, August 9, 1860.

28 "Arrest for Conspiracy to Burn a Bridge," *New York Times*, August 9, 1860.

29 *Chicago Press and Tribune*, August 9, 1860.

30 "A Plot to Burn the Rock Island Railroad Bridge," *Geneseo [Illinois] Republic*, August 16, 1860, quoting from *Chicago Press and Tribune*, August 9, 1860.

31 Ibid.

32 DG, August 10, 1860.

33 CT, December 12, 1860.

34 CT, December 18, 1860.

35 *Hurd, Jacob, et al., vs. Chicago R. I. & P. R. R. et al*, File No. 440, Clerk's Index of Civil Cases, Circuit Court of McDonough County, Macomb, Illinois. Record Book I, pp. 501, 544, 599; Book L, pp. 10, 81. Disposed of Sept. 1875, Judgment Book 28, p. 75; Fee Book R, p. 88.

36 PAL:LDC 3:310n8; Way, *Way's Packet Directory, 1848–1994*, 326, 477.

13. THE GREAT AND DURABLE QUESTION

1 Guelzo, *Lincoln and Douglas: The Debates That Defined America*, 56.
2 Donald, *Lincoln*, 205.
3 CWL 2:461–62 (emphasis in original, but division into paragraphs ignored). The biblical phrase is from Matthew 12:25 and Mark 3:25.
4 CWL 2:399.
5 CWL 2:400–409.
6 CWL 2:522.
7 Burlingame, *Abraham Lincoln: A Life* 1:484.
8 CWL 3:177.
9 CWL 3:322. One transcript of this statement quotes Douglas here as using the word "nigger" rather than "Negro." Both Douglas and Lincoln were frequently (although not consistently) quoted as having used that word. Although it is clear that Douglas used it to derogate African-Americans, it is not as clear that Lincoln did so.
10 CWL 3:145–46.
11 CWL 3:276.
12 CWL 3:226.
13 CWL 3:249.
14 CWL 3:254.
15 CWL 3:112.
16 CWL 3:231.
17 *McCulloch v. Maryland*, 17 U.S. [4 Wheaton] 316 (1819).
18 CWL: 3:28, 232, 278.
19 CWL 3:255.
20 Guelzo, *Lincoln and Douglas*, 116–17; Holzer, *The Lincoln-Douglas Debates*, 10–11. Both Binmore and Hitt had assistants who helped them with the reports.
21 Donald, *Lincoln*, 227–28.
22 CWL 3:339.
23 Leroy, *Mr. Lincoln's Book*, 73–77, 145, 149.
24 CWL 3:397n1.
25 CWL 3:396–97.
26 Dodge, *Personal Recollections*, 11.
27 Ibid.
28 *The Lincoln Log*, August 15, 1859, http://www.thelincolnlog.org.
29 Holzer, *Lincoln at Cooper Union*, 8–10.
30 Ibid., 119–48.
31 CWL 3:555.
32 Holzer, *Lincoln at Cooper Union*, 157.
33 Ibid., 210–11.
34 See *Jones v. Johnston*, 59 U.S. [18 Howard] 150–58 (1855).
35 PAL:LDC 3:442.
36 *Johnston v. Jones*, 66 U.S. [1 Black] 209–27 (1861); PAL:LDC 3:452.
37 Burlingame, *Abraham Lincoln: A Life* 1:621–24.

14. HISTORY'S VERDICT

1 "Republican Platform of 1860," May 17, 1860, *American Presidency Project*, http://www.presidency.ucsb.edu/ws/index.php?pid=29620.
2 CWL 4:52.
3 CWL 7: 17; 5:537.
4 12 Stat. 392–93.
5 12 Stat. 489–98. For the variety of gauges before the Civil War and the difficulties they presented to travelers and shippers, see White, *Railroaded*, 2–3, 8–9.
6 12 Stat. 503–5.
7 Stat. 537; Slattery, *Illustrated History of the Rock Island Arsenal and Arsenal Island: Part Two*, 16–20.
8 CWL 6:68.
9 12 Stat. 807; CWL 6:68n1. The congressional vote in favor of four feet eight and a half inches was largely the result of eastern lobbying. The final vote in the Senate was 26 to 9, with only three senators east of the Mississippi supporting five feet. Starr, *Lincoln and the Railroads*, 224.
10 CWL 7:16; see also CWL 7:228.
11 CWL 7:382n.
12 13 Stat. 356–64; see Borneman, *Rival Rails: The Race to Build America's Greatest Transcontinental Railroad*, 40; White, *Railroaded: The Transcontinentals and the Making of Modern America*, 22–26 (described the 1864 amendment as "the worst act money could buy").
13 Faust, *Historical Times Illustrated Encyclopedia of the Civil War*, 383.
14 Long, *The Civil War Day by Day*, 723–24; McPherson, *Battle Cry of Freedom*, 318–19.
15 Long, *The Civil War Day by Day*, 724; Wolmar, *The Great Railroad Revolution*, xxii.
16 Riebe, "The Government Bridge," 71–73.
17 DG, March 10–14, 1868.
18 DG, March 13, 14, 16, 1868; April 9, 14, 1868.
19 DG, March 17, 18, 1868.
20 Brayton, "The Crossing of the River," 49; Nothstein, "The First Railroad Bridge to Cross the Mississippi," 20.
21 DG, April 23, 24, 1868.
22 DG, April 23, 1868.
23 14 Stat. 75–76; Hayes, *High Road to Empire*, 70–71. The act authorized the secretary of war to fix the location of the bridge.
24 Hayes, *High Road to Empire*, 53, 70–71; Flagler, *History of the Rock Island Arsenal*, 166–68.
25 15 Stat. 485–87.
26 15 Stat. 258–59.
27 Switzler, *Report on the Internal Commerce of the United States*, 22.
28 Warren, *Report on Bridging the Mississippi River*, 1001, states that the width of the river between the Illinois and Iowa shore was 1,650 feet at the site of the bridge.
29 Riebe, "The Government Bridge," 73.

30 Flagler, *History of the Rock Island Arsenal*, 179; Slattery, *Illustrated History of the Rock Island Arsenal and Arsenal Island: Part Two*, 67–68; *War's Greatest Workshop*, 98; Hayes, *High Road to Empire*, 72, 86.

31 Weingardt, *Engineering Legends*, 61–62; Petroski, *Engineers of Dreams*, 170–75, 214–15, 338–39; see Głomb, *A Man Who Spanned Two Eras*.

32 Pfeiffer, "Bridging the Mississippi," 6.

33 Tweet, *History of Transportation on the Upper Mississippi and Illinois Rivers*, 34.

34 14 Stat. 244–46; Warren, *Report on Bridging the Mississippi River between Saint Paul, Minn., and St. Louis, Mo.*, 197.

35 14 Stat. 244–46.

36 PAL:LDC 3:383.

37 Tweet, *History of Transportation on the Upper Mississippi and Illinois Rivers*, 38.

38 Ibid.

39 Hunter, *Steamboats on the Western Rivers*, 595; Switzler, *Report on the Internal Commerce of the United States*, 25.

40 Primm, *Lion of the Valley*, 279–82.

41 Ibid., 282.

42 Jackson, *Great American Bridges and Dams*, 194.

43 Primm, *Lion of the Valley*, 291–92.

44 Tweet, *History of Transportation on the Upper Mississippi and Illinois Rivers*, 38.

45 Costello, *Climbing the Mississippi River Bridge by Bridge*, vol. 2.

46 Tweet, *History of Transportation on the Upper Mississippi and Illinois Rivers*, 13.

47 Ibid.

BIBLIOGRAPHY

MANUSCRIPTS

Benjamin B. Brayton Jr. to Hilon A. Parker, Davenport, Iowa, February 10, 1903. Parker Papers, Clements Library, University of Michigan.

Frank Fuller Fowle, 1877–1946. Correspondence relative to "A Famous Interference Case," 1924–33. Abraham Lincoln Presidential Library, Springfield, Illinois.

George E. Hubbell and Charles H. Hubbell. Letters and newspaper clippings concerning Abraham Lincoln as counsel in two lawsuits brought against the Bridge Company of Davenport, Iowa. Lillian Goldman Law Library, Yale University.

Elwin L. Page. "Who Was 'Effie Afton'?" Mariners' Museum, Newport News, Virginia, 1956.

ARCHIVES

Robert R. Hitt Papers, Manuscript Division, Library of Congress, Washington, DC.

Jacob Hurd, et al., v. Chicago and Rock Island and Pacific Railroad, et al. Circuit Court of McDonough County, Macomb, Illinois. Index of Civil Cases, Record Book K, pages 501, 544, 599, Book L, pages 10, 81. Judgment Book 28, p. 75.

Jacob S. Hurd Papers. Cincinnati Room, Public Library of Cincinnati and Hamilton County, Cincinnati, Ohio.

"Railroad Bridge across the Mississippi River at Rock Island," April 15, 1858. 35th Congress, 1st Session, House Report No. 250, Records of the House of Representatives, Center for Legislative Archives, National Archives, Washington, DC.

James Ward v. The Mississippi and Missouri Railroad Company, District Court of the United States for the District of Iowa, Middle Division, RG 21, National Archives and Records Administration, Central Plains Region, Kansas City, MO.

CASE REPORTS

American Publishing Co. v. Fisher, 166 U.S. 464 (1897).

Bridges v. Armour, 46 U.S. [5 Howard] 91 (1847).

Charles River Bridge v. Warren Bridge, 36 U.S. [11 Peters] 420 (1837).

Colgrove v. Battin, 413 U.S. 149 (1873).

Columbus Insurance Co. v. Curtenius, 6 McLean 209 (7th Cir. 1853).

Columbus Insurance Company v. Peoria Bridge Company, 6 McLean 70 (7th Cir. 1853).

Dred Scott v. Sandford, 60 U.S. [19 Howard] 393 (1857).

Illinois Central Rail Road v. County of McLean, 17 Illinois 291 (1856).

Johnston v. Jones, 66 U.S. [1 Black] 209 (1861).

Jones v. Johnston, 59 U.S. [18 Howard] 150 (1855).

Lewis v. Lewis, 48 U.S. [7 Howard] 776 (1849).

McCormick v. Talcott, 61 U.S. [20 Howard] 402 (1857).

McCulloch v. Maryland, 17 U.S. [4 Wheaton] 316 (1819).

Mississippi and Missouri Railroad v. Ward, 67 U.S. [2 Black] 485 (1863).

Pennsylvania v. Wheeling and Belmont Bridge Company, 54 U.S. [13 Howard] 518 (1852).

Pennsylvania v. Wheeling and Belmont Bridge Company, 59 U.S. [18 Howard] 421 (1855).

The Rock Island Bridge, 73 U.S. [6 Wallace] 213 (1867).

Springville City v. Thomas, 166 U.S. 707 (1897).

United States v. Railroad Bridge Company, 6 McLean 517 (7th Cir. 1855).

PUBLISHED PRIMARY SOURCES

Basler, Roy P., ed. *The Collected Works of Abraham Lincoln.* 9 vols. New Brunswick, NJ: Rutgers University Press, 1953–55.

Crist, Lynda Lasswell, ed., and Mary Seaton Dix, assoc. ed. *The Papers of Jefferson Davis.* Vol. 5, 1853–55. Baton Rouge: Louisiana State University Press, 1985.

Stowell, Daniel W., Susan Krause, John A. Lupton, Stacy Pratt McDermott, Christopher A. Schnell, Dennis E. Suttles, Kelley B. Clausing, and R. Dan Monroe, eds. *The Papers of Abraham Lincoln: Legal Documents and Cases.* 4 vols. Charlottesville: University of Virginia Press, 2008.

ONLINE SOURCES

Britton, Rick. "'What a Beautiful Country It Is': Robert E. Lee on the Mississippi." March 25, 2007. http://leearchive.wlu.edu/reference/addresses/britton/index.html.

Cayton, Andrew. "Abraham Lincoln and the Problem of Progress." 2005 Railroad Symposium: Lincoln and the Railroads. Indiana Historical Society. http://www.indianahistory.org/our-services/books-publications/railroad-symposia-essays-1.

Ely, James W., Jr. "Abraham Lincoln as a Railroad Attorney." 2005 Railroad Symposium: Lincoln and the Railroads. Indiana Historical Society. http://www.indianahistory.org/our-services/books-publications/railroad-symposia-essays-1.

———. "Lincoln and the Rock Island Bridge Case." 2005 Railroad Symposium: Lincoln and the Railroads. Indiana Historical Society. http://www.indianahistory.org/our-services/books-publications/railroad-symposia-essays-1.

The Law Practice of Abraham Lincoln. 2nd ed. http://www.lawpracticeofabrahamlincoln.org/Search.aspx.

The Lincoln Log: A Daily Chronology of the Life of Abraham Lincoln. http://www.thelincolnlog.org.

Morsman, Jenry. "Collision of Interests: The *Effie Afton,* the Rock Island Bridge, and the Making of America." *Common-Place* 6, no. 4 (July 2006). http://www.common-place.org/vol-06/no-04/morsman/.

The Papers of Abraham Lincoln. http://www.papersofabrahamlincoln.org.

"Republican Party Platform of 1860," May 17, 1860. *American Presidency Project.* http://www.presidency.ucsb.edu/ws/index.php?pid=29620.

Roseman, Curtis C. "History of First Railroad Bridge Crossing of the Mississippi River: A Pictorial History of the First Railroad Bridge across the Mississippi River and Its Three Successors." *River Action.* http://www.riveraction.org/node/121.

When Lincoln Fought for a Bridge. Chicago: Rock Island Lines, 1922 https://archive.org/details/whenlincolnfoughtooalle.

BOOKS AND ARTICLES

Adams, Charles Francis. *History of Braintree, Massachusetts.* Cambridge, MA: Riverside Press, 1891.

Afton, Effie [Sarah Elizabeth Harper Monmouth]. *Eventide: A Series of Tales and Poems.* Boston: Fetridge and Company, 1854.

Agnew, Dwight L. "Iowa's First Railroad." *Iowa Journal of History* 48 (1950): 1–26.

———. "Jefferson Davis and the Rock Island Bridge." *Iowa Journal of History* 47 (1949): 3–14.

"A. Lincoln v. Timothy D. Lincoln," *Lincoln Lore,* October 1956, 4.

Andreas, A. T. *History of Chicago from the Earliest Period to the Present Time.* 3 vols. Chicago: A. T. Andreas, 1884.

Anfinson, John O. *The River We Have Wrought: A History of the Upper Mississippi.* Minneapolis: University of Minnesota Press, 2003.

Angle, Paul M. *"Here I Have Lived": A History of Lincoln's Springfield, 1821–1865.* Springfield, Illinois: Abraham Lincoln Association, 1935.

Arnold, Isaac N. *The Life of Abraham Lincoln.* Chicago: Jansen, McClurg, 1885.

Autobiography of Ma-Ka-Tai-Me-She-Kia-Kiak, or Black Hawk. St. Louis: Continental Printing Company, 1882.

Bannister, Dan. W. *Lincoln and the Illinois Supreme Court.* Ed. Barbara Hughett. Springfield, IL: Dan W. Bannister, 1995.

Beltrami, Giacomo C. *A Pilgrimage in America, Leading to the Discovery of the Sources of the Mississippi and Bloody Rivers; with a Description of the Whole Course of the Former, and of the Ohio.* 1828; Chicago: Quadrangle Books, 1962.

Benedict, Erastus C. *The American Admiralty, Its Jurisdiction and Practice.* New York: Banks and Brothers, 1870.

Beveridge, Albert J. *Abraham Lincoln, 1809–1858.* 2 vols. Boston: Houghton Mifflin, 1928.

Billings, Roger, and Frank J. Williams, eds. *Abraham Lincoln, Esq.: The Legal Career of America's Greatest President.* Lexington: University Press of Kentucky, 2010.

Boorstin, Daniel J. *The Americans: The Democratic Experience.* New York: Random House, 1965.

Boritt, Gabor S. *Lincoln and the Economics of the American Dream.* Urbana and Chicago: University of Illinois Press, 1994.

Borneman, Walter R. *Rival Rails: The Race to Build America's Greatest Transcontinental Railroad.* New York: Random House, 2010.

Borrett, George Tuthill. *Out West: Letters from Canada and the United States.* London: J. E. Adlard, 1865.

Botkin, B. A., and Alvin F. Harlow, eds. *A Treasury of Railroad Folklore: The Stories, Tall Tales, Traditions, Ballads and Songs of the American Railroad Man.* New York: Crown Publishers, 1953.

Brayton, B. B. "The Crossing of the River: The Turning Point for the Railroad and the West." *Davenport Democrat and Leader, Half-Century Edition,* October 22, 1905, 49.

Brock, William R. *Parties and Political Conscience: American Dilemmas, 1840–1850.* Millwood, NY: KTO Press, 1979.

Burlingame, Michael. *Abraham Lincoln: A Life.* 2 vols. Baltimore, MD: Johns Hopkins University Press, 2008.

Cahan, Richard. *A Court That Shaped America: Chicago's Federal District Court from Abe Lincoln to Abbie Hoffman.* Evanston, IL: Northwestern University Press, 2002.

Campanella, Richard. *Lincoln in New Orleans: The 1828–1831 Flatboat Voyages and Their Place in History.* Lafayette: University of Louisiana at Lafayette Press, 2010.

Cincinnati: A Guide to the Queen City and Its Neighbors. American Guide Series. Cincinnati, OH: Wiesen-Hart Press, 1943.

Cooper, William J., Jr. *Jefferson Davis, American.* New York: Alfred A. Knopf, 2000.

Costello, Mary Charlotte Aubry. *Climbing the Mississippi River Bridge by Bridge,* vol. 2, *All the Minnesota Bridges across the Mississippi River from the Iowa Border to Lake Itasca, the Source of the Mississippi River.* Davenport, IA: Mary C. Costello, 2002.

Davis, William C. *Jefferson Davis: The Man and His Hour.* New York: HarperCollins, 1991.

———. *Portraits of the Riverboats.* San Diego, CA: Thunder Bay Press, 2001.

Death of Lincoln: Proceedings in the Supreme Court of Illinois. Chicago: J. W. Middleton, 1865.

DeRose, Chris. *Congressman Lincoln: The Making of America's Greatest President.* New York: Threshold Editions, 2013.

Dickson, W. M. "Abraham Lincoln at Cincinnati." *Harper's New Monthly Magazine,* June 1884, 62–66.

Dirck, Brian R. "A. Lincoln, Respectable 'Prairie Lawyer.'" In *Abraham Lincoln, Esq.: The Legal Career of America's Greatest President,* ed. Roger Billings and Frank J. Williams, 65–80. Lexington: University Press of Kentucky, 2010.

———. *Lincoln and the Constitution.* Carbondale and Edwardsville: Southern Illinois University Press, 2012.

———. *Lincoln the Lawyer.* Urbana and Chicago: University of Illinois Press, 2007.

Dix, Morgan, comp. *Memoirs of John Adams Dix.* 2 vols. New York: Harper and Brothers, 1883.

Dodge, Grenville M. *Personal Recollections of President Abraham Lincoln, General Ulysses S. Grant and General William T. Sherman.* Council Bluffs, IA: Monarch Printing Company, 1914.

Donald, David Herbert. *Lincoln.* New York: Simon and Schuster, 1995.

———. *"We Are Lincoln Men": Abraham Lincoln and His Friends.* New York: Simon and Schuster, 2003.

Dooley, Raymond N. "Lincoln and His Namesake Town." *Journal of the Illinois State Historical Society* 52 (1959): 130–45.

Dorsey, Florence L. *Master of the Mississippi: Henry Shreve and the Conquest of the Mississippi.* Boston: Houghton Mifflin, 1941.

Duff, John J. *A. Lincoln: Prairie Lawyer.* New York: Bramhall House, 1960.

Emerson, Jason. *Lincoln the Inventor.* Carbondale: Southern Illinois University Press, 2009.

———. *Giant in the Shadows: The Life of Robert T. Lincoln.* Carbondale and Edwardsville: Southern Illinois University Press, 2012.

Faulk, Odie B. *Too Far North, Too Far South.* Los Angeles: Westernlore Press, 1967.

Faust, Patricia L., ed. *Historical Times Illustrated Encyclopedia of the Civil War.* New York: Harper and Row, 1986.

Fehrenbacher, Don. E. *The Dred Scott Case: Its Significance in American Law and Politics.* New York: Oxford University Press, 1978.

Finkelman, Paul. "Abraham Lincoln: Prairie Lawyer." In *America's Lawyer-Presidents from Law Office to Oval Office*, ed. Norman Gross. Evanston, IL: Northwestern University Press and the American Bar Association Museum of Law, 2004.

———. "John McLean: Moderate Abolitionist and Supreme Court Politician." *Vanderbilt Law Review* (2009): 519–66.

Flagler, D. W. *A History of the Rock Island Arsenal from Its Establishment in 1863 to December, 1876; and of the Island of Rock Island, the Site of the Arsenal, from 1804 to 1863*. Washington: Government Printing Office, 1877.

Fowle, Frank F. "A Famous Interference Case: Lincoln and the Bridge." *National Electric Light Association Bulletin* 14, no. 10 (October 1927): 613–22.

———. "The Original Rock Island Bridge across the Mississippi River." *Railway and Locomotive Historical Society Bulletin No. 56* [Railway and Locomotive Historical Society, Baker Library, Harvard Business School], October 1941, 55–63.

Fraker, Guy C. *Lincoln's Ladder to the Presidency: The Eighth Judicial Circuit.* Carbondale and Edwardsville: Southern Illinois University Press, 2012.

Frank, John P. *Lincoln as a Lawyer.* Urbana: University of Illinois Press, 1961.

Fremling, Calvin R. *Immortal River: The Upper Mississippi in Ancient and Modern Times.* Madison: University of Wisconsin Press, 2005.

Frey, Robert L., ed. *Encyclopedia of American Business History and Biography: Railroads in the Nineteenth Century.* New York and Oxford: Facts on File, 1988.

Gary, Ralph. *Following in Lincoln's Footsteps: A Complete Annotated Reference to Hundreds of Historical Sites Visited by Abraham Lincoln.* New York: Carroll and Graf, 2001.

Goodwin, Doris Kearns. *Team of Rivals: The Political Genius of Abraham Lincoln.* New York: Simon and Schuster, 2005.

Greenleaf, Simon. *A Treatise on the Law of Evidence.* 5th ed. Boston: Charles C. Little and James Brown, 1850.

Greve, Charles Theodore. *Centennial History of Cincinnati and Representative Citizens.* Chicago: Biographical Publishing Company, 1904.

Gridley, Eleanor. *The Story of Abraham Lincoln; or, The Journey from the Log Cabin to the White House.* Chicago: M. A. Donohue, 1927.

Głomb, Józef. *A Man Who Spanned Two Eras: The Story of Bridge Engineer Ralph Modjeski.* Trans. Peter J. Obst. Philadelphia: Kosciuszko Foundation, 2002.

Guelzo, Allen C. *Abraham Lincoln: Redeemer President.* Grand Rapids, MI: William B. Eerdmans Publishing Company, 1999.

———. *Lincoln and Douglas: The Debates That Defined America.* New York: Simon and Schuster, 2008.

Hayes, William Edward. *Iron Road to Empire: The History of 100 Years of the Progress and Achievements of the Rock Island Lines.* New York: Simmons-Boardman, 1953.

Heidler, David S., and Jeanne T. Heidler. *Henry Clay: The Essential American.* New York: Random House, 2010.

Hill, Frederick Trevor. *Lincoln the Lawyer.* New York: Century, 1906.

Holt, Michael F. *The Rise and Fall of the American Whig Party: Jacksonian Politics and the Onset of the Civil War.* New York and Oxford: Oxford University Press, 1999.

Holzer, Harold. *Lincoln President-Elect.* New York: Simon and Schuster, 2008.

———. "Reassessing Lincoln's Legal Career." In *Abraham Lincoln, Esq.: The Legal Career of America's Greatest President,* ed. Roger Billings and Frank J. Williams, 5–18. Lexington: University Press of Kentucky, 2010.

———, ed. *The Lincoln-Douglas Debates: The First Complete, Unexpurgated Text.* New York: Fordham University Press, 2004.

Hughes, Robert M. *Handbook of Admiralty Law.* 2nd ed. St. Paul, MN: West Publishing Company, 1920.

Hunter, Louis C. *Steamboats on the Western Rivers: An Economic and Technological History.* New York: Dover, 1993.

Hurlbut, Henry H. *Chicago Antiquities: Comprising Original Items and Relations, Letters, Extracts, and Notes, Pertaining to Early Chicago; Embellished with Views, Portraits, Autographs, Etc.* Chicago: Printed for the author, 1881.

Jackson, Donald C. *Great American Bridges and Dams.* Great American Places Series. Washington, DC: Preservation Press, National Trust for Historic Preservation, 1988.

Jackson, Robert W. *Rails across the Mississippi: A History of the St. Louis Bridge.* Urbana: University of Illinois Press, 2001.

Jervis, John B. *Report of John B. Jervis, Civil Engineer, in Relation to the Railroad Bridge over the Mississippi River, at Rock Island.* New York: Wm. C. Bryant, 1857.

Johannsen, Robert W. *Stephen A. Douglas.* Urbana and Chicago: University of Illinois Press, 1997.

Judd, Mrs. Norman. "An Evening with Mr. Lincoln." In *The Lincoln Memorial: Album-Immortelles,* ed. Osborn H. Oldroyd, 520–24. New York: G. W. Carleton, 1882.

Kane, Adam I. *The Western River Steam-Boat.* College Station: Texas A&M University Press, 2004.

King, Willard L. *Lincoln's Manager: David Davis.* Cambridge, MA: Harvard University Press, 1960.

Knecht, William L. "The Bridge." *BYU Studies* 7 (Autumn 1965): 53–60.

Larkin, F. Daniel. *John B. Jervis: An American Engineering Pioneer.* Ames: Iowa State University Press, 1990.

Latrobe, J. H. B. *The First Steamboat Voyage on the Western Waters.* Baltimore: Maryland Historical Society, 1871.

Leonard, L. O. "Lincoln Was at the Bridge." *Rock Island Magazine,* February 1929: 21–22.

Leroy, David H. *Mr. Lincoln's Book: Publishing the Lincoln-Douglas Debates.* New Castle, DE: Oak Knoll Press; Chicago: Abraham Lincoln Book Shop, 2009.

"Lincoln and the Bridge Case." *Palimpsest* 3, no. 5 (May 1922): 142–54.

"Lincoln's Visit to the Rock Island Bridge." Bulletin of the Abraham Lincoln Association 44, no. 1 (September 1936): 9–10.

Lloyd, James T. *Lloyd's Steamboat Directory, and Disasters on the Western Waters.* Cincinnati, OH: James T. Lloyd; Chicago: D. B. Cook, 1856.

Long, E. B., with Barbara Long. *The Civil War Day by Day: An Almanac, 1861–1865.* New York: Doubleday, 1971.

Lupton, John A. "A. Lincoln, Esquire: The Evolution of a Lawyer." In *A. Lincoln, Esquire: A Shrewd, Sophisticated Lawyer in His Time,* by Allen D. Spiegel, 18–50. Macon, GA: Mercer University Press, 2002.

———. "Basement Barrister: Abraham Lincoln's Practice before the United States Supreme Court." *Lincoln Herald* 101 (Summer 1999): 47–58.

———. "The Power of Lincoln's Legal Words." In *Abraham Lincoln, Esq.: The Legal Career of America's Greatest President,* ed. Roger Billings and Frank J. Williams, 105–18. Lexington: University Press of Kentucky, 2010.

Lyford, James Otis. *History of the Town of Canterbury, New Hampshire, 1727–1912.* Concord, NH: Rumford Press, 1912.

Lynch, Charles J., Jr. "Lincoln and the Effie Afton Bridge Case." In *The Bollinger Lectures: Addresses Given at the Dedication of the Lincoln Library Collected by James W. Bollinger, November 19, 1951,* ed. Clyde C. Walton, Jr. 46–67. Iowa City: State University of Iowa Libraries, the Bollinger Lincoln Foundation, 1953.

Magee, David. *The John Deere Way: Performance That Endures.* Hoboken, NJ: John Wiley and Sons, 2005.

Magliocca, Gerard N. *Andrew Jackson and the Constitution: The Rise and Fall of Generational Regimes.* Lawrence: University Press of Kansas, 2007.

Martin, Albro. *Railroads Triumphant: The Growth, Rejection, and Rebirth of a Vital American Force.* New York: Oxford University Press, 1992.

Matthews, Elizabeth W. *Lincoln as a Lawyer: An Annotated Bibliography.* With a foreword by Cullom Davis. Carbondale and Edwardsville: Southern Illinois University Press, 1991.

McDermott, Stacy Pratt. *The Jury in Lincoln's America.* Athens: Ohio University Press, 2012.

McGinty, Brian. *The Body of John Merryman: Abraham Lincoln and the Suspension of Habeas Corpus.* Cambridge, MA: Harvard University Press, 2011.

———. *Lincoln and the Court.* Cambridge, MA: Harvard University Press, 2008.

McPherson, James M. *Battle Cry of Freedom: The Civil War Era.* New York: Oxford University Press, 1988.

Merrick, George Byron. *Old Times on the Upper Mississippi: Recollections of a Steamboat Pilot from 1854 to 1863.* 1909; Minneapolis and London: University of Minnesota Press, 2001.

Meyers, Marvin. *The Jacksonian Persuasion: Politics and Belief.* Stanford, CA: Stanford University Press, 1957.

Miers, Earl Schenck, ed. *Lincoln Day by Day.* 3 vols. Washington: Lincoln Sesquicentennial Commission, 1960.

Monette, John. "The Progress of Navigation and Commerce on the Waters of the Mississippi River and the Great Lakes, A.D. 1700 to 1846." *Publications of the Mississippi Historical Society* 7 (1903): 479–523.

Monroe, Elizabeth Brand. *The Wheeling Bridge Case: Its Significance in American Law and Technology*. Boston: Northeastern University Press, 1992.

Neely, Mark E., Jr. *Lincoln and the Triumph of the Nation: Constitutional Conflict in the American Civil War*. Chapel Hill: University of North Carolina Press, 2011.

Nevins, F. J. "Seventy Years of Service: From Grant to Gorman." *Rock Island Magazine* 17, no. 10 (October 1922): 5–45.

Nothstein, Ira O. "The First Railroad Bridge to Cross the Mississippi." *Museum Quarterly* 1, no. 2 (April 1956): 1–10.

———. "Rock Island and the Rock Island Arsenal." *Journal of the Illinois State Historical Society* 33 (1940): 304–40.

Oates, Stephen B. *With Malice toward None: The Life of Abraham Lincoln*. New York: New American Library, 1977.

Oldroyd, Osborn H., ed. *The Lincoln Memorial: Album-Immortelles*. New York: G. W. Carleton, 1882.

Olson, James S. *Encyclopedia of the Industrial Revolution in America*. Westport, CT: Greenwood Press, 2002.

Page, Elwin L. "The *Effie Afton* Case." *Lincoln Herald* 58, no. 3 (Fall 1956): 3–10.

Palmer, John M., ed. *The Bench and Bar of Illinois*. 2 vols. Chicago: Lewis Publishing, 1899.

Paludan, Philip Shaw. "'Dictator Lincoln': Surveying Lincoln and the Constitution." *Organization of American Historians Magazine of History* (2007) 21, no. 1: 8–13.

———. *The Presidency of Abraham Lincoln*. Lawrence: University Press of Kansas, 1994.

Papaioannou, Helen Iles, and Daniel W. Stowell. "Dr. Charles A. Leale's Report on the Assassination of Abraham Lincoln." *Journal of the Abraham Lincoln Association* 34 (2013): 40–53.

Parish, John C. "The First Mississippi Bridge." *Palimpsest* 3, no. 5 (May 1922): 133–41.

Parker, N. Howe. *Iowa as It Is in 1855: A Gazeteer for Citizens, and a Hand-book for Emmigrants [sic]*. Chicago: Keen and Lee, 1855.

Parkinson, Robert Henry. "The Patent Case That Lifted Lincoln into a Presidential Candidate." *Abraham Lincoln Quarterly* 4, no. 3 (September 1946): 105–22.

The Past and Present of Rock County, Ill. Chicago: H. F. Kett, 1877.

Petersen, William J. "The Grand Excursion of 1854." *Palimpsest* 14, no. 6 (August 1933): 301–16.

———. "The Rock Island Comes." *Palimpsest* 14, no. 6 (August 1933): 285–300.

———. "The 'Virginia,' the 'Clermont' of the Upper Mississippi." *Minnesota History* 9 (1928): 347–62.

Petroski, Henry. *Engineers of Dreams: Great Bridge Builders and the Spanning of America*. New York: Alfred A. Knopf, 1995.

Pfeiffer, David A. "Bridging the Mississippi: The Railroads and Steamboats Clash at the Rock Island Bridge." *Prologue* 36, no. 2 (Summer 2004): 40–47.

Pratt, Harry E. "The Genesis of Lincoln the Lawyer." *Bulletin of the Abraham Lincoln Association* 57 (September 1939): 3–10.

———. *The Personal Finances of Abraham Lincoln.* Springfield, IL: Abraham Lincoln Association, 1943.

Prevost, Lewis M., Jr. "Description of Howe's Patent Truss Bridge, Carrying the Western Railroad over the Connecticut River at Springfield, Massachusetts." *Journal of the Franklin Institute of the State of Pennsylvania*, 3rd ser., 3 (1982): 289–92.

Primm, James Neal. *Lion of the Valley: St. Louis, Missouri, 1764–1980.* 3rd ed. St. Louis: Missouri Historical Society Press, 1998.

The Rail-Roads, History and Commerce of Chicago. 2nd ed. Chicago: Democratic Press Job and Book Steam Printing Office, 1854.

Rice, Allen Thorndike, ed. *Reminiscences of Abraham Lincoln by Distinguished Men of His Time.* New York: North American Review, 1888.

Richards, John T. *Abraham Lincoln, the Lawyer-Statesman.* Boston: Houghton Mifflin, 1916.

Riddle, Donald W. *Congressman Abraham Lincoln.* Urbana: University of Illinois Press, 1957.

Riebe, William. "The Government Bridge." *Rock Island Digest* [Rock Island Technical Society, Silvis, IL] 2 (1982): 68–92.

Riney, Larry A. *Hell Gate of the Mississippi: The* Effie Afton *Trial and Abraham Lincoln's Role in It.* Geneseo, IL: Talesman Press, 2006.

Roseman, Curtis C., and Elizabeth M. Roseman, eds. *Grand Excursions on the Upper Mississippi River: Places, Landscapes, and Regional Identity after 1854.* Iowa City: University of Iowa Press, 2004.

Ross, Michael A. *Justice of Shattered Dreams: Samuel Freeman Miller and the Supreme Court during the Civil War Era.* Baton Rouge: Louisiana State University Press, 2003.

Russell, Charles Edward. *A-Rafting on the Mississip'.* 1928; Minneapolis: University of Minnesota Press, 2001.

Saltonstall, F. G. "A Recollection of Lincoln in Court." *Century* 53, no. 4 (February 1897): 636–37.

Sedgwick, Catharine Maria. "The Great Excursion to the Falls of St. Anthony." *Putnam's Monthly Magazine* 4, no. 21 (September 1854): 320–25.

Skilton, John S. "Abraham Lincoln: A Lawyer 'for the Ages.'" *Wisconsin Law Review* 2011 (2011): 1–26.

Slattery, Thomas J. *An Illustrated History of the Rock Island Arsenal and Arsenal Island: Parts One and Two.* Rock Island, IL: Historical Office, U.S. Army Armament, Munitions and Chemical Command, 1990.

Smith, John William. *A Selection of Leading Cases on Various Branches of the Law.* 6th American ed. 2 vols. Philadelphia: T. and J. W. Johnson, 1866.

Spiegel, Allen D. *A. Lincoln, Esquire: A Shrewd, Sophisticated Lawyer in His Time.* Macon, GA: Mercer University Press, 2002.

Stampp, Kenneth M. *America in 1857: A Nation on the Brink*. New York: Oxford University Press, 1990.

Starr, John W., Jr. *Lincoln and the Railroads: A Biographical Study*. New York: Dodd, Mead, 1927.

Steiner, Mark E. "Abraham Lincoln and the Rule of Law Books." *Marquette Law Review* 93 (2009–10): 1283–324.

———. "Does Lawyer Lincoln Matter?" In *Abraham Lincoln, Esq.: The Legal Career of America's Greatest President*, ed. Roger Billings and Frank J. Williams, 45–64. Lexington: University Press of Kentucky, 2010.

———. *An Honest Calling: The Law Practice of Abraham Lincoln*. DeKalb: Northern Illinois University Press, 2006.

———. "'The Sober Judgement of Courts': Lincoln, Lawyers, and the Rule of Law." *Northern Kentucky Law Review* 36 (2009): 279–93.

"Stephen T. Logan Talks About Lincoln," *Bulletin of the Abraham Lincoln Association* 12, no. 1 (September 1928): 1–8.

Stewart, David O. *The Summer of 1787: The Men Who Invented the Constitution*. New York: Simon and Schuster, 2007.

Stickney, William, ed. *The Autobiography of Amos Kendall*. Boston: Lee and Shepard, 1872.

Stover, John F. *The Routledge Historical Atlas of the American Railroads*. New York and London: Routledge, 1999.

Swisher, Carl B. *The Taney Period, 1863–64*. Vol. 5 of *The Oliver Wendell Holmes Devise History of the Supreme Court of the United States*. New York: Macmillan, 1974.

Switzler, William F. *Report on the Internal Commerce of the United States*. Washington: Government Printing Office, 1888.

Tarbell, Ida M. *Life of Abraham Lincoln, Drawn from Original Sources and Containing Many Speeches, Letters and Telegrams*. 2 vols. New York: Lincoln Memorial Association, 1900.

Temple, Wayne C. *Lincoln's Connections with the Illinois and Michigan Canal, His Return from Congress in '48, and His Invention*. Springfield, IL: Illinois Bell, 1986.

———. "Mary Todd Lincoln's Travels." *Journal of the Illinois State Historical Society* 52, no. 1 (Spring 1959): 180–94.

Thomas, Benjamin P. "Abe Lincoln, Country Lawyer" and "Lincoln and the Courts, 1854–61." In Benjamin P. Thomas, *"Lincoln's Humor" and Other Essays*, ed. Michael Burlingame, 139–52, 153–88. Urbana and Chicago: University of Illinois Press, 2002.

Thomas, Emory M. *Robert E. Lee: A Biography*. New York: W. W. Norton, 1995.

Thornton, Richard H. *An American Glossary*, vol. 2. Philadelphia: J. B. Lippincott, 1912.

Trescott, Paul B. "The Louisville and Portland Canal Company, 1825–1874. " *Mississippi Valley Historical Review* 44 (1958): 686–708.

Twain, Mark. *Autobiography of Mark Twain*, vol. 1. Ed. Harriet Elinor Smith. Berkeley and Los Angeles: University of California Press, 2010.

———. *Life on the Mississippi*. 1883; New York: Barnes and Noble, 2010.

Tweet, Roald D. *History of Transportation on the Upper Mississippi and Illinois Rivers*. N.p.: National Waterways Study, U.S. Army Engineer Water Resources Support Center, Institute for Water Resources, 1983.

VanderVelde, Lea. *Mrs. Dred Scott: A Life on Slavery's Frontier*. New York: Oxford University Press, 2009.

Vile, John R. *The Constitutional Convention of 1787: A Comprehensive Encyclopedia of America's Founding*. Santa Barbara, CA: ABC-CLIO, 2005.

Vincent, Francis. *Vincent's Semi-Annual United States Register...Events Transpiring Between the 1st of January and 1st of July, 1860*. Philadelphia: Francis Vincent, 1860.

Warren, G. K. *Report on Bridging the Mississippi River between Saint Paul, Minn., and St. Louis, Mo.* Washington: Government Printing Office, 1878.

War's Greatest Workshop: Rock Island Arsenal, Historical, Topographical and Illustrative. [Rock Island, IL:] Arsenal Publishing Co. of the Tri-Cities, 1922.

Washburne, Elihu B. "Abraham Lincoln in Illinois, Part I." *North American Review* 141, no. 347 (October 1885): 307–20.

Way, Frederick, Jr. *Way's Packet Directory, 1848–1994: Passenger Steamboats of the Mississippi River System Since the Advent of Photography in Mid-Continent America*. Athens: Ohio University Press, 1994.

Weingardt, Richard H. *Engineering Legends: Great American Civil Engineers—32 Profiles of Inspiration and Achievement*. Reston, VA: American Society of Civil Engineers, 2005.

White, Richard. *Railroaded: The Transcontinentals and the Making of Modern America*. New York: W. W. Norton, 2011.

Whitney, Henry Clay. *Life on the Circuit with Lincoln*. 1892. Ed. Paul M. Angle. Caldwell, Idaho: Caxton Printers, 1940.

Wiecek, William M. "*Somerset*: Lord Mansfield and the Legitimacy of Slavery in the Anglo-American World." *University of Chicago Law Review* 42 (1974): 86–146.

Wigmore, John Henry. *Select Cases on the Law of Evidence*. 2nd ed. Boston: Little, Brown, 1913.

Williams, Frank J. "Abraham Lincoln: The Making of the Attorney-in-Chief." In *Lincoln's America: 1809–1865*, ed. Joseph R. Fornieri and Sara Vaughn Gabbard, 115–34. Carbondale and Edwardsville: Southern Illinois University Press, 2008.

———. *Judging Lincoln*. Carbondale and Edwardsville: Southern Illinois University Press, 2002.

———. *Lincoln as Hero*. Carbondale and Edwardsville: Southern Illinois University Press, 2012.

———. "Lincoln's Lessons for Lawyers." In *Abraham Lincoln, Esq.: The Legal Career of America's Greatest President,* ed. Roger Billings and Frank J. Williams, 19–44. Lexington: University Press of Kentucky, 2010.

Wilson, Douglas L. *Lincoln's Sword: The Presidency and the Power of Words.* New York: Alfred A. Knopf, 2006.

Wilson, Douglas L., and Rodney O. Davis, eds., with the assistance of Terry Wilson. *Herndon's Informants: Letters, Interviews, and Statements about Abraham Lincoln.* Urbana and Chicago: University of Illinois Press, 1998.

Wilson, Douglas L., and Rodney O. Davis, eds. *Herndon's Lincoln by William H. Herndon and Jesse W. Weik.* Urbana and Chicago: Knox College Lincoln Studies Center and University of Illinois Press, 2006.

Wilson, Rufus Rockwell, ed. *Intimate Memories of Lincoln.* Elmira, NY: Primavera Press, 1945.

Woldman, Albert A. *Lawyer Lincoln.* Boston: Little, Brown, 1937; rpt. New York: Carroll and Graf, 1994.

Wolmar, Christian. *The Great Railroad Revolution: The History of Trains in America.* New York: Public Affairs, 2012.

Wood, David Ward, ed. *History of the Republican Party and Biographies of Its Supporters, Illinois Volume.* Chicago: Lincoln Engraving and Publishing, 1895.

Wood, F. J. "New England Toll Bridges," *Stone and Webster Journal,* September 1917, 163–79.

Zobrist, Benedict K. "Steamboat Men versus Railroad Men: The First Bridging of the Mississippi River." *Missouri Historical Review* 59, no. 2 (January 1965): 159–72.

ILLUSTRATION CREDITS

1. Abraham Lincoln Presidential Library and Museum, Springfield, Illinois
2. Engraving by A.H. Ritchie. Brian McGinty Collection
3. Technical Library of the U.S. Army Corps of Engineers, Rock Island District, Rock Island, Illinois
4. Brian McGinty Collection
5. Putnam Museum of History and Natural Science, Davenport, Iowa
6. *Ballou's Pictorial Drawing-Room Companion*, December 18, 1858
7. Courtesy of William Riebe
8. Engraving by Wellstood & Peters as printed in *The Ladies' Repository*, Cincinnati, January 1855
9. Engraving by W. Wellstood from *The Ladies' Repository*, Cincinnati, February 1856
10. Putnam Museum of History and Natural Science, Davenport, Iowa
11. Brian McGinty Collection
12. Library of Congress, Prints and Photographs Division
13. Brian McGinty Collection
14. *History of Cook County, Illinois: From the Earliest Period to the Present Time* by Alfred Theodore Andreas (Chicago: 1884)
15. *Frank Leslie's Illustrated Newspaper*, June 27, 1857
16. Rock Island County Historical Society
17. Rock Island County Historical Society
18. Wood engraving by Alfred R. Waud in *Picturesque America* by William Cullen Bryant (1874)
19. U.S. Army photo provided by Rock Island Arsenal, Rock Island, Illinois
20. Brian McGinty Collection
21. Mapcraft, Woodstock, Illinois

INDEX

ABOUT THE AUTHOR

BRIAN McGINTY is an attorney and writer who specializes in American history and law. Born and raised in Southern California, he attended the University of California in Berkeley, where he earned his BA in American history and his JD from Boalt Hall, the school of law at the same university. He practiced law in Monterey County for ten years before beginning a writing career in which he produced ten books and more than 150 articles in popular magazines and scholarly journals. His awards include the Best Writing Prize from the National Historical Society, the Editor's Award for Historic Scholarship from the Sonoma County (California) Historical Society, a nomination for the One Book Arizona prize for 2008, and Honorable Mention in the 2010 Scribes Book Award of the American Society of Legal Writers. For a dozen years he was a writer and editor at a large national legal publisher. His most recent books include *Strong Wine: The Life and Legend of Agoston Haraszthy* (Stanford University Press, 1998), *The Oatman Massacre: A Tale of Desert Captivity and Survival* (University of Oklahoma Press, 2005), *Lincoln and the Court* (Harvard University Press, 2008), *John Brown's Trial* (Harvard University Press, 2009), *The Body of John Merryman: Abraham Lincoln and the Suspension of Habeas Corpus* (Harvard University Press, 2011), and *A Toast to Eclipse: Arpad Haraszthy and the Sparkling Wine of Old San Francisco* (University of Oklahoma Press, 2012).